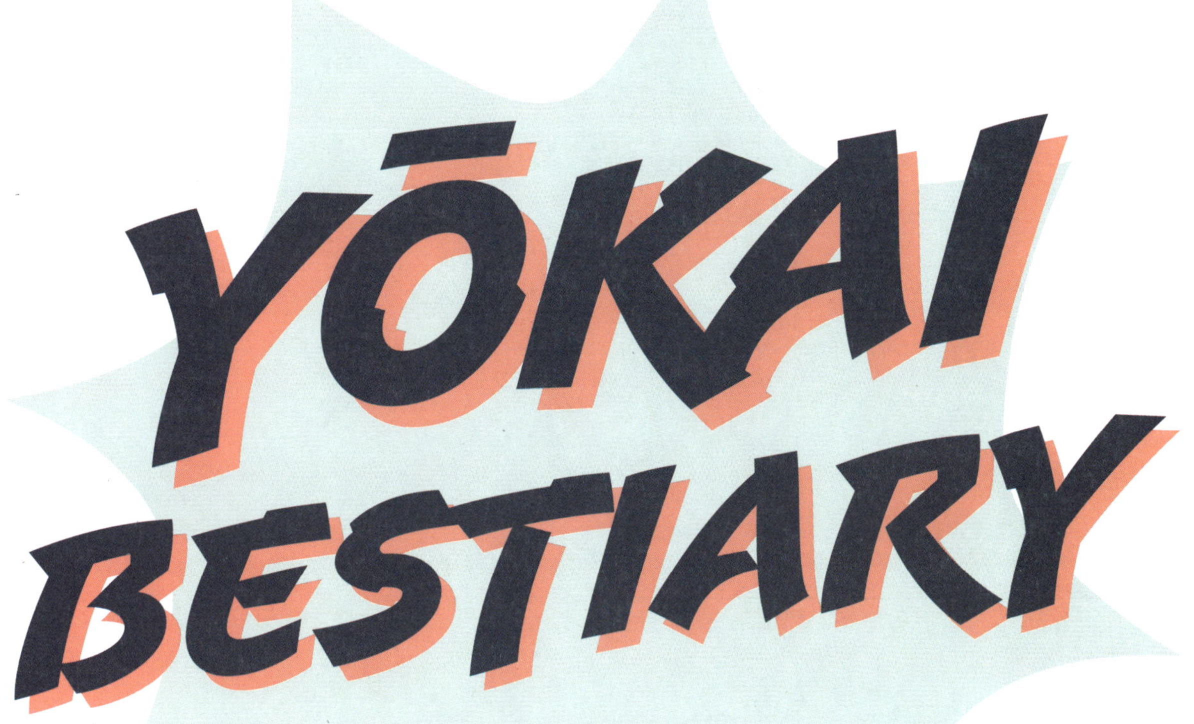

HOW to DRAW EERIE and ENCHANTING JAPANESE GHOULS and MONSTERS

Lance Red

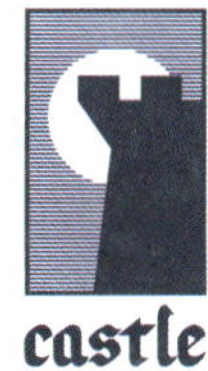

castle

Welcome!

In this book I seek to guide you through the drawing of many monstrous *yōkai*, from the most well-known iconic creatures like the mischievous tanuki to the more frightening oni. Know that the yōkai in this book are but a small portion of the vast variety of yōkai out there. I hope this book helps to captivate your interest in not only yōkai and the folklore around them, but also in Japanese culture, which gave birth to these strange and wonderful creatures. I hope you find inspiration in these pages and are challenged by them to grow your drawing skills.

As you work through each chapter the yōkai are designed to start with the easiest to draw, then progress in difficulty. Though some yōkai may look intimidating, with all the layers of details, take your time working through each step carefully. You can do it. Enjoy the process and know that drawing, like any skill, takes diligence and practice to improve.

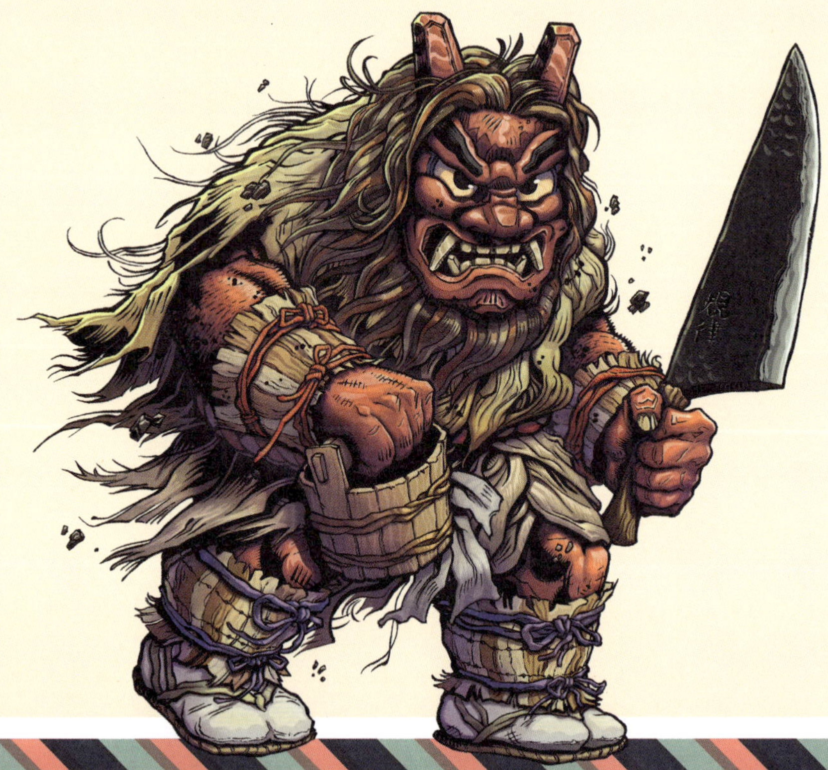

Introduction

WHAT ARE YŌKAI?

Bakekujira haunting dark shores, once-cherished heirlooms now neglected coming to life. A glimpse of a fin as a *ningyo* disappears beneath the waves. Unexplained sounds in the night, glowing wisps of light flitting just at the edge of sight, or that fox watching you from the tree line with deep intelligence in its eyes.

These are all examples of yōkai, creatures from Japanese folklore and tradition. Yōkai exist in the in-between places, where the supernatural meets the everyday, born from the fears and feelings of awe from the Japanese people of the past. In that twilight land where day meets night, life meets death; where the fantastical intrudes upon the mundane: this is where yōkai exist. However, yōkai are not just creatures, but also phenomena, especially earlier yōkai. They served as explanations for mysterious events, such as unexplained sounds, storms, and pestilence. During this early time, yōkai mainly existed in oral tradition and it was not until artists took hold of yōkai that they gained concrete visual forms and became more like creatures.

Many yōkai are born directly from Japanese history and tradition, while others stem from or intersect with religious beliefs (Shintoism, Buddhism). Others still originate from foreign cultures, having been imported from countries such as China or India and adapted into Japanese culture.

YŌKAI PAST & PRESENT

Once the embodiment of peoples' fears and curiosity, during the Edo period (1603–1868), yōkai began to shift from creatures of fear to entertainment thanks to the work of artists such as Toriyama Sekien.

He and other artists began illustrating yōkai for the masses in the form of books and prints. People grabbed hold of yōkai and craved more. In turn, artists began to look at the world around them and imagine, giving birth to more and more yōkai, going beyond the original legends and folklore in order to feed this growing yōkai craze.

Artists gave yōkai visual form, taking them from oral concepts to creatures of comics, spurring on a cultural interest in yōkai that has only grown over the centuries. Even this book is a small piece born forth from this wave of ever-growing interest in yōkai, as foreign artists like myself seek to learn more about them, Japanese culture, and the stories from which they are born.

Today, yōkai are everywhere in Japanese culture. They serve as a deep well of inspiration for artists and other creators. Many of the creatures and monsters you see in anime, manga, and Japanese video games are inspired in some way by yōkai, further spurring on international interest in these bizarre and astounding creatures.

YŌKAI AND MY OWN ARTIST JOURNEY

I've been interested in and a part of Asian culture all my life, growing up in a Filipino American household. In middle school, I had the opportunity to travel to Japan when my aunt took me along on a trip one summer to visit our family in Tokyo, who had emigrated there from the Philippines. It was during this trip that I fell in love with Japanese culture. For a month we visited temples, districts in Tokyo, museums, and the countryside. In high school I went on to study Japanese. Now, as a fantasy artist working in the gaming field, many of the projects I have worked on have been based on Tolkien-esque fantasy rooted in European folklore and culture. So, in my personal art I love diving into Japanese yōkai with all their unique forms and diverse stories; it offers a whole new world of visually unique creatures to explore.

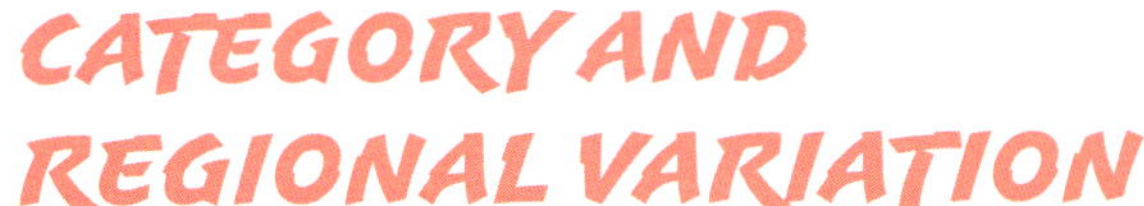

CATEGORY AND REGIONAL VARIATION

The categories used in this book are a tool to help make the vast world of the yōkai more approachable and easier to understand. Many of the yōkai shown in these pages could be placed in multiple categories. So, please do not take these as writ for how to organize the vast pantheon of yōkai, but more like guideposts for the content of this book.

Yōkai vary from region to region, village to village, story to story. For example, the famous kappa yōkai has numerous variations throughout Japan. So, know that the forms presented in this book are more general interpretations and that should your interest be piqued, there is much more to discover.

Here are the tools and materials I use in my studio on a daily basis when drawing: the workhorses of my art practice. Before we dive in, I want to note that not all of these are needed. When it comes to drawing, you essentially just need something to make a mark on a surface and a surface to mark upon. That is one of the beauties of drawing. At its core it is a straightforward, expressive experience.

IN MY STUDIO

Pencils

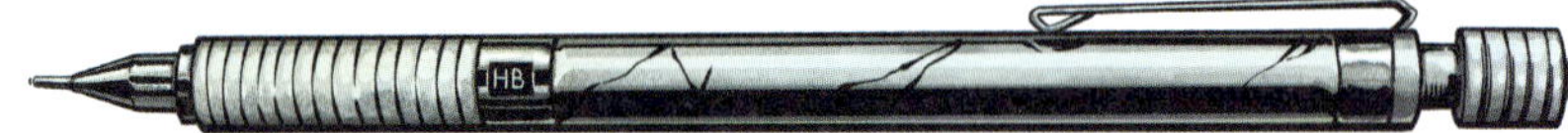

Mechanical pencil: The main pencil I use is the Staedtler 925, 0.5 mm. It has great weight, so it feels nice in the hand to hold—not too heavy nor too light. I have multiple versions of this pencil, each with a different lead weight. I use 2H to start a drawing (if I'm not using Col-Erase pencils, see below), HB for the final lines, and sometimes 2B if I need to go darker.

Col-Erase colored pencil: These are soft, erasable, colored pencils. I enjoy using these sometimes during the initial block-in stages of a drawing because I find I am able to be a little more loose and free-flowing with them.

Other Pencil Options

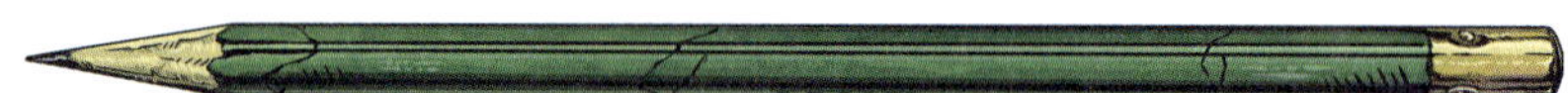

General's Drawing Pencils (2H, HB, 2B): These are fantastic, straightforward drawing pencils, and are great alternatives to the Staedtler pencils.

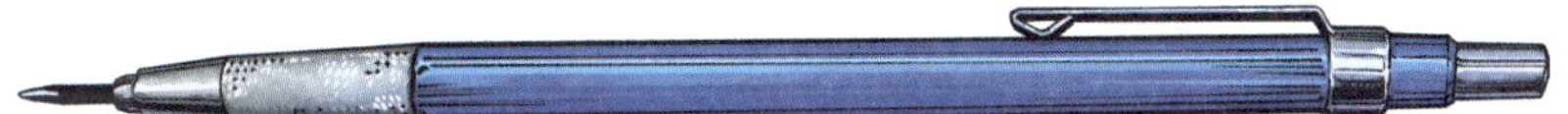

2mm lead holder (2H, HB, 2B): I used this as my main drawing tool for years before switching to mechanical pencils. You can attain a sharp, fine point on these by using a lead pointer. The main reason I switched is that I grew tired of having to sharpen my pencil all the time in a single drawing session. Still awesome to use.

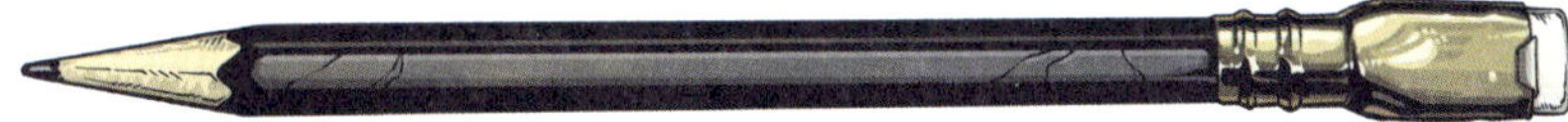

Blackwing pencils: These have a nice, wonderful soft lead that allows you to draw from very light to very dark depending on the pressure you apply. Sometimes I get in the mood to draw with a traditional pencil and these Blackwing pencils are one of my go-tos.

Drawing Board

This is a giant **clipboard for drawing**. I like these because I am constantly rotating my drawing as I work, and by placing it on a drawing board I can rotate the board without having to touch my actual drawing. This helps to protect my drawing from any smudging as I work on it. Smudging equals the death of drawing! One must keep the white areas clean! Habits drilled into me from back in my drafting days.

Pencil Sharpener

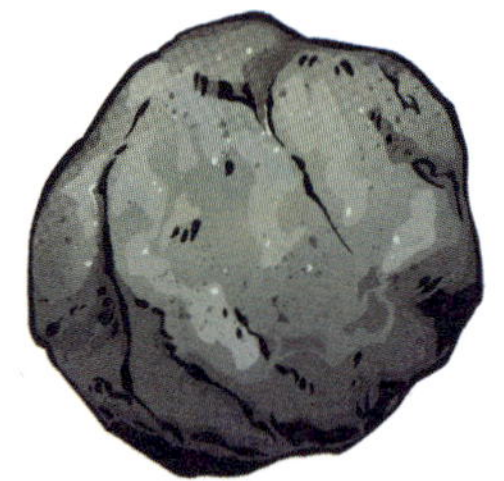

I am not too particular here. There are the **crank kind** with a handle, **electric sharpeners**, or the **small, cheap, plastic handheld ones**. I use all of them. It just needs to be sharp.

Erasers

Kneaded erasers: These rubbery, bendy erasers are great for lightening lines that you may have drawn too dark, but do not want to erase completely.

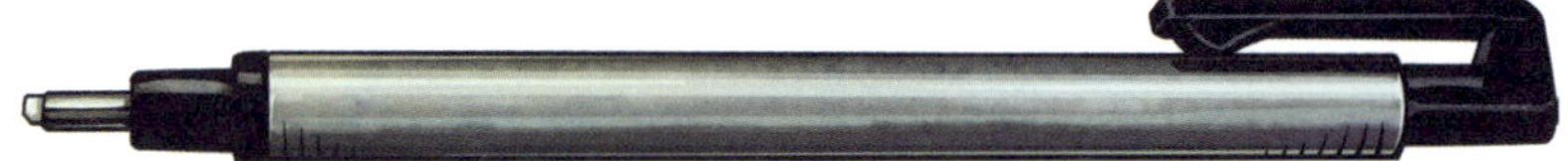

Pen-style erasers: These are perfect for precision-detail erasing, as you can hold them like a pencil. My current favorite is the Tombow MONO Zero eraser, as it has a very fine point compared to other erasers.

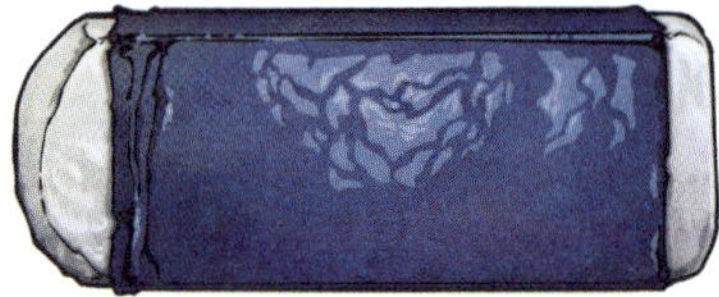

White plastic block erasers: Block erasers are great for fully erasing large areas. The erasers on the Blackwing pencils are similar, just smaller.

Eraser shields: If you want to be really cool, eraser shields are great if you do detailed drawings. They work well in isolating only what you want to erase, while protecting the rest of a drawing. Eraser shields work best in conjunction with a block eraser; with newer, smaller pen-style erasers they may be unneeded.

Paper

Printer paper: Since you are probably still in the learning phase of your artist journey, you do not need anything fancy. In fact, back in art school this was the go-to drawing paper for students.

Smooth bristol paper: However, for more finished drawings, the best, most wonderful, heavenly paper in the world is smooth bristol, in particular comic smooth bristol. I hate having to fight with paper texture when drawing tight details and this paper is glass smooth.

A NOTE ON DIGITAL MATERIALS

If you are drawing digitally, I would recommend that you practice traditionally too, as being able to manipulate physical drawing tools will increase your overall skill even more. I find the better I get traditionally, the better I get digitally.

My digital drawing setup consists of:
- iPad Pro (as big as I possibly can get—the 12.9", or 327 mm, model)
- Apple Pencil and full-screen protector with just a slight tooth/texture to it
- Drawing glove
- Procreate app
- Your favorite digital drawing brush

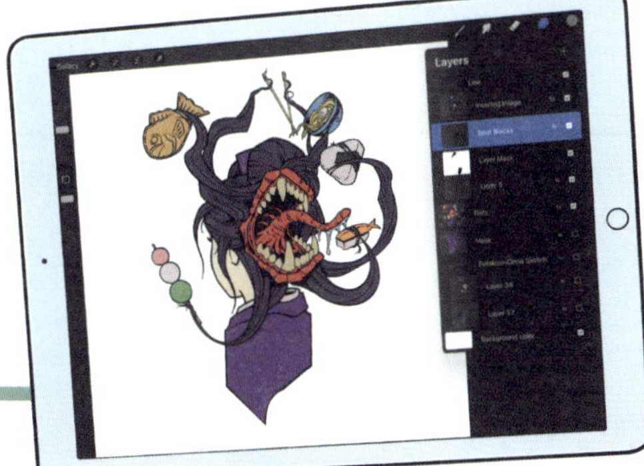

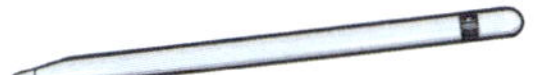

DRAWING TIPS

'll start with the single most important piece of art advice I have received in my career thus far. I was at IlluxCon, a traditional fantasy art show focused on Imaginative Realism, as a young professional. At the time, I enjoyed making art, but having been trained as a commercial artist, to me, art was all about making assets for products. I humbly approached one of my favorite artists in the fantasy art field, Steve Prescott, who makes incredible illustrations. His work has beautiful linework, bold graphic shading, expressive strokes, and characters that feel alive: the whole shebang. I asked him for his #1 tip for making art. I was expecting perhaps a certain technique, maybe a particular process or studio practice, but he gave me two words:

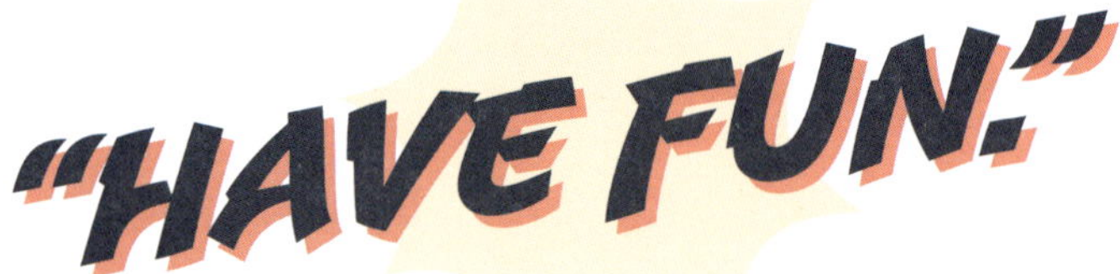

This may sound trite or too simple, but for me, at the time, I was so focused on the work side of being an artist—clients, deadlines, portfolio updates—that "fun" was not even on my radar. I remember thinking to myself, "Is that even allowed?" He went on to explain (I'm paraphrasing here): "We make fantasy art for books, games, and people's homes. If we aren't having fun, it will show through our work, and our viewers won't have any fun when viewing our art. If you are not having fun making art, what's the point? There are better, easier ways to make money out there."

Boom! Mind blown.

So, I pass this sage wisdom on to you: "Have fun." Give yourself permission to make bad drawings. It does not have to be perfect because we are still learning and growing.

DRAWING TIPS

Here are a few drawing tips and techniques to keep in mind and practice incorporating as you work through this book.

Start drawing lightly. The initial lines in a drawing are just the foundation upon which we will build the finished drawing and not the final lines that people will see. So they should be light and erasable.

Draw with confidence (no hairy lines). Many early artists draw lines with a seesaw motion going back and forth because they are not confident they can draw the line with one stroke. Go for it and throw that line! You can always erase if you need to.

Use your whole arm. Bouncing off the previous technique, another bad drawing habit is to draw while only bending at your wrist. While it may seem to give you more control, that is only because you probably have not practiced enough drawing using your whole arm.

Fill the page. Aim to fill the whole page with your drawing. Be brave, draw BIG!

Follow the order of steps. Outside to inside. Big to small. General to specific. This is the usual order when working on a drawing. Start with the largest shape and work toward the center or focal point of a figure. For example, draw in the shape of the head before adding in the features.

Note repeating shapes. In many of these drawings we will be working through, you will be using what are called repeating shapes, which help to simplify more complex designs. It is an artistic trick to break a larger, more complex image into smaller, similar pieces and redrawing them so we can create a visual shorthand. An example of this would be when drawing the vertebrae of the bakekujira (page 118) or the eyes on the hyaku-me (page 146).

Read and research. This book is just a toe-dip into the wonderful world of yōkai and drawing. Don't stop here. Dive into Japanese culture: Read about the country's mythology, history, and folklore. Go read all you can on whatever interests you. Fill your creative well so that you have more to draw on when you need ideas. One of my favorite parts about being an artist is that I am always researching and learning about new things!

I touched on this already, but it bears repeating: When learning to draw, give yourself permission to fail and grow. Not every drawing you make will be a masterpiece, and that is okay. Let's have fun learning to draw yōkai! At first you may want to follow my steps exactly as I have drawn them, but as you build your skills, feel more confident, and learn more about yōkai, I encourage you to try adding your own twist. Maybe it's new poses or perhaps a different variation of a yōkai (of which there are many, depending on the region of Japan the yōkai originates from or the story it is pulled from).

Drawing Process Overview

The yōkai drawings in this book are broken down into multiple steps. Here is the general art process you should follow when working your way through these steps. These are not set-in-stone absolutisms to follow, but guiding thoughts on what to focus on during each stage of the drawing process. You will also notice that each step is broken down with purpose to effectively build on what came before. We do not begin with the final linework, but instead work our way up to it through multiple passes, building up the basic shapes of the yōkai before drawing in the final line and details.

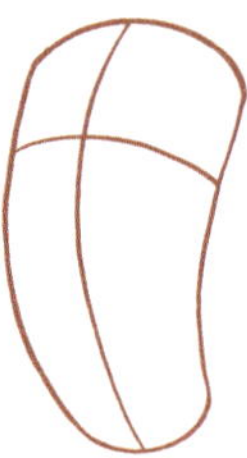

Foundation for the Drawing

In this first step we will draw the main line of action. A line of action is a single line that captures the general flow of the pose for a given figure. We are boiling down the action of a character into a single gesture, a single line. On this line we will then place the major shapes of the figure, usually starting with the basic head shape and center lines for the facial features.

Basic Shape and Structure

Think of this stage as hanging the skeleton on the line of action upon which we will construct the rest of the drawing. We will simplify the major forms of the figure into basic shapes.

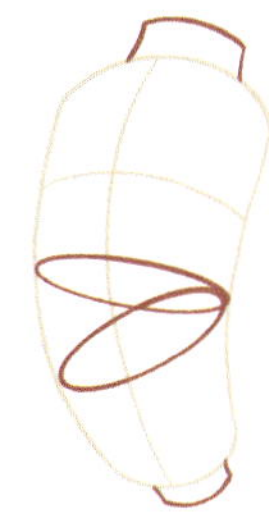

Refined Outlines and Secondary Forms

With the major shapes established, we now start to render the actual forms of the figure, turning the basic shapes into actual limbs and costume, starting with the outlines. Working outside to inside, we will add in the secondary forms, like facial features, to already-drawn head shapes.

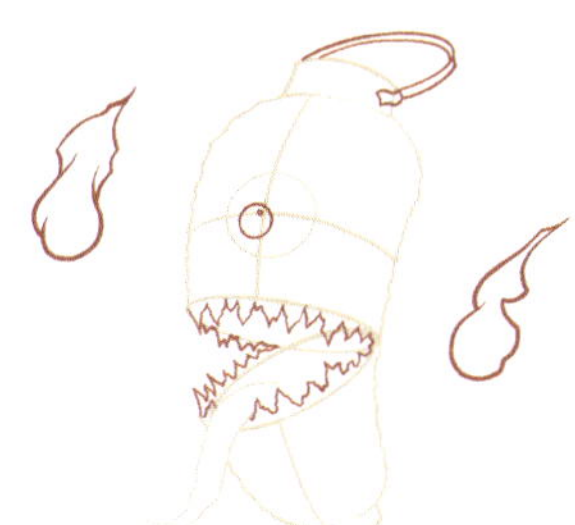

The Yōkai Comes to Life

Now we will start to turn the shapes we have been drawing into a character by adding in textures, expression, and details. Having established the forms of the character, now we go inside to draw the details, turning a generic grouping of shapes into a specific character. It is also at this stage that we can erase the guidelines we used at the beginning of our drawing.

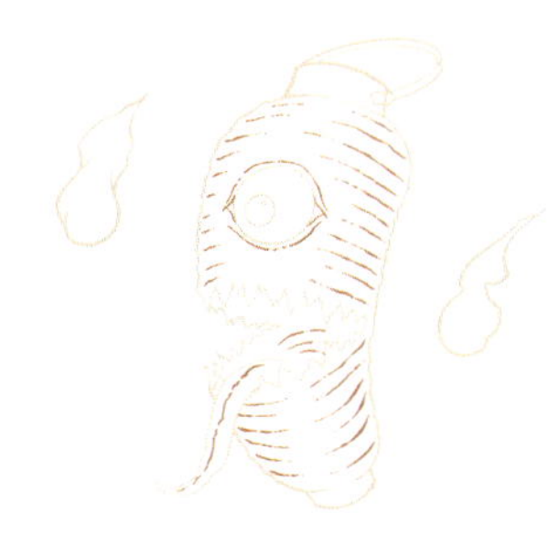

Final Touches and Styling

These last steps are where style can come into play with final touches such as minor details, shading, or variation in line weight. For example, I like to thicken the major outlines and holding lines, especially those away from the light source.

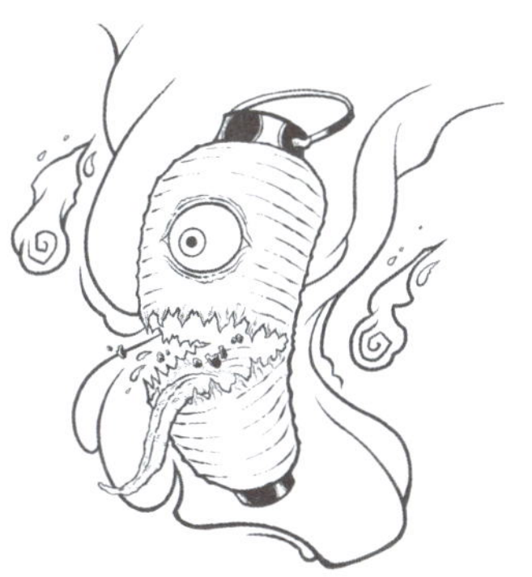

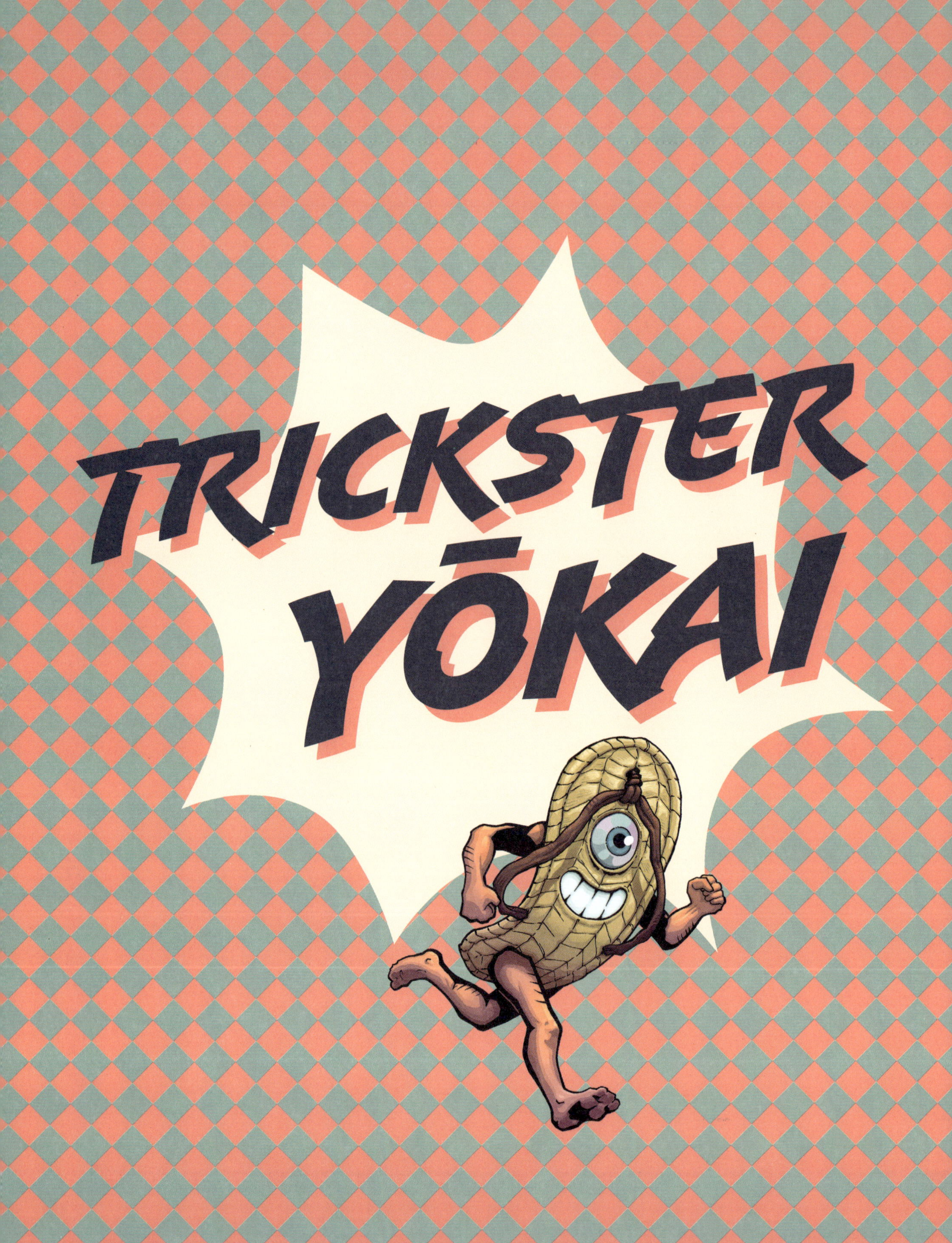

TRICKSTER
YŌKAI

While some yōkai are monstrous, others vengeful, some divine, this first group of yōkai have no such lofty aspirations. These yōkai are known to be tricksters and pranksters, from shapeshifting animals to sandals that run away leaving you with cold bare feet, and still other yōkai that will sneak up on you just to give you a big slobbery lick. These yōkai are typically lighthearted, silly creatures out for their own amusement. Many are often depicted as comedic relief in modern anime and manga.

TANUKI (たぬき)

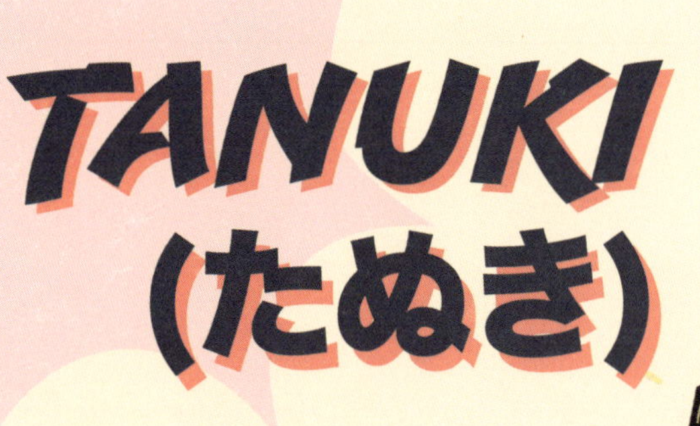

Tanuki are whimsical tricksters known for their playful antics, who will often shapeshift into household items, trees, and people to surprise unsuspecting travelers. They revel in transforming leaves into money or antiques to reward people, only for the illusion to vanish when the tanuki sneaks away. Tanuki have a fondness for sake, adding to their jovial reputation, which is also why statues of tanuki are often shown holding sake jugs.

The tanuki is based on an animal native to Japan, similar in appearance to a racoon. It is also one of the most beloved and iconic figures in Japanese folklore, and statues of tanuki can be found in storefronts, temples, and homes throughout Japan as they are symbols of good fortune.

This yōkai is designed as a shape-building exercise. In each step we will be drawing shapes on top of one another in order to build up the character.

1

Start with a squat, round shape for the head and a bent box for the body, capturing the flow of the pose. Draw in the center lines.

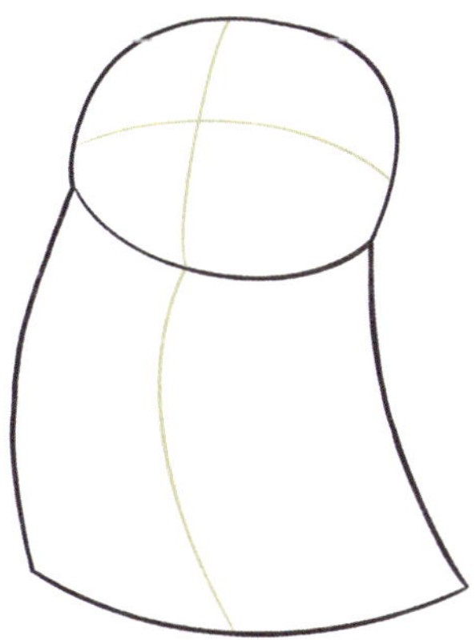

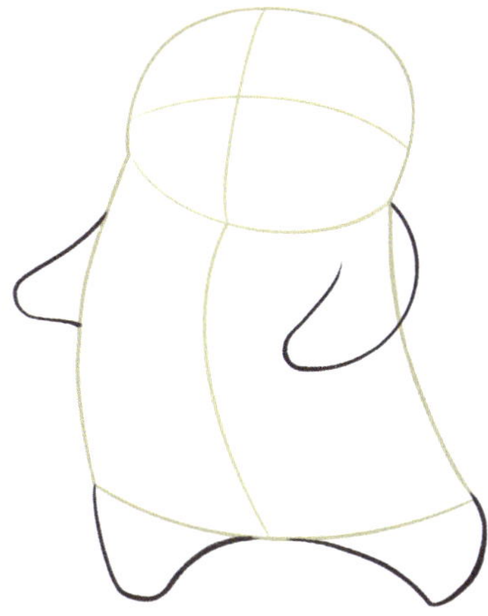

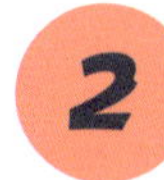

2

Extending from the edge of the body shape, draw curves for the short arms and legs.

3

With the body blocked in, now add in the secondary shapes. Draw a large curve for the tail and rounded triangles for the ears and feet.

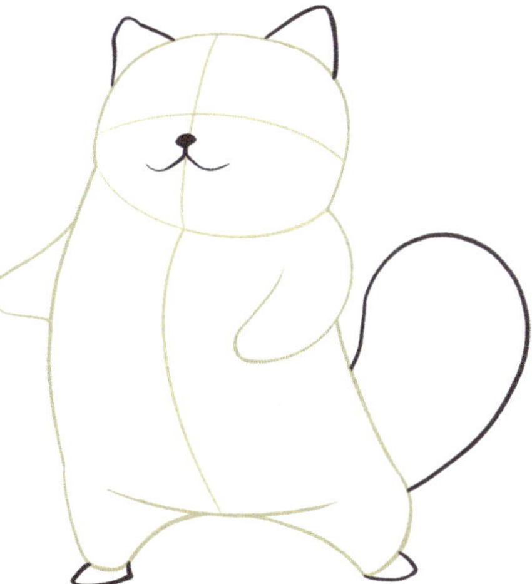

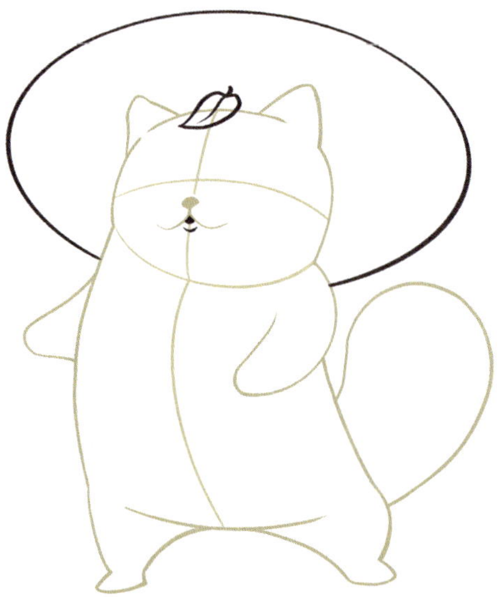

Draw a large oval for the *sugegasa* hat. Add a leaf to the tanuki's forehead. Add the tanuki's tiny mouth and lip.

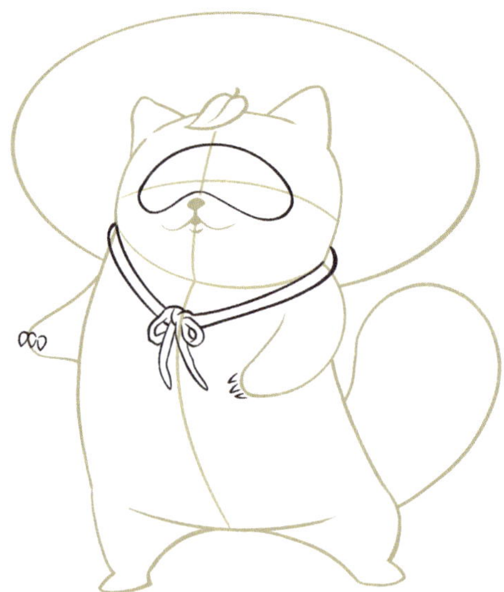

Use curved tube shapes to form the rope holding his hat on. Start with the rope that circles the neck, add the rounded loops for the bow, and finally the two ends of the rope dangling down in the middle. Draw a long bean shape for the dark fur patch around the eyes.

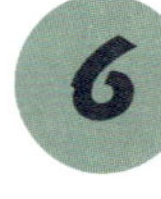
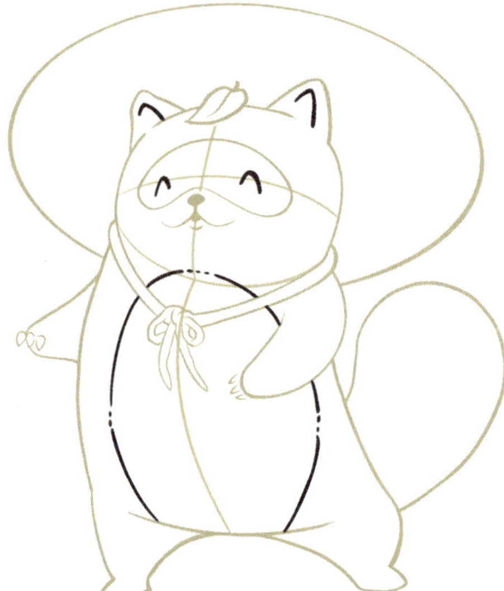

Draw triangular curves for the eyes and inner ears. Using a broken line, add a large oval for his tummy.

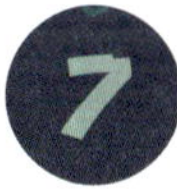

7

Using curved rectangles, draw in the paper lantern and handle.

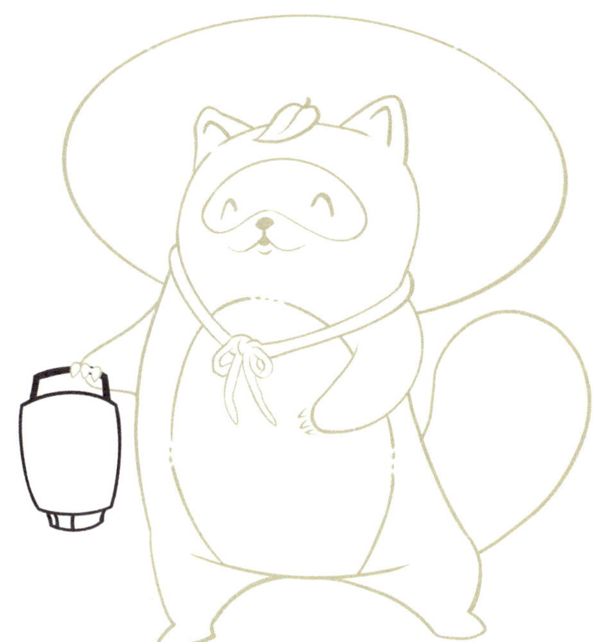

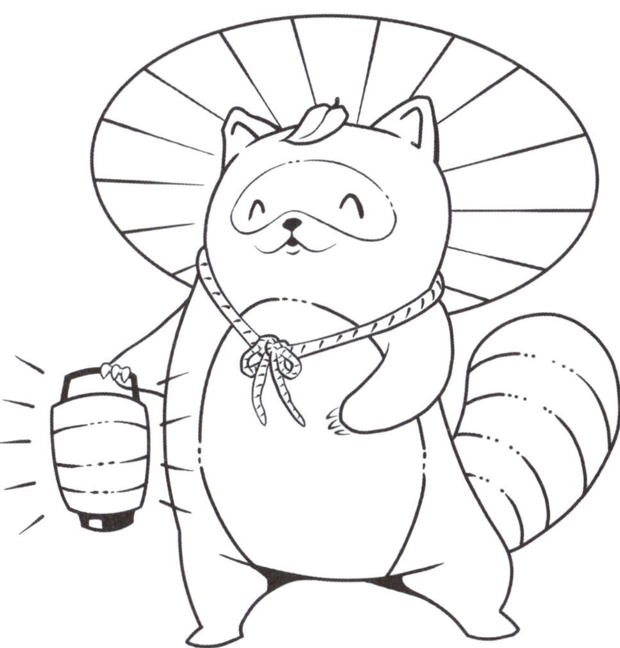

8

To finish the drawing, use evenly spaced, curved lines to draw the ribs on the lantern, stripes on the tail, and the rope. Use straight lines for the ribs of the sugegasa.

CHŌCHIN-OBAKE (ちょうちんおばけ)

The chōchin-obake is a type of *tsukumogami*, which are yōkai born from everyday objects. This mischievous lantern flies about the night sky swooping down at its victims in the hopes of scaring them, but it means no real harm. Some versions have a long tongue they use to lick their targets, further startling them. Others have arms too.

Paper lanterns were one of the main sources of light at night in ancient Japan. These lanterns often appeared to float eerily on their own, their light too weak to illuminate the people holding them. You can imagine where the idea for this yōkai came from. Paper lanterns are still common in modern Japan and can be seen adorning the entrances to many shops and restaurants.

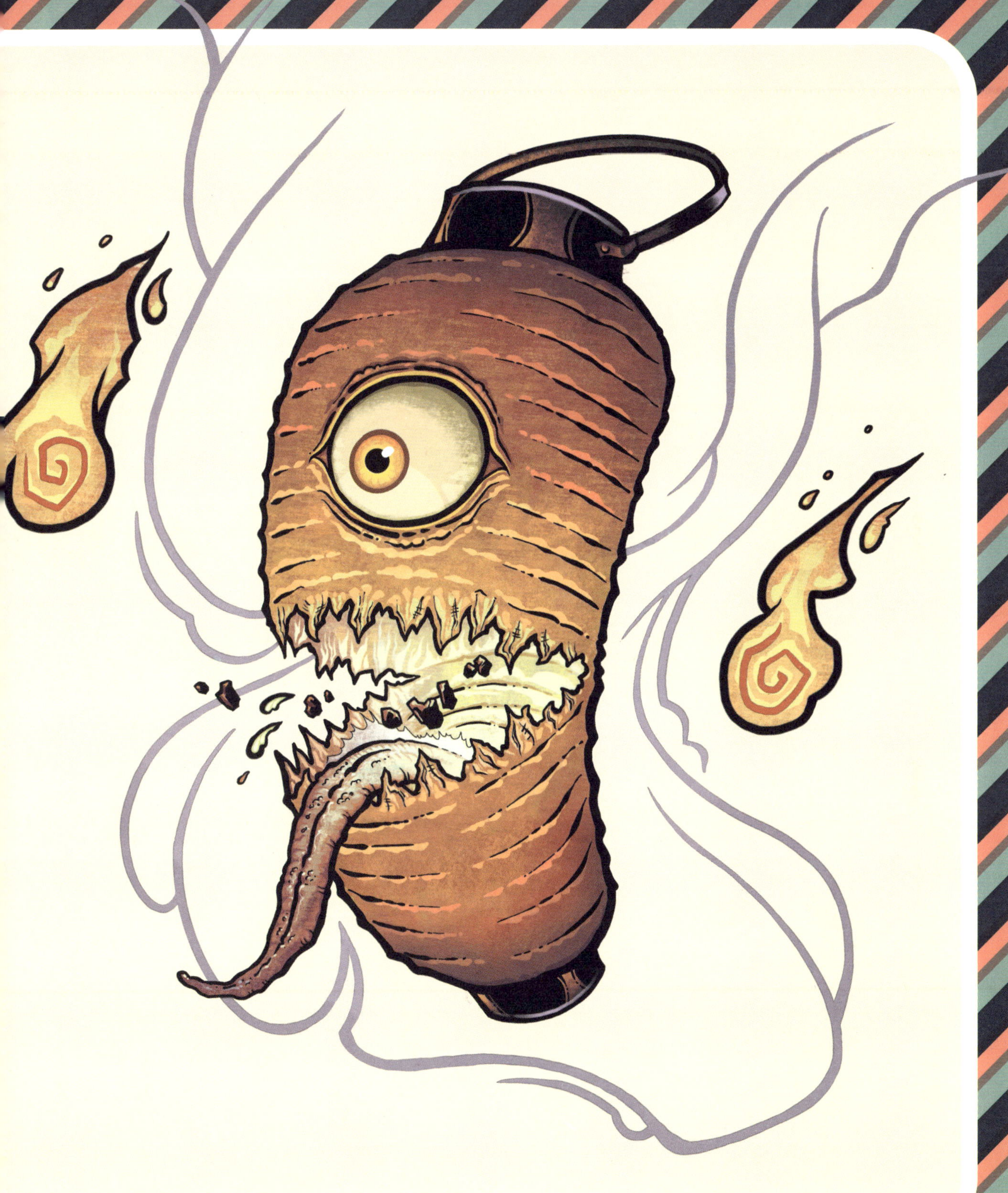

1

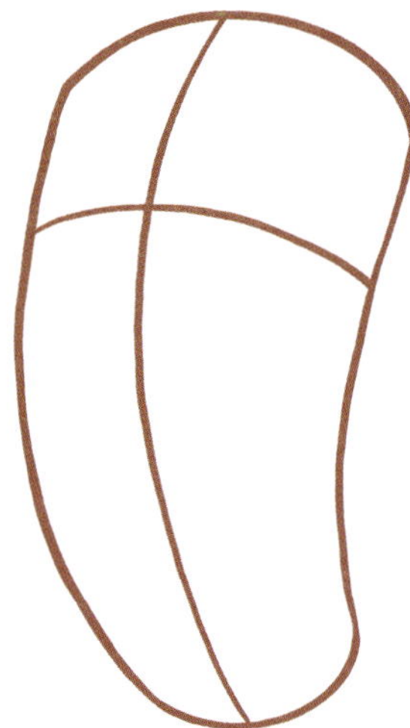

Lightly draw the curved, rectangular body of the lantern. The curves will add a sense of motion to our yōkai, as if it were flying through the air. Draw two center lines. These lines indicate the center of the face and will help guide the placement of the facial features.

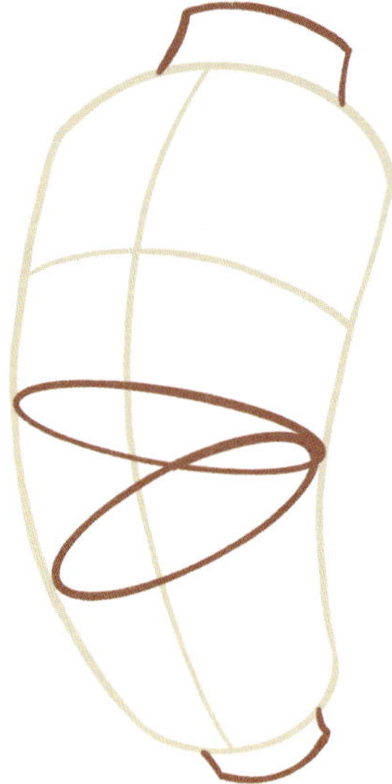

2

Add curved caps at the top and bottom of the lantern. Then draw two overlapping elliptical shapes inside the lantern's body. These circles will guide where we draw the top and bottom of the mouth.

3

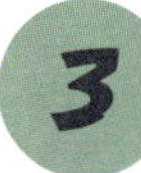

Using the center lines as a guide, draw a circle for the eyeball. Draw a scalloped line going all the way around the body. This type of line helps to show that the paper lantern is made of paper stretched over bamboo ribs. Add in the shape of the tongue.

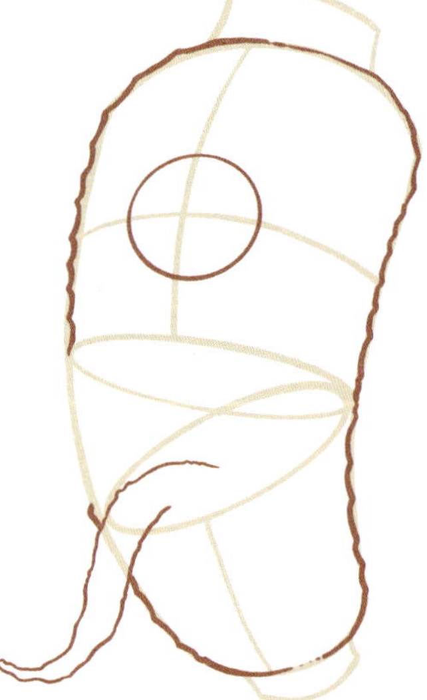

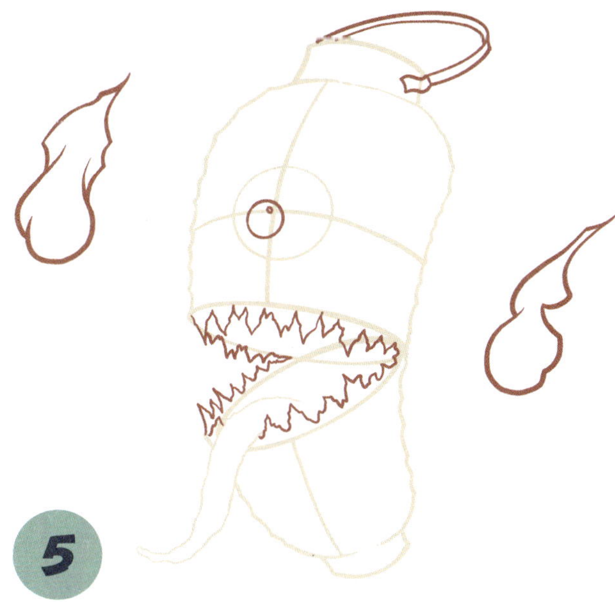

4

With all the major shapes established, we can start to add secondary forms. Draw in the teeth along the lines of the ellipses drawn in step 2. Make the teeth ragged, as if they are made from torn paper. Lastly, add in two floating spirit-fire balls, the pupil, and curved handle.

5

To really pull off the paper-lantern look, use broken lines to draw the bamboo ribs showing through the paper. Since this is a monster and handmade, we do not want these lines to be solid and straight. Give them a little character.

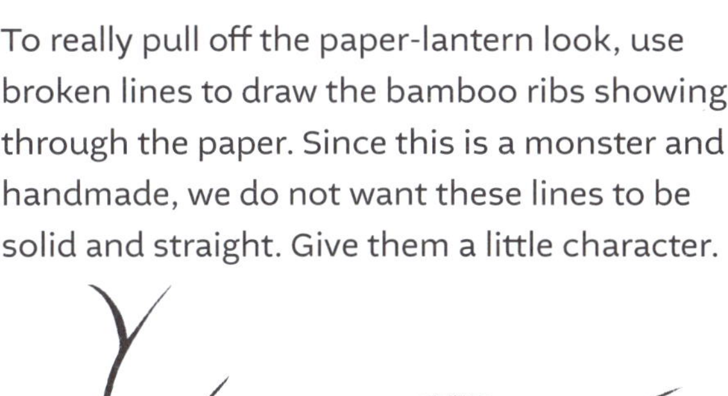

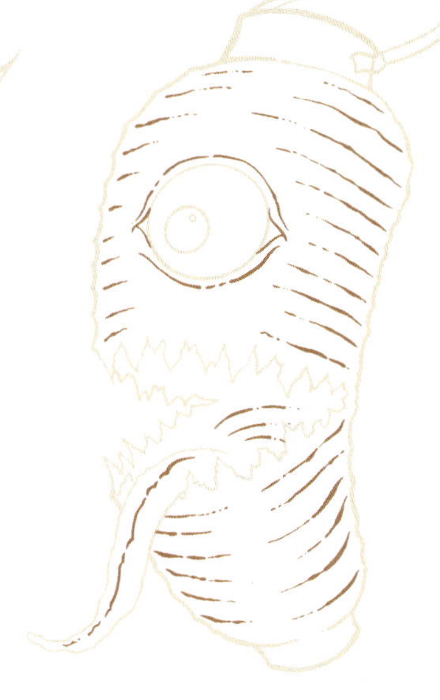

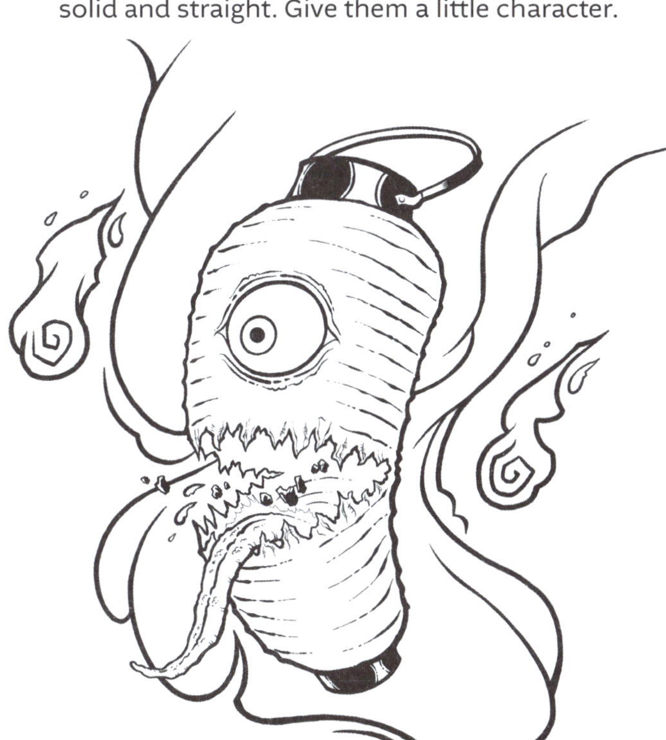

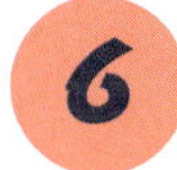

6

Lastly, draw curved lines around the chōchin-obake, as if the lantern is breathing out smoke. Draw a few final details, like the taste buds on its tongue to make the tongue look more gross, as well as spit coming out of its mouth.

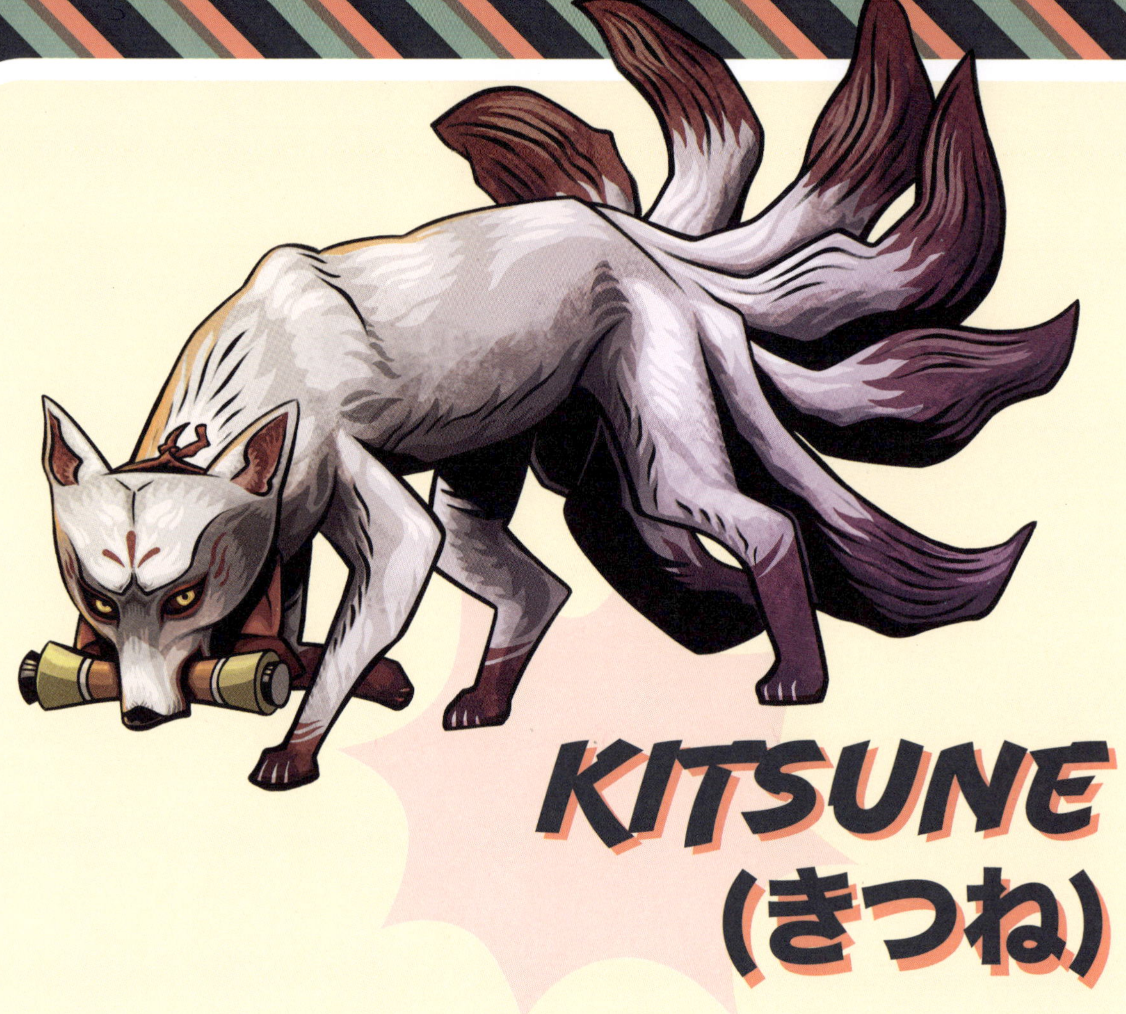

KITSUNE
(きつね)

In Japanese folklore, it is believed that when anything reaches one hundred years of age, it can gain supernatural powers. The kitsune is a fox that grows a new tail for each century of life it has lived. The most powerful kitsune have nine tails, which has served as inspiration for many anime and video game characters.

Whereas tanuki are comical in nature, kitsune are generally more cunning. Kitsune are sometimes portrayed with various items under their paws or being carried in their mouths. Each item symbolizes a different aspect of the kitsune. In this version, the kitsune is shown with a scroll in its mouth, signifying its role as a messenger for Inari, the Japanese god of rice.

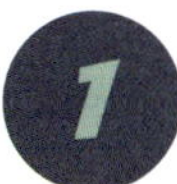

Draw the curved line of action. Notice how it changes direction once you get to the tail. Draw a semicircular shape for the head, adding in the center lines for the face. Add triangles to the top of the semi-circle for the kitsune's ears.

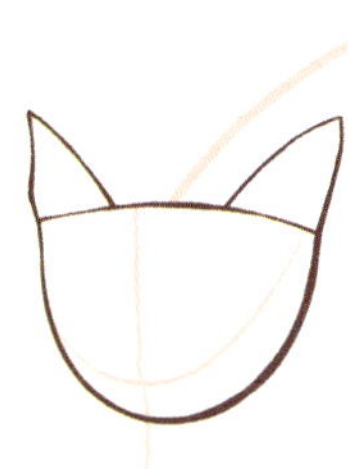

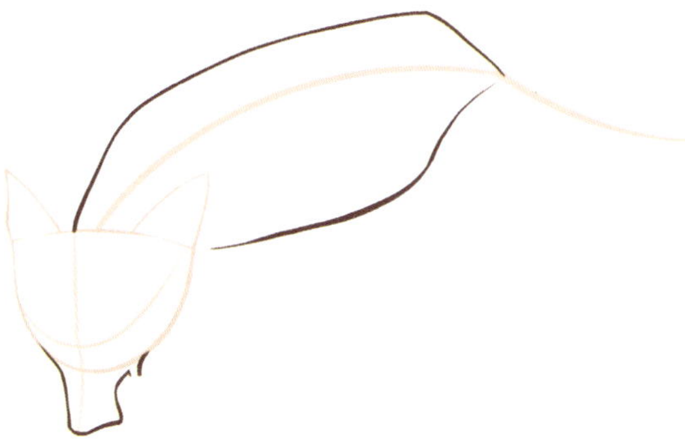

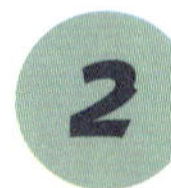

Following the center line of the face, draw in the fox's muzzle. In a similar manner, draw the general shape of the kitsune's body by following the line of action.

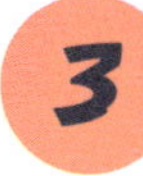

Use angled lines to draw the legs of the kitsune, paying attention to the joint locations. Refine the top edge of the body.

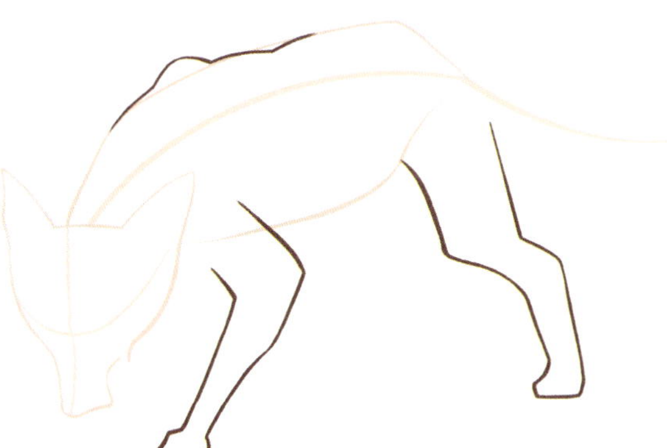

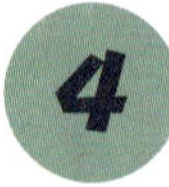

Draw the scroll in the fox's mouth. Add in the back leg using the same shapes from step 3. Draw the downward, flowing tail.

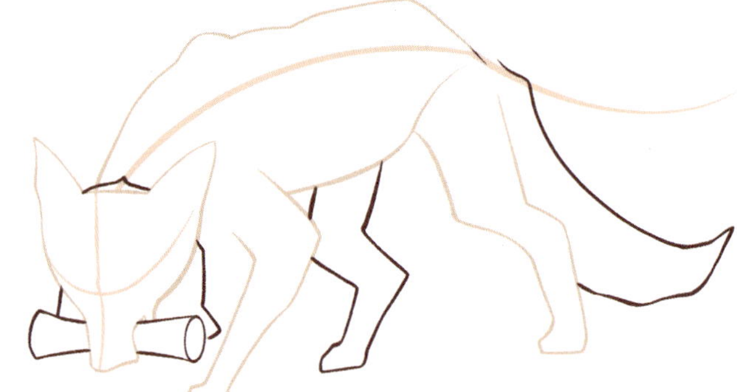

Let's keep building from step 4. Make leaf shapes for the kitsune's eyes, and add more details to the scroll. Draw in three more tails starting in the front and spiraling back.

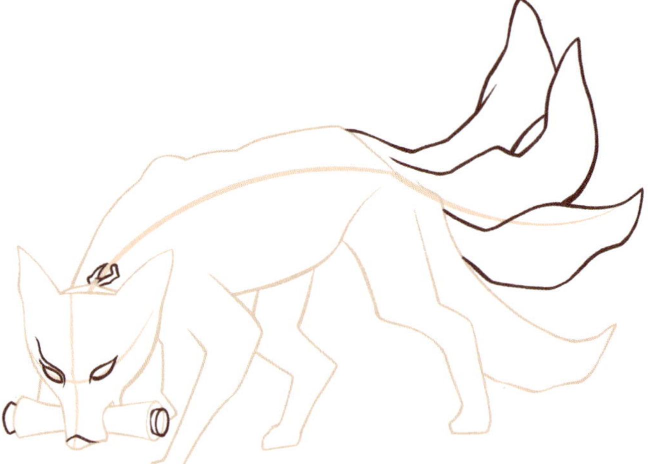

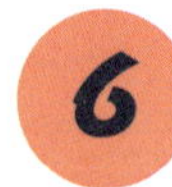

Add two more tails. Observe how the tails spiral around the body counterclockwise. Draw in the last leg, bent at 90 degrees to show the fox walking forward.

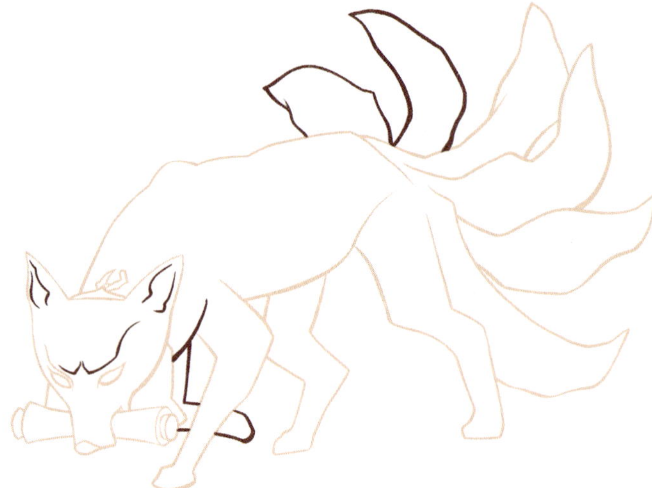

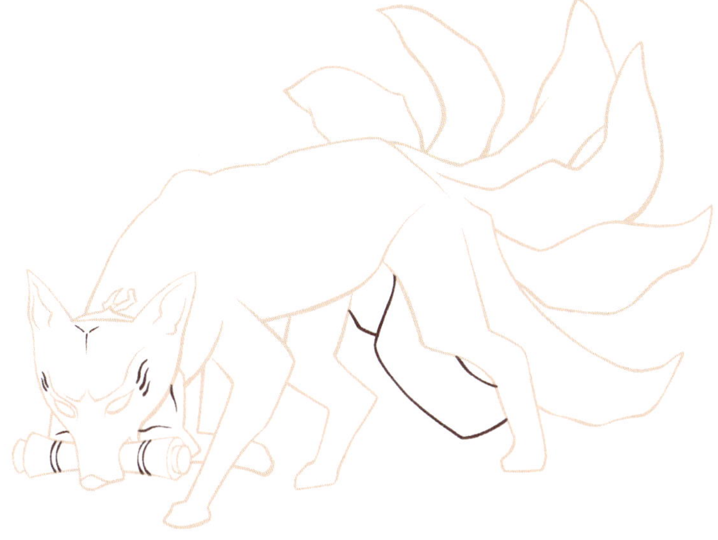

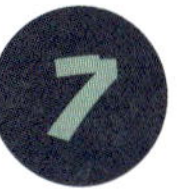

Draw in the last two tails between the legs. Add in the final details around the face.

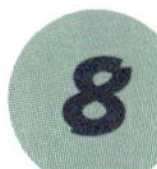

Finish the kitsune, using long and short curves to indicate the texture of the fox's fur. I like to do so near the ends of the tails and along the underbelly of the fox.

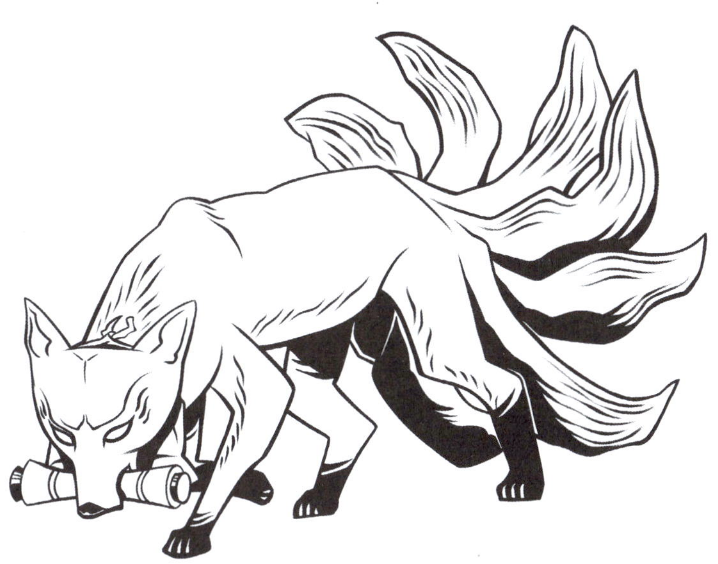

BAKEZŌRI (ばけぞうり)

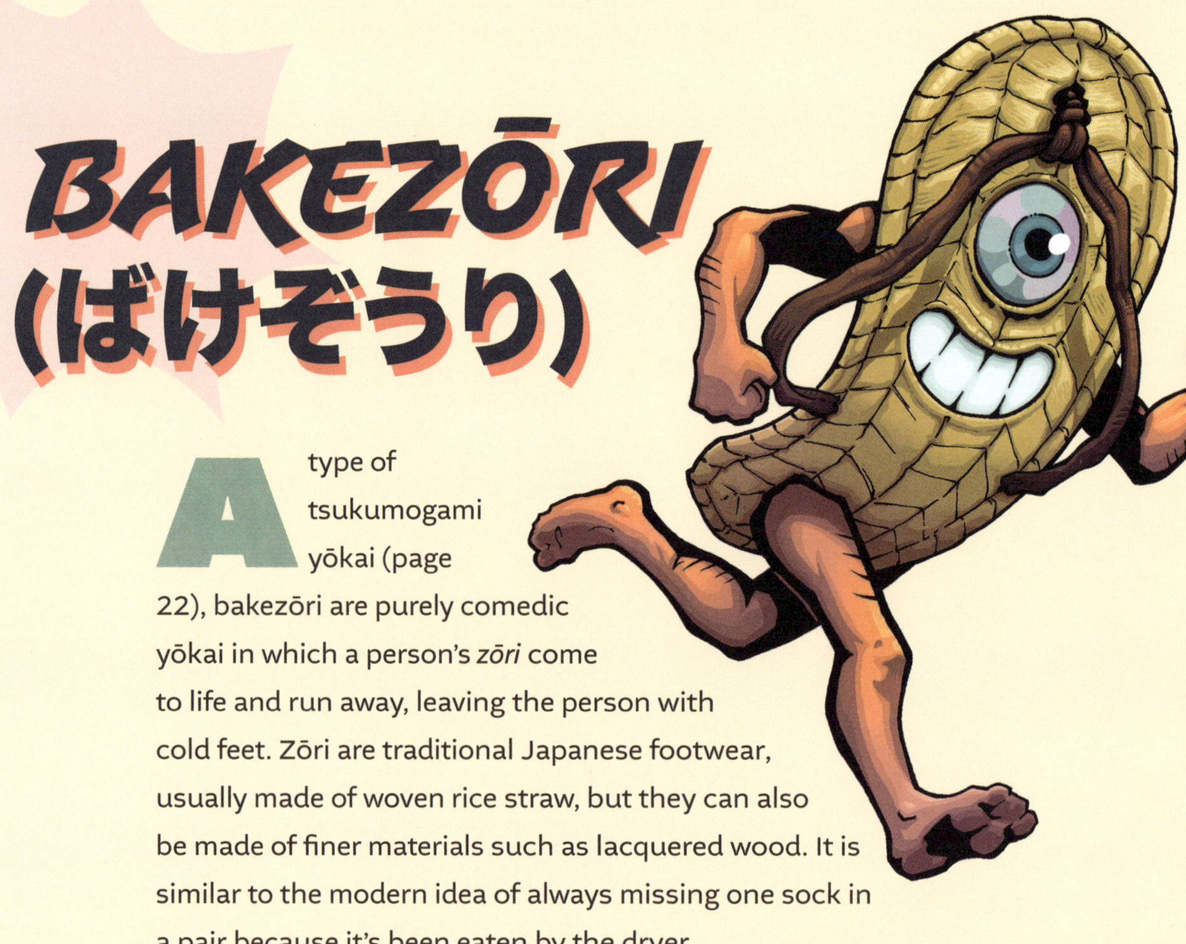

A type of tsukumogami yōkai (page 22), bakezōri are purely comedic yōkai in which a person's *zōri* come to life and run away, leaving the person with cold feet. Zōri are traditional Japanese footwear, usually made of woven rice straw, but they can also be made of finer materials such as lacquered wood. It is similar to the modern idea of always missing one sock in a pair because it's been eaten by the dryer.

Tsukumogami are yōkai that are real-world items that have come to life. This usually happens in two ways: they reach the grand age of one hundred years old and so gain supernatural powers or, should the owners of the object not treat it well, disregard it, ignore it, or throw it away, the object may come to life in order to haunt its disrespectful owners. Before tsukumogami, yōkai were creatures of the night, lurking in the dark and to be feared, but tsukumogami brought yōkai into the home right where people lived and at the same time began transitioning yōkai into creatures of entertainment.

1

Lightly draw a curved line of action. Centered on this line, draw a bean-like shape. This will be the body of the bakezōri. Lastly, draw a horizontal center line for the eye.

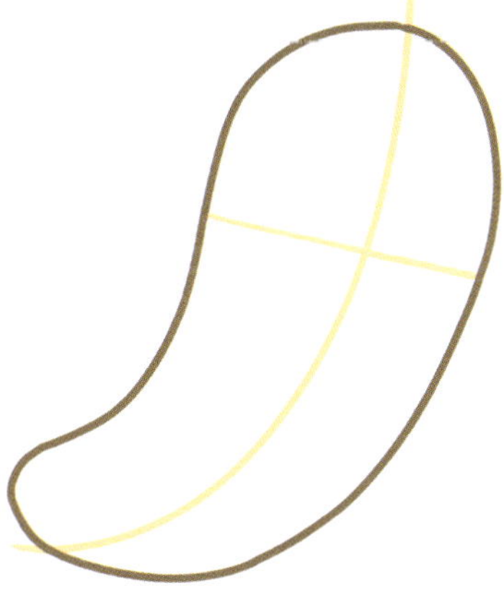

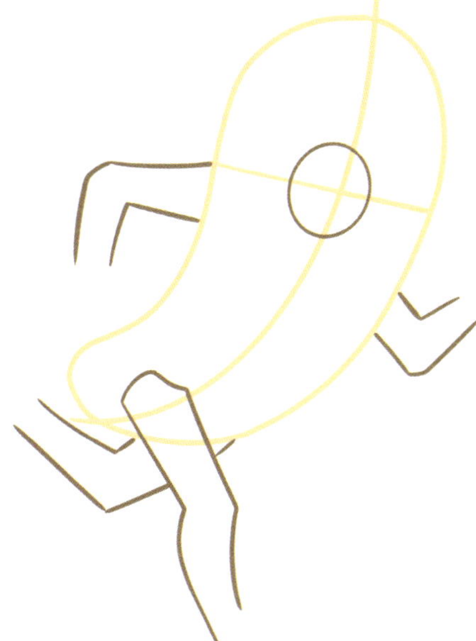

2

Using mainly straight lines, draw in the arms and legs. Pay attention to the bends of the knees and elbows. Draw a circle for its large eye.

3

With the center lines as a guide, use flowing, curved lines to draw the *hanao*—thong straps—which will frame the face. Draw bent ovals to indicate the hands and feet.

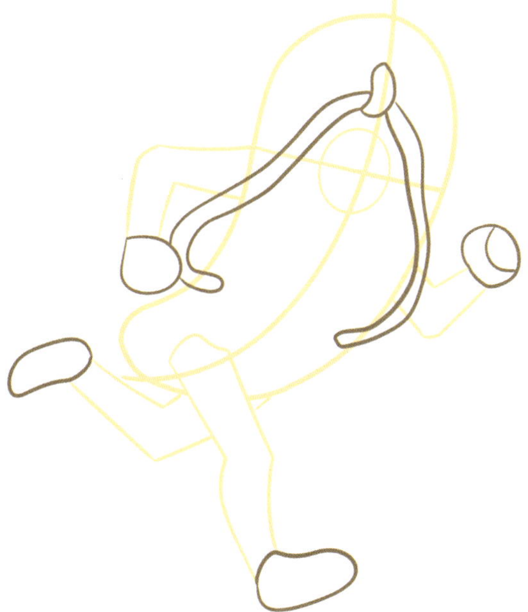

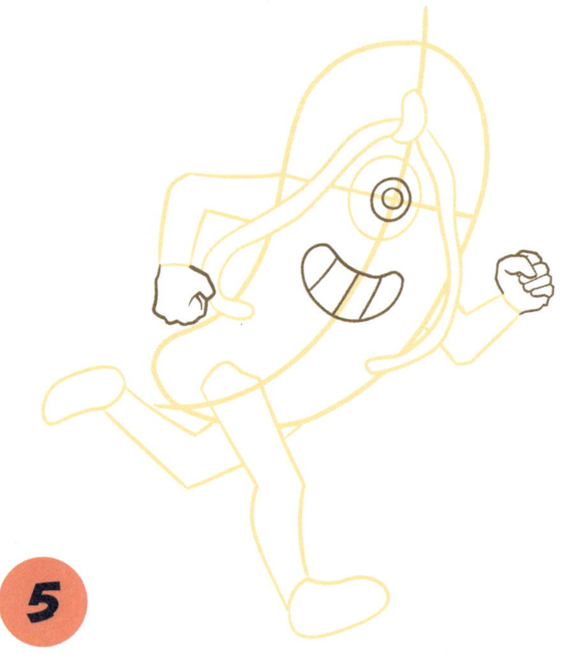

4

Draw a curved bean shape to create a big, cartoonish grin for this comical character. Add smaller circles to the eye for its pupil and iris. Refine the shape of the hands and add the fingers.

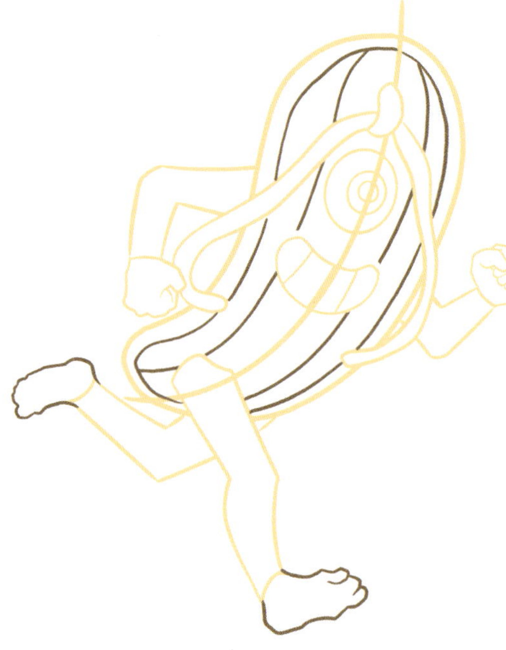

5

Zōri were traditionally made from woven rice straw, so we should indicate that in the drawing. Start by drawing the inner rim of the sandal around the inside of the body. Add two more vertical lines, similar to the center line. Refine the feet by adding in heels and bumps to indicate toes.

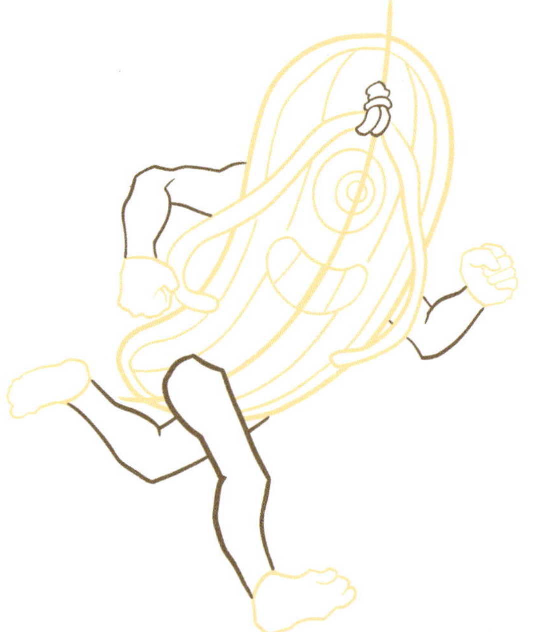

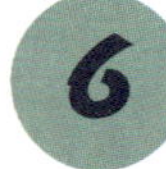

6

Refine the shapes of the arms and legs, adding bulges to indicate muscles, since this yōkai is a runner. With curved lines, form the knot of the hanao.

7

With the lines in the body from step 5 as a guide, use broken diagonal lines to create a woven pattern. Note how the columns go in opposing directions. Refine the shapes of the hanao straps.

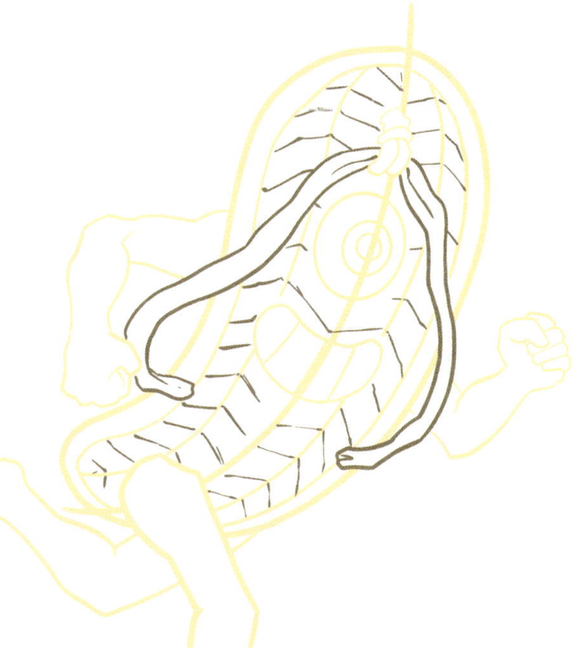

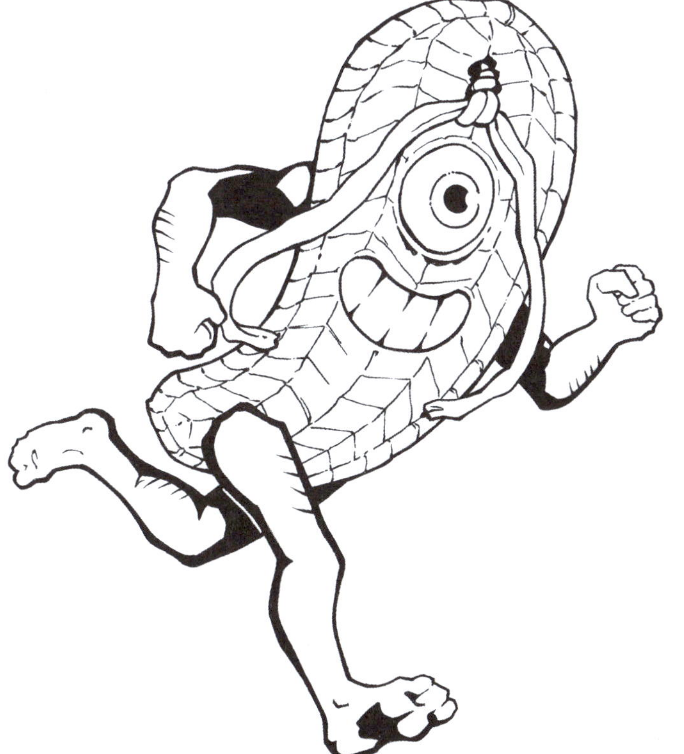

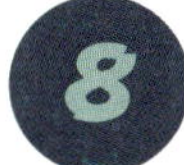

8

Using more broken diagonal lines, draw the woven texture in the rim going around the zōri. To finish, thicken the major outlines of the zōri body and its limbs.

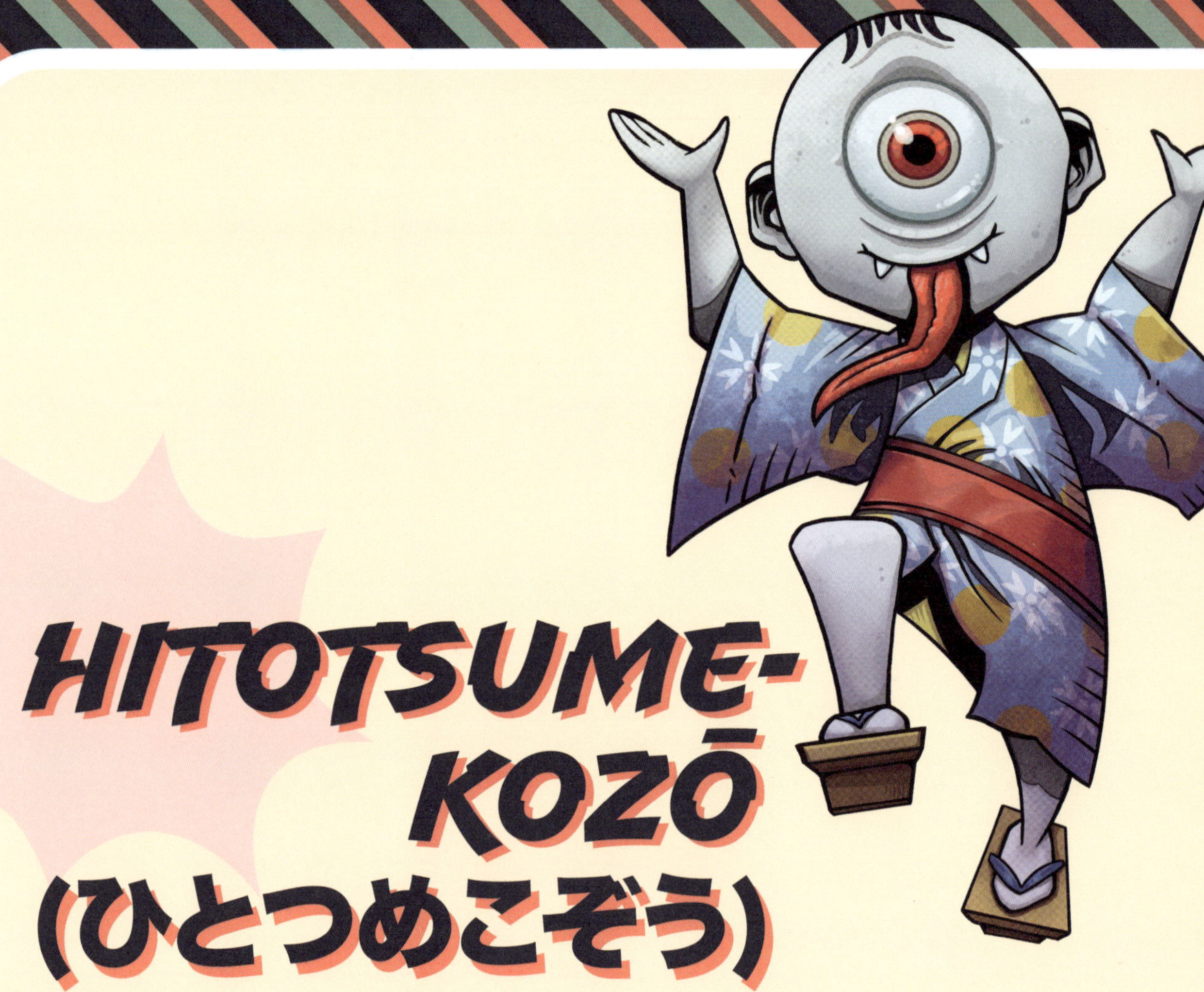

HITOTSUME-KOZŌ
(ひとつめこぞう)

The hitotsume-kozō is a harmless, small, childlike yōkai with a single large eye in the center of its face and sometimes a long tongue. They often approach people on the street pretending to be normal children, then turn to show their bizarre appearance, causing people to faint. In traditional yōkai art, hitotsume-kozō are often depicted wearing the robes of a monk and used as comedic relief.

Similar to the tanuki, this yōkai will be an exercise in using shapes to build up a character.

1

Start with a curved line of action. Draw a circle for the head and a curved box for the body, following the flow of the line of action.

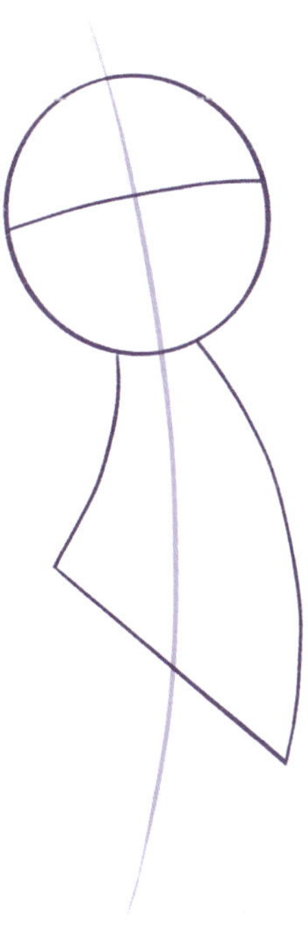

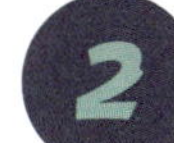

2

Draw lines for the tops of the arms. Hanging from these lines, draw the sleeve shapes on either side of the body.

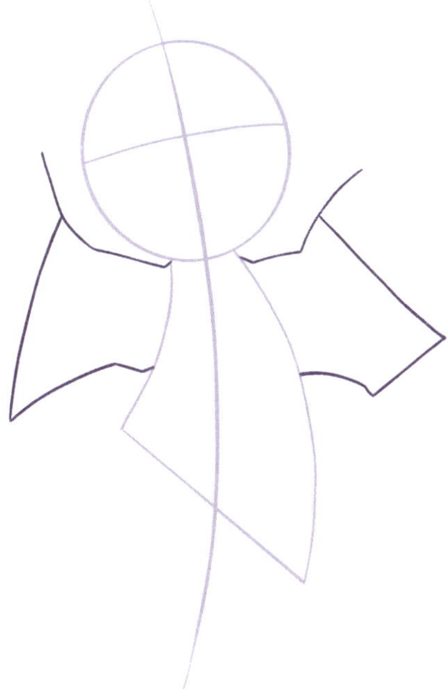

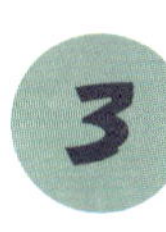

3

On the bottom of the figure, draw the legs. To show that the figure is dancing, one leg is kicked back, while the other is lifted toward us.

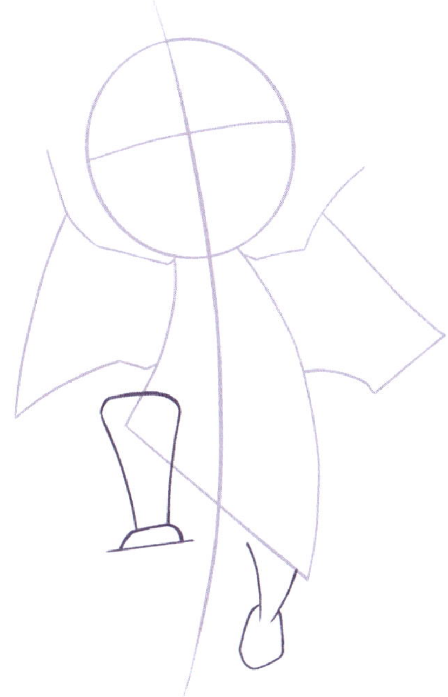

4

Building off the feet shapes from step 3, draw the hitotsume-kozō's *geta*, traditional Japanese sandals, using stacked box shapes. Follow the curves of the arms to finish drawing in the shape of the hands.

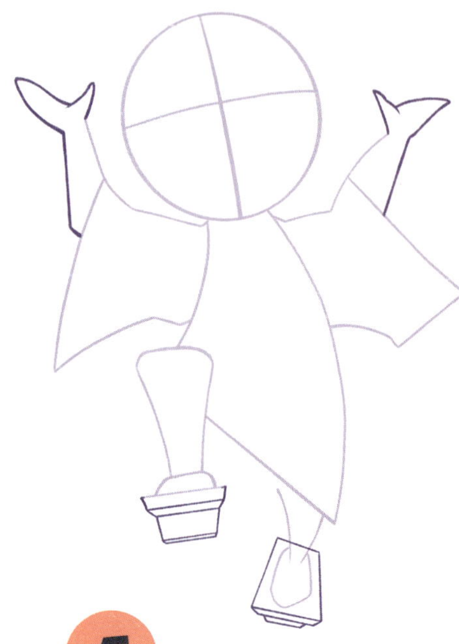

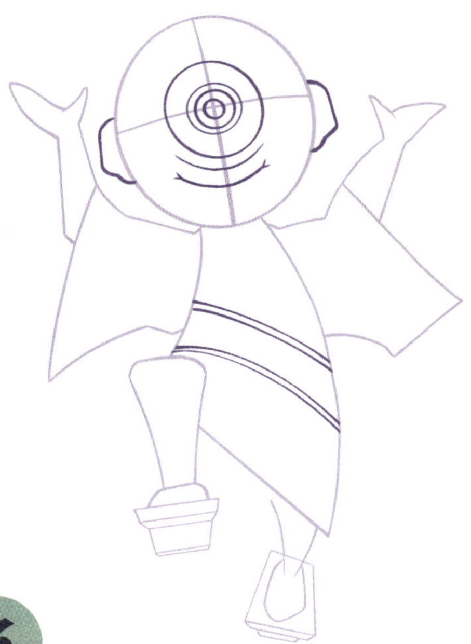

5

Draw the eye with concentric circles. Using similar curves, add the ears, mouth, and *obi* sash going across the body.

6

Refine the face. Add details such as the long sweeping tongue, rounded fangs, and the shapes of the inner ear. Draw the wrinkle at the top of the hitotsume-kozō's head and lines to indicate the fingers on his hands.

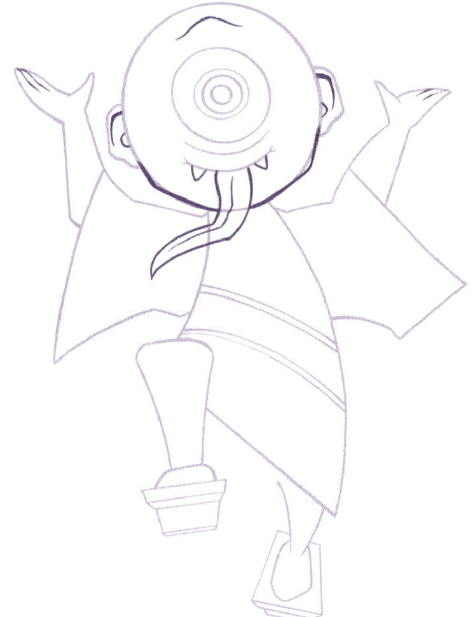

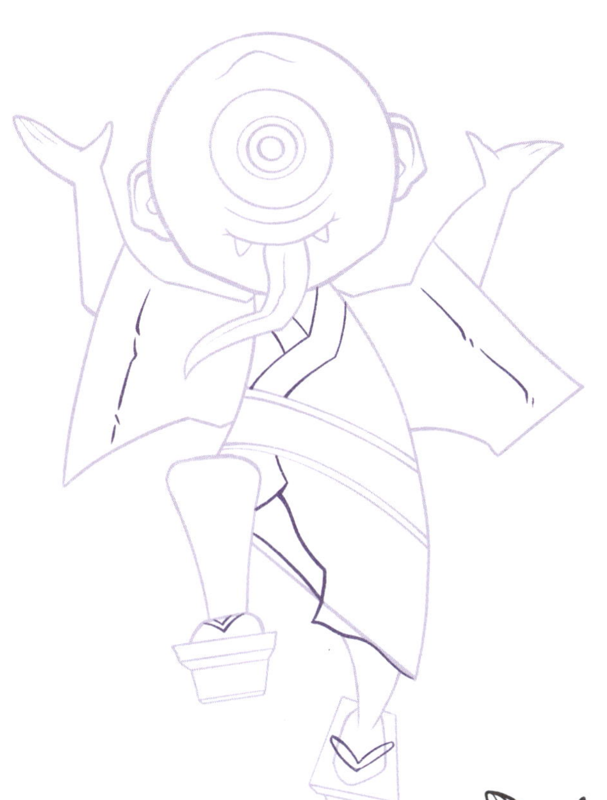

Starting at the obi, draw the center folds of the kimono, including the wide collar. Add the sleeve hems and thongs of the sandals.

To finish your hitotsume-kozō, draw short, wide hairs on the top of its head. If you would like to, draw wrinkles into the armpit areas to help push his chest forward.

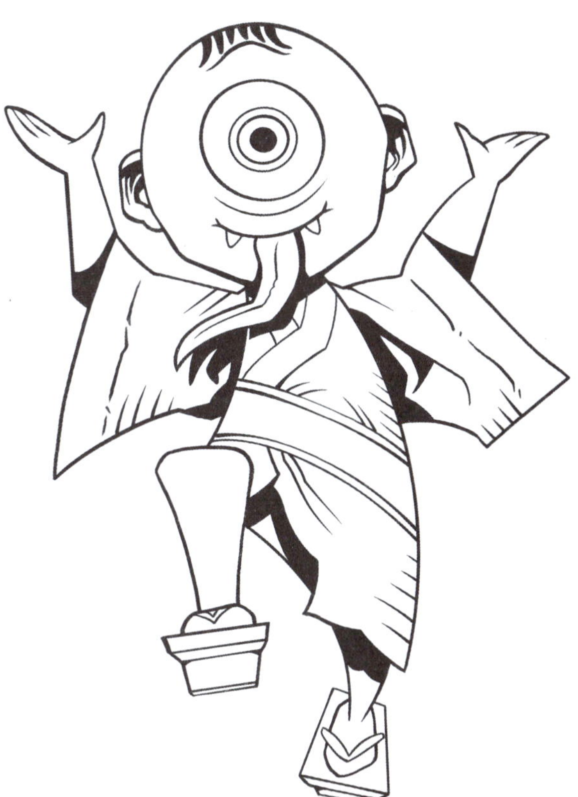

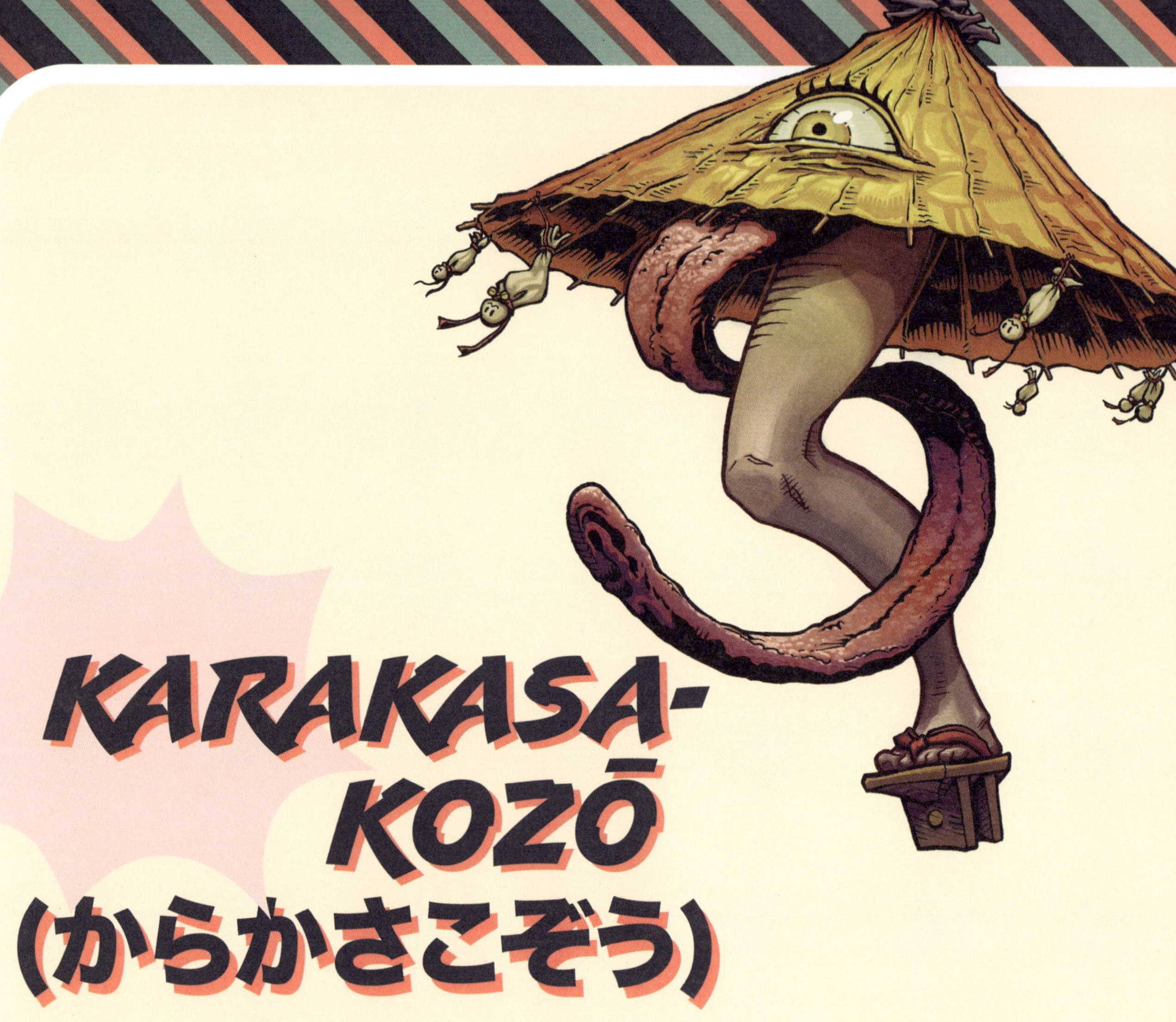

KARAKASA-KOZŌ (からかさこぞう)

The karakasa-kozō is another type of tsukumogami yōkai. It is born from a traditional oil-paper umbrella. The karakasa-kozō hops around on its single leg seeking to surprise and startle its victims, possibly giving them a big lick with its long tongue. Often seen with the chōchin-obake (page 22), it shares a similar lighthearted personality. This yōkai, like its appearance, is silly in nature.

While there are no particular legends about this yōkai, it has appeared in artwork since 1625. This yōkai has different variations; some have arms and/or a mouth in the torn paper.

Draw a curved line of action. Using it as a center point, draw the top of a wide triangle, which will serve as the top of the *kasa* (Japanese for "umbrella"). Connect the bottom points of the triangle with a tilted circle, indicating the open bottom of the kasa.

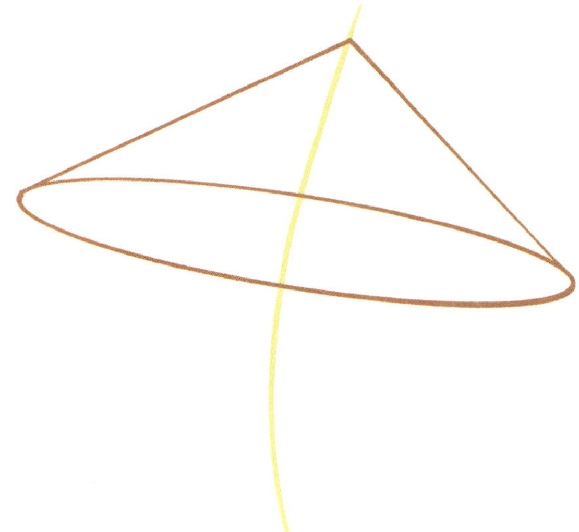

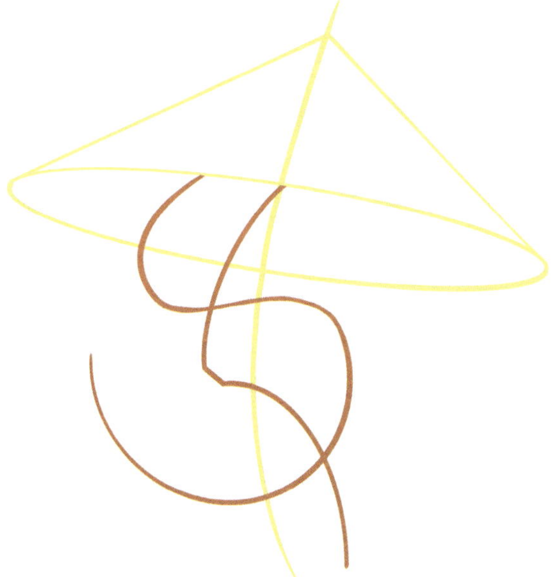

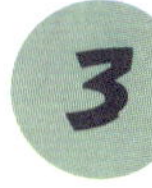

Next, draw lines of action for the tongue and leg, aiming to capture the hopping motion of the leg and of the tongue whipping around.

To complete the foundation, draw a half circle and lower lid for where the eyeball will go. Draw curved lines hanging off the end of the kasa.

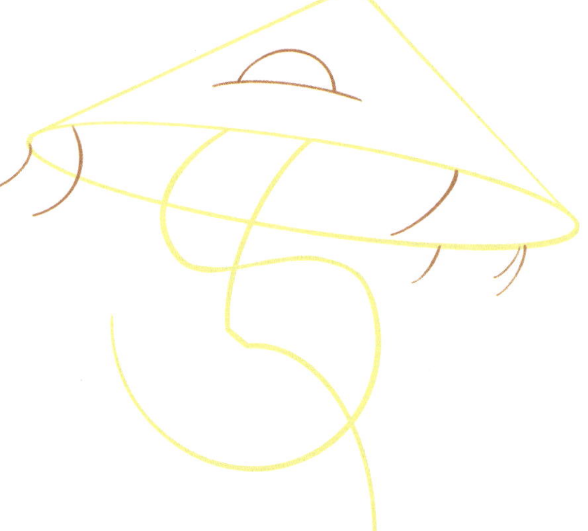

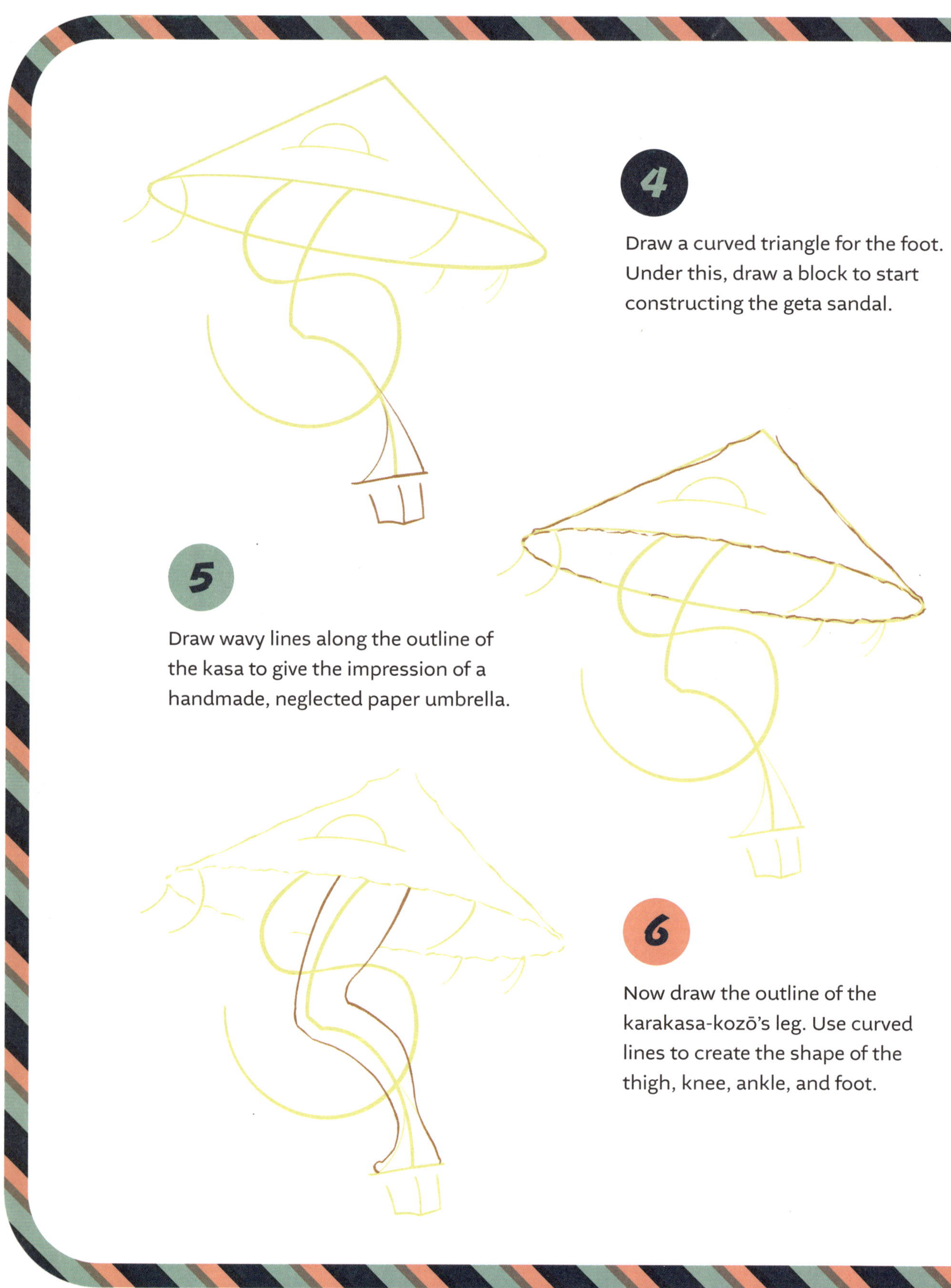

4

Draw a curved triangle for the foot. Under this, draw a block to start constructing the geta sandal.

5

Draw wavy lines along the outline of the kasa to give the impression of a handmade, neglected paper umbrella.

6

Now draw the outline of the karakasa-kozō's leg. Use curved lines to create the shape of the thigh, knee, ankle, and foot.

7

Teru teru bōzu are traditional dolls to ward off rain and will be adorning the kasa. They will be hanging upside down to attract rain instead, so that the karakasa-kozō can go out and stalk people. Use smaller wavy lines to outline the bodies of the dolls and draw circles at the end to indicate their heads.

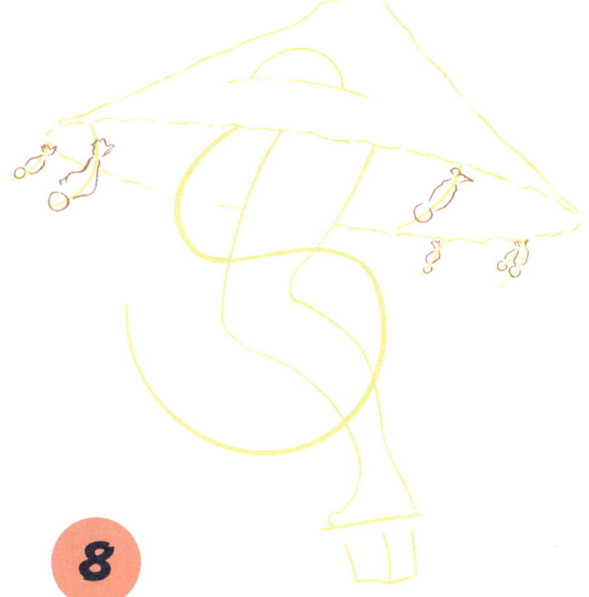

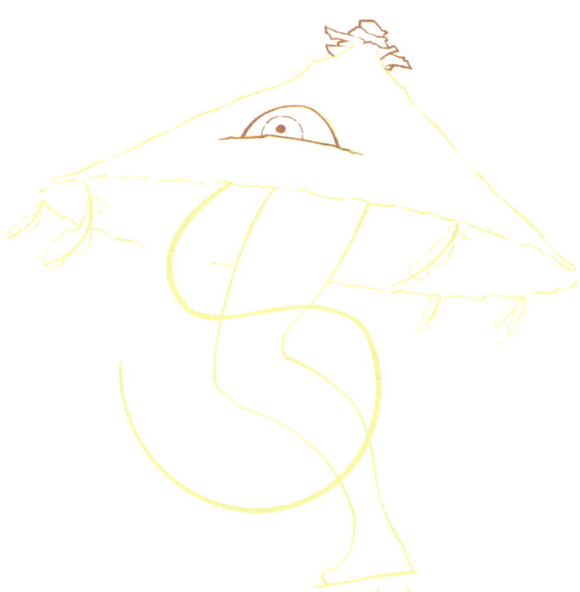

8

Add in details following the structure we have built so far. Starting at the top, draw the *zukami*, a piece of paper that covers the top of the kasa. Add the pupil and iris of the karakasa-kozō's large eye.

9

Use curved lines to create the uneven, wavy body of the tongue. Notice how it swings behind, then in front of the leg.

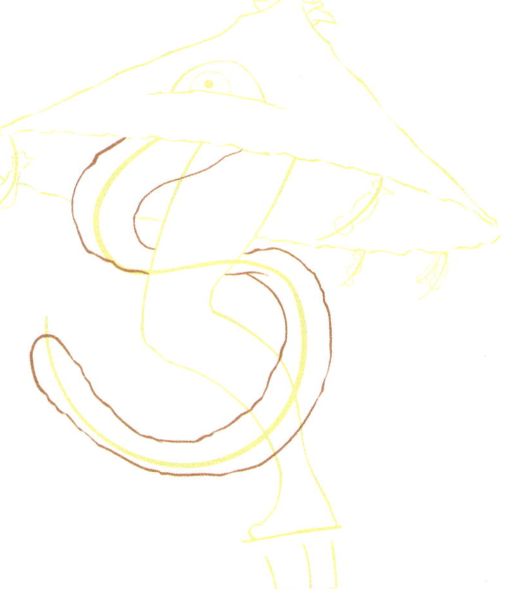

Draw small, rectangular sticks around the edge of the kasa to indicate the ends of the kasa's bamboo ribs poking out.

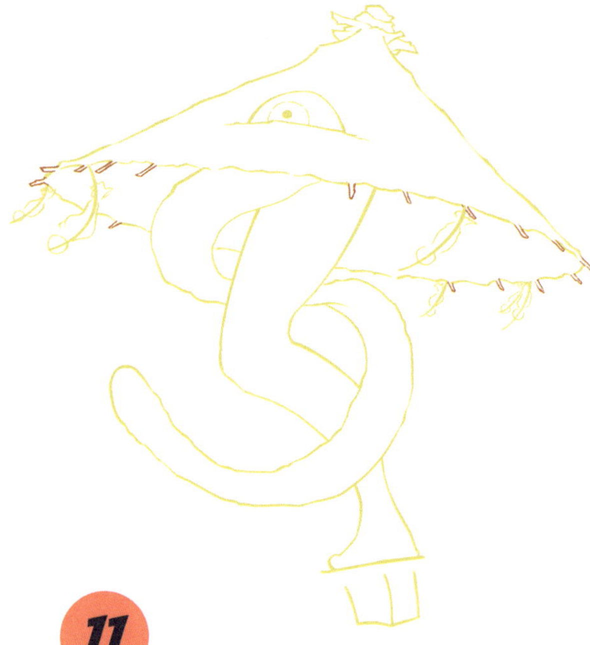

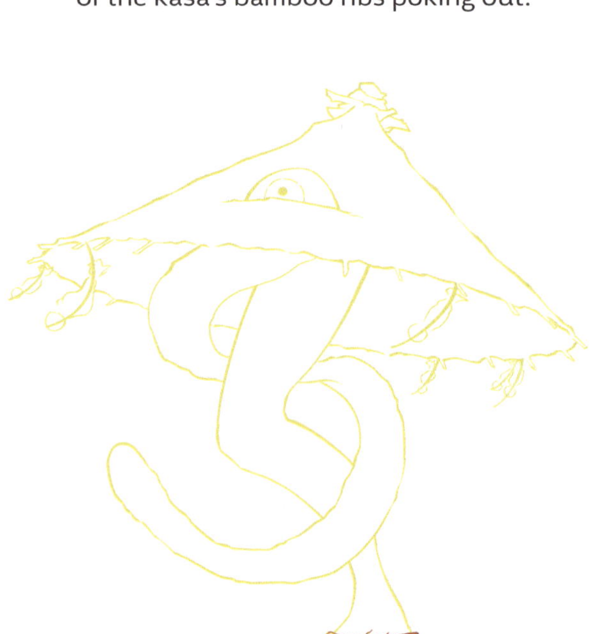

To create the karakasa-kozō's geta, draw a flat thin box under the foot for the sole and then two thin vertical boxes to support the sole.

Begin adding details: Use broken, uneven lines to draw the rib lines of the kasa, extending from the top center and radiating around its body. Add in the ropes tying the teru teru bōzu to the umbrella. Draw the eyelashes and the strap of the geta.

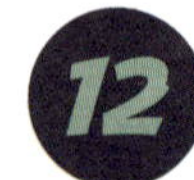

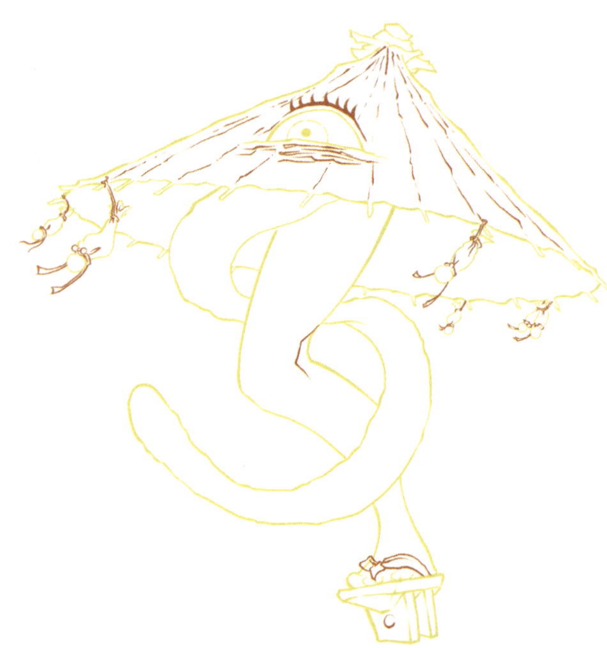

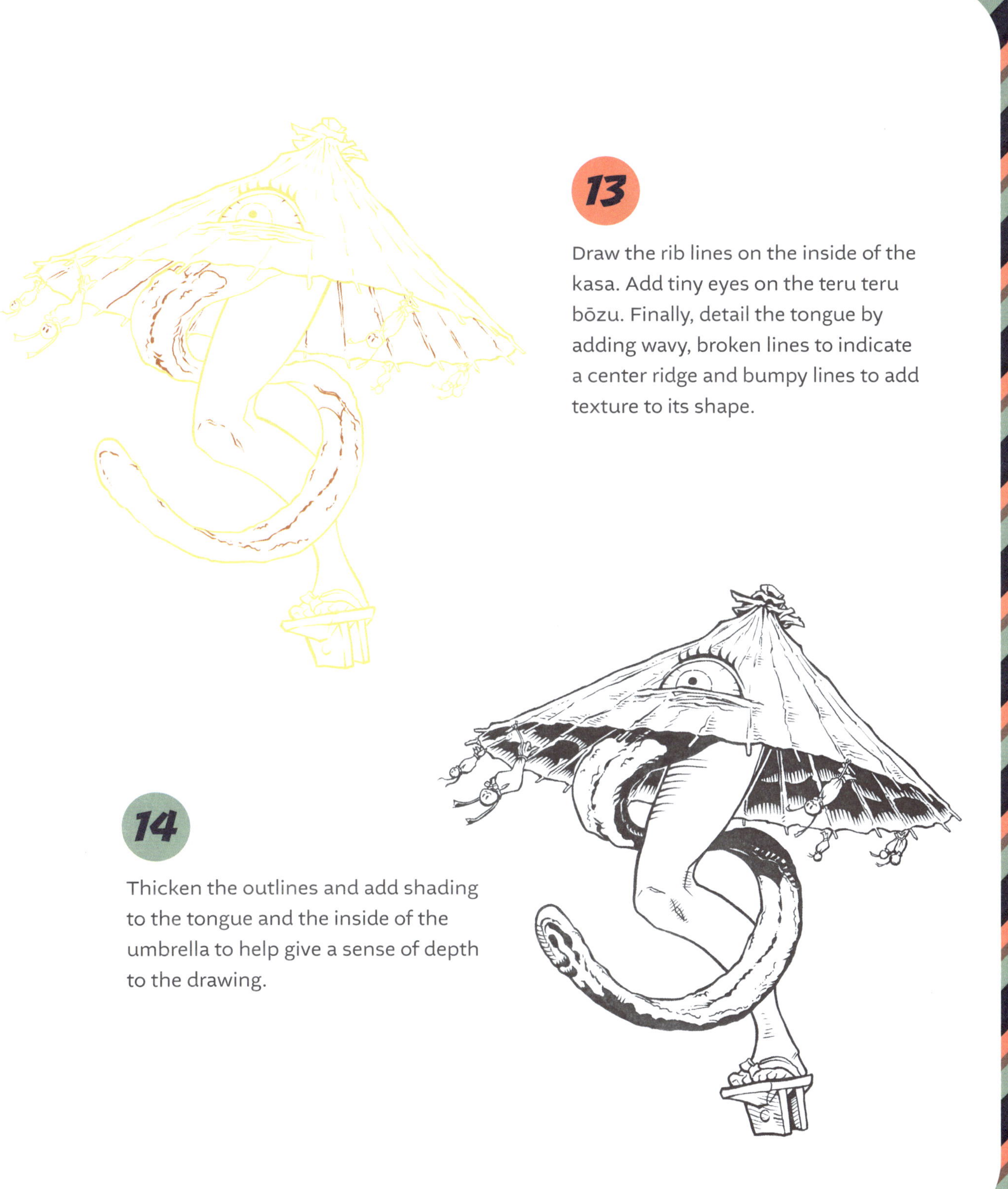

13

Draw the rib lines on the inside of the kasa. Add tiny eyes on the teru teru bōzu. Finally, detail the tongue by adding wavy, broken lines to indicate a center ridge and bumpy lines to add texture to its shape.

14

Thicken the outlines and add shading to the tongue and the inside of the umbrella to help give a sense of depth to the drawing.

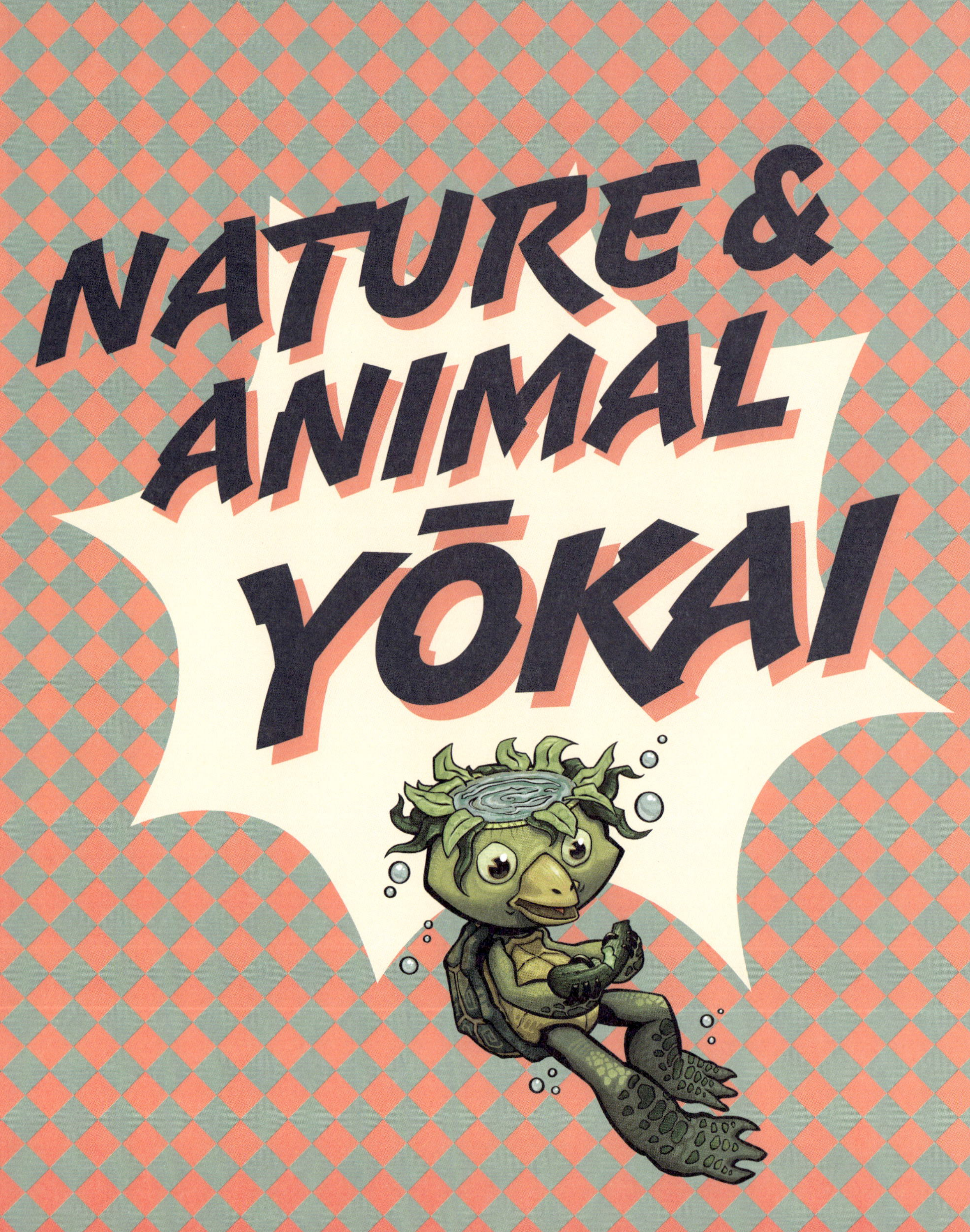

NATURE &
ANIMAL
YŌKAI

From mist-shrouded mountains to old-growth forests and out to the mighty seas, Japan is a country of rugged natural beauty with deep cultural connections to nature and the animals that live there. These values are rooted in the Shinto beliefs that all plants, animals, and objects have a spirit, and the even-older practices of nature worship. It is no surprise, then, that in the wide-ranging world of yōkai, many of these creatures originate from everyday animals and plants, or from aspects of nature come to life. In this section we will draw a few of these mysterious yōkai born from the natural world.

KODAMA
（こだま）

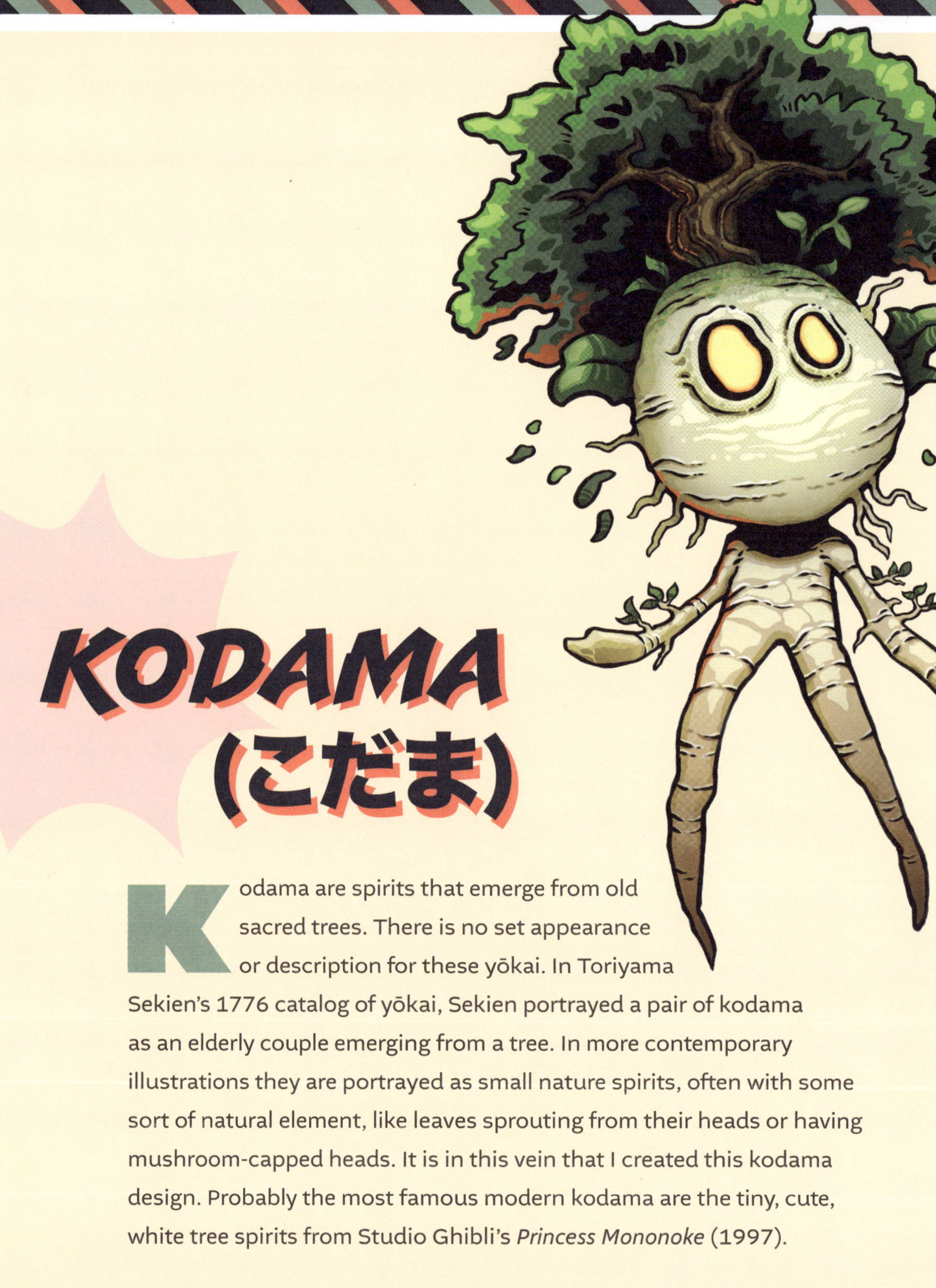

Kodama are spirits that emerge from old sacred trees. There is no set appearance or description for these yōkai. In Toriyama Sekien's 1776 catalog of yōkai, Sekien portrayed a pair of kodama as an elderly couple emerging from a tree. In more contemporary illustrations they are portrayed as small nature spirits, often with some sort of natural element, like leaves sprouting from their heads or having mushroom-capped heads. It is in this vein that I created this kodama design. Probably the most famous modern kodama are the tiny, cute, white tree spirits from Studio Ghibli's *Princess Mononoke* (1997).

Draw a long, curved line of action. Add the circular head shape with center lines.

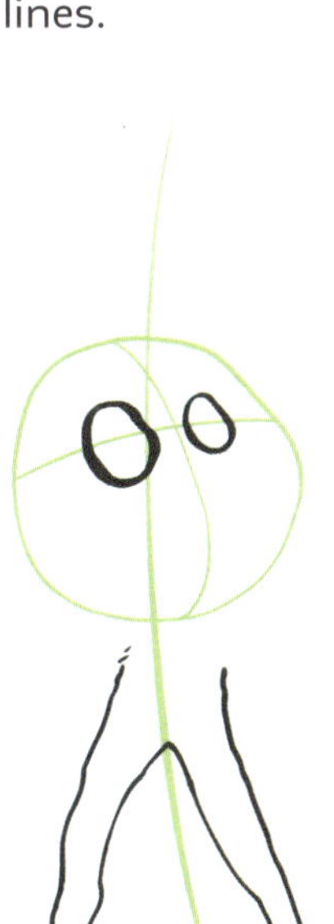

Draw the legs, using wavy lines to capture the shape of roots. Add the uneven eyes.

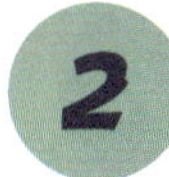

Draw the arms using the same wavy lines, but round the shapes at the end to give them the feel of hands. Add leaves to either side of the head to mimic ears.

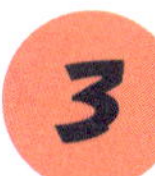
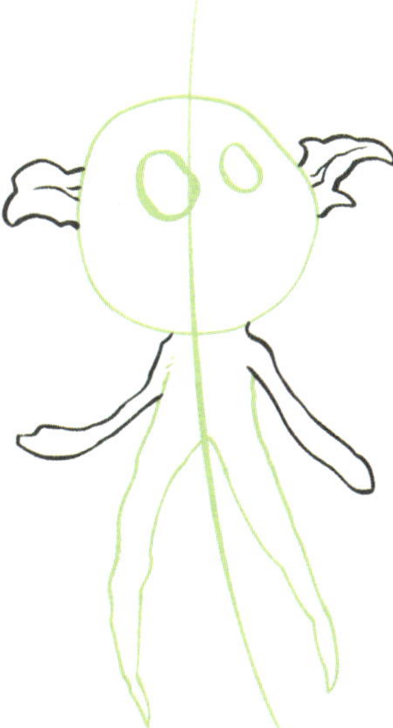

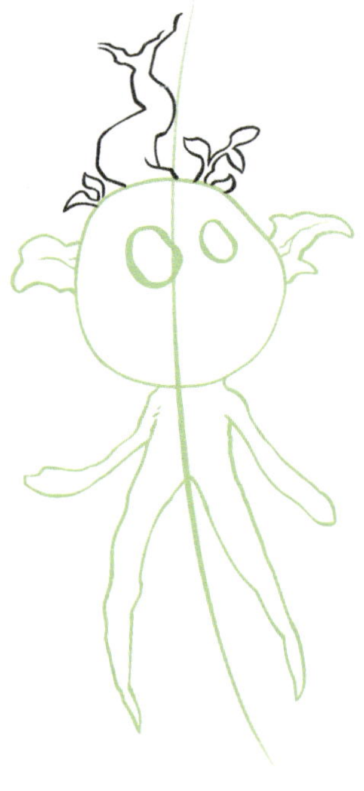

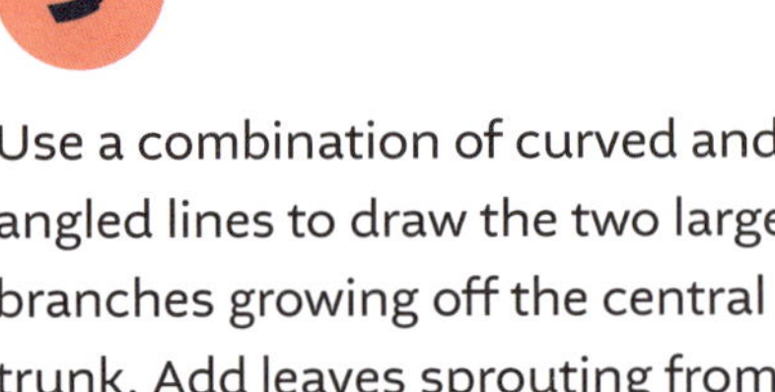

Start building the bonsai on the kodama's head by drawing in the bent central trunk of the tree, along with a few leaves on either side.

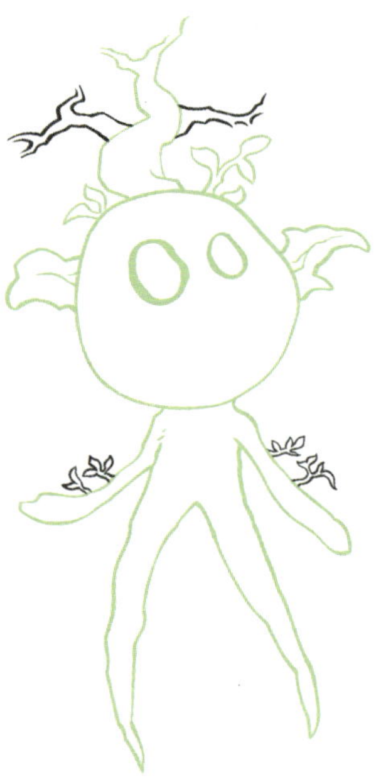

Use a combination of curved and angled lines to draw the two large branches growing off the central trunk. Add leaves sprouting from the tops of its arms.

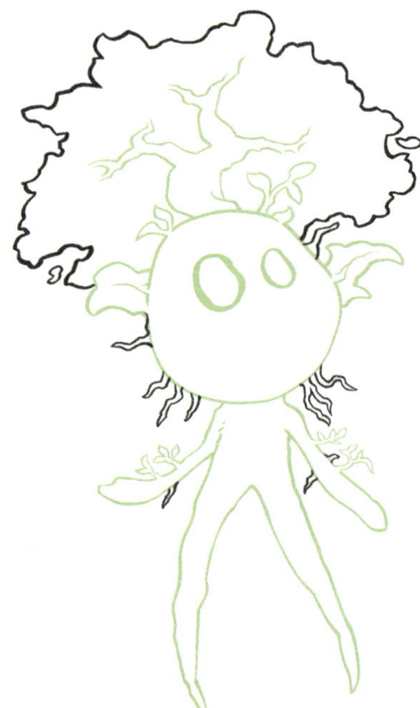

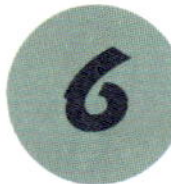

Draw in a large, broccoli-like shape around the tree and head to show the leaves of the bonsai. Add roots to the bottom of the face and arms using similar shapes to the legs.

7

Add another layer of leaves inside the broccoli-like shape from step 6. Draw leaves and petals floating in the air.

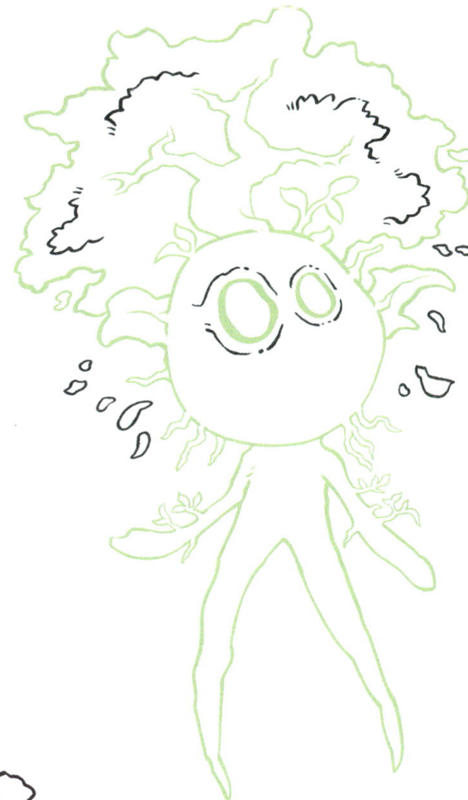

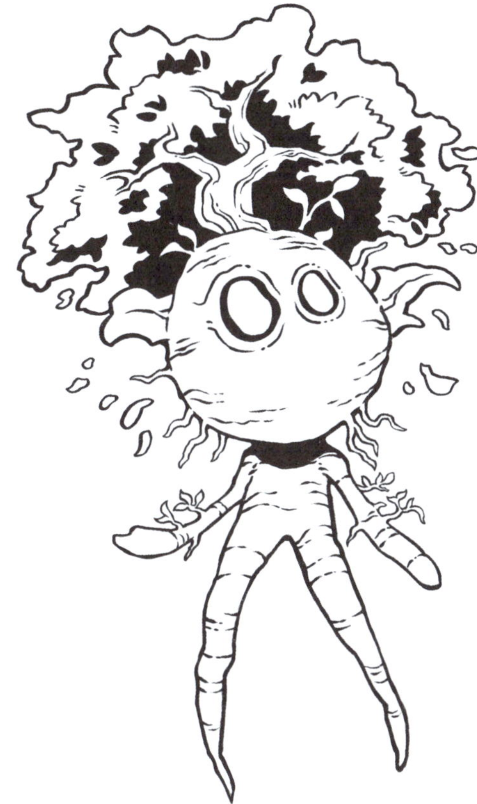

8

Finish off the kodama by giving its body a parsnip- or carrot-like texture. Do so by using short lines that follow the curve of the head, body, and arms.

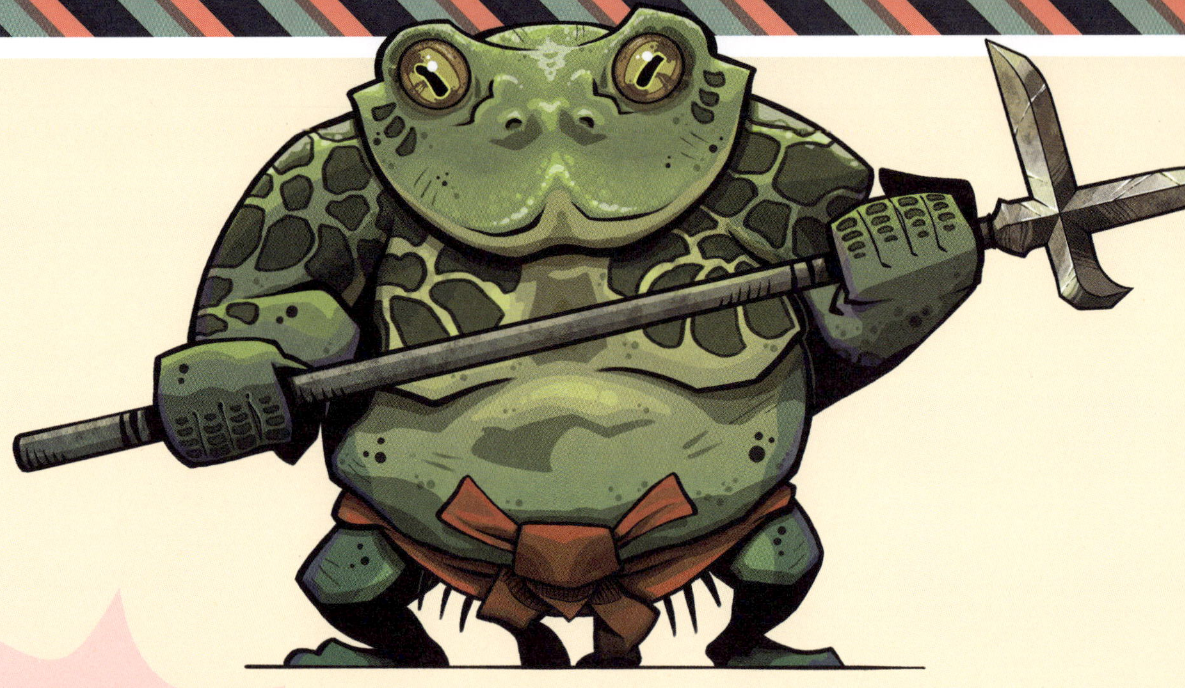

ŌGAMA
(おおがま)

The ōgama is a toad that has lived for one thousand years and, having reached such a venerable age, has attained supernatural powers. Ōgama continue to grow as they age, so the older the ōgama, the larger and more dangerous they are. The larger, ancient ōgama hunt not only bigger animals to eat, but also humans. They live deep in the mountains, in rivers, and in streams. These older, smarter toads have also been known to wield spears and be able to shapeshift, enabling them to disguise themselves as humans in order to stalk their prey.

Start with a vertical line of action and a horizontal line for the ground. Draw a tall, wide oval for our toad's body.

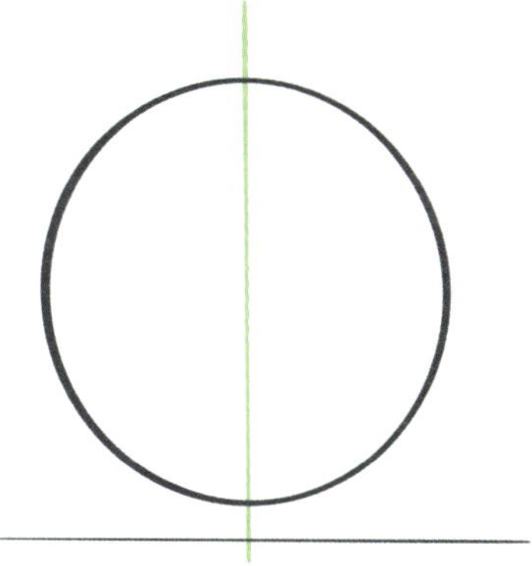

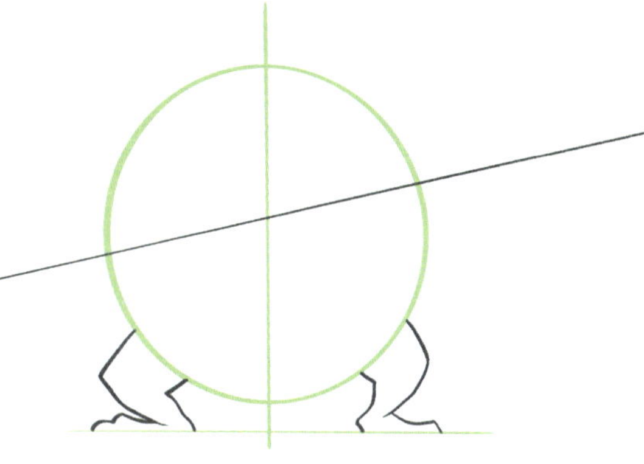

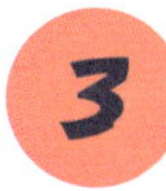

Add a long, diagonal line showing where the spear will go. Draw the short, bent legs of the toad.

Draw rounded boxes that will be the ōgama's hands holding the spear. Draw a large, curved shape for the head; take note of the notch for the mouth in the bottom center of this shape.

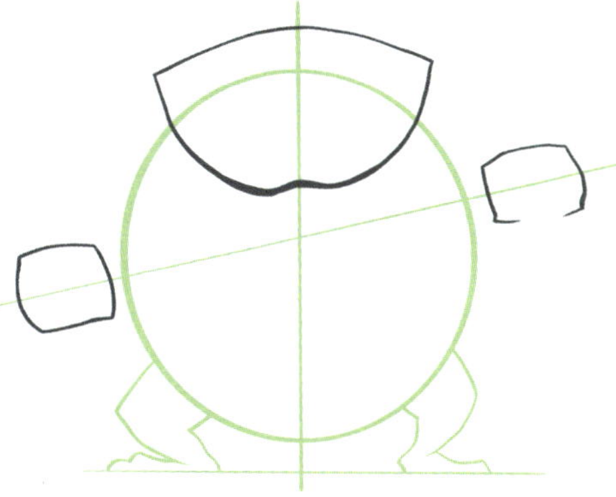

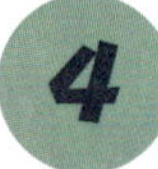

4

Use curved lines to draw the ōgama's large, strong arms, connecting the hand shapes to the body. Add angled ovals for the eyes and a rectangle for the spear shaft.

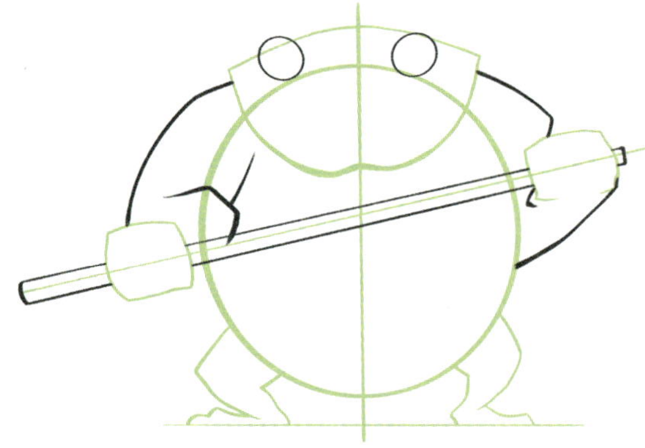

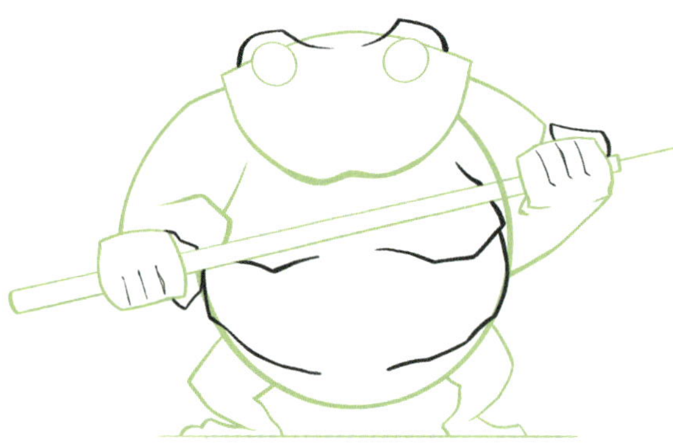

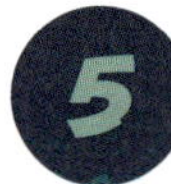

5

Refine the overall body shape by adding ridges above the eyes. Use these same ridged lines to indicate the chest. Draw curved lines to create the thumbs and to indicate fingers.

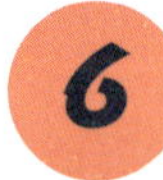

6

Add details to the face, such as the rectangular pupils that are a distinct feature of some toads. Draw the bow of the ōgama's waist wrap, which is inspired by the *mawashi* loincloth that sumo wrestlers wear. Create the spearhead using a pointed tube shape.

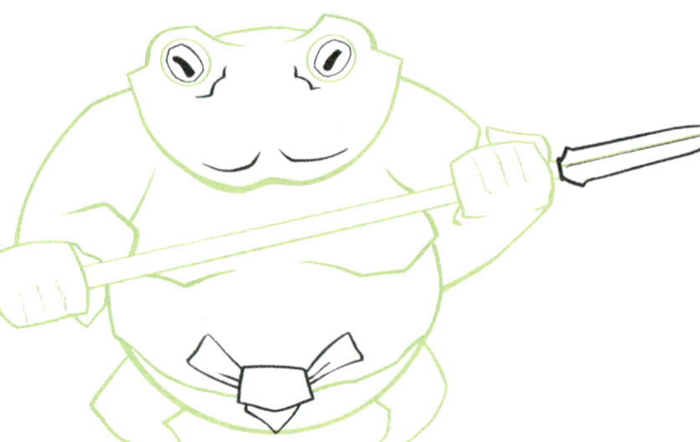

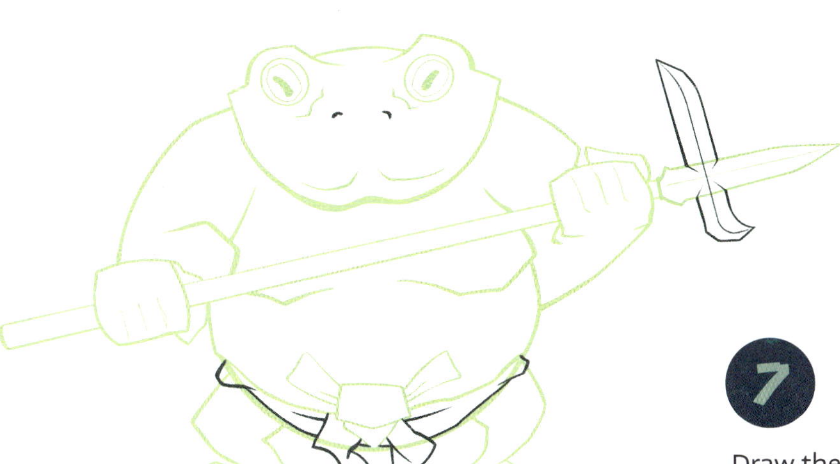

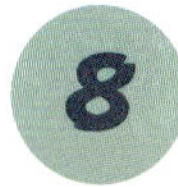

7

Draw the cross blade to the spearhead. This type of Japanese cross-bladed spear is called a *katakama yari*. Continue to build up the waist wrap and have the two ends hang to the ground, like the legs.

8

To finish, draw the spots of the toad however you wish to give yours a unique pattern. Here, the spots are drawn to loosely mimic the shapes you would see in traditional Japanese chest-tattoo designs.

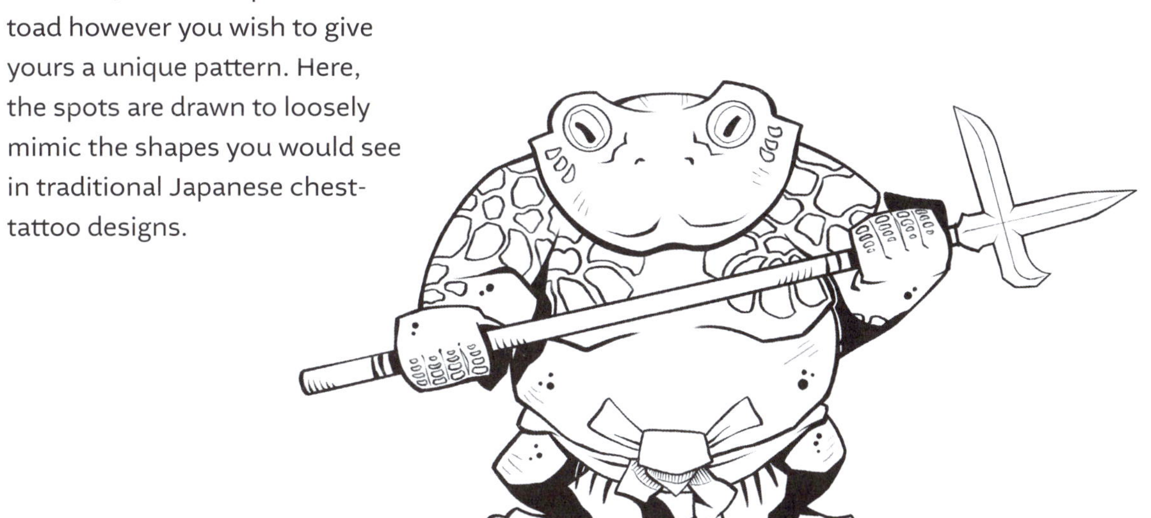

KAMA-ITACHI
(かまいたち)

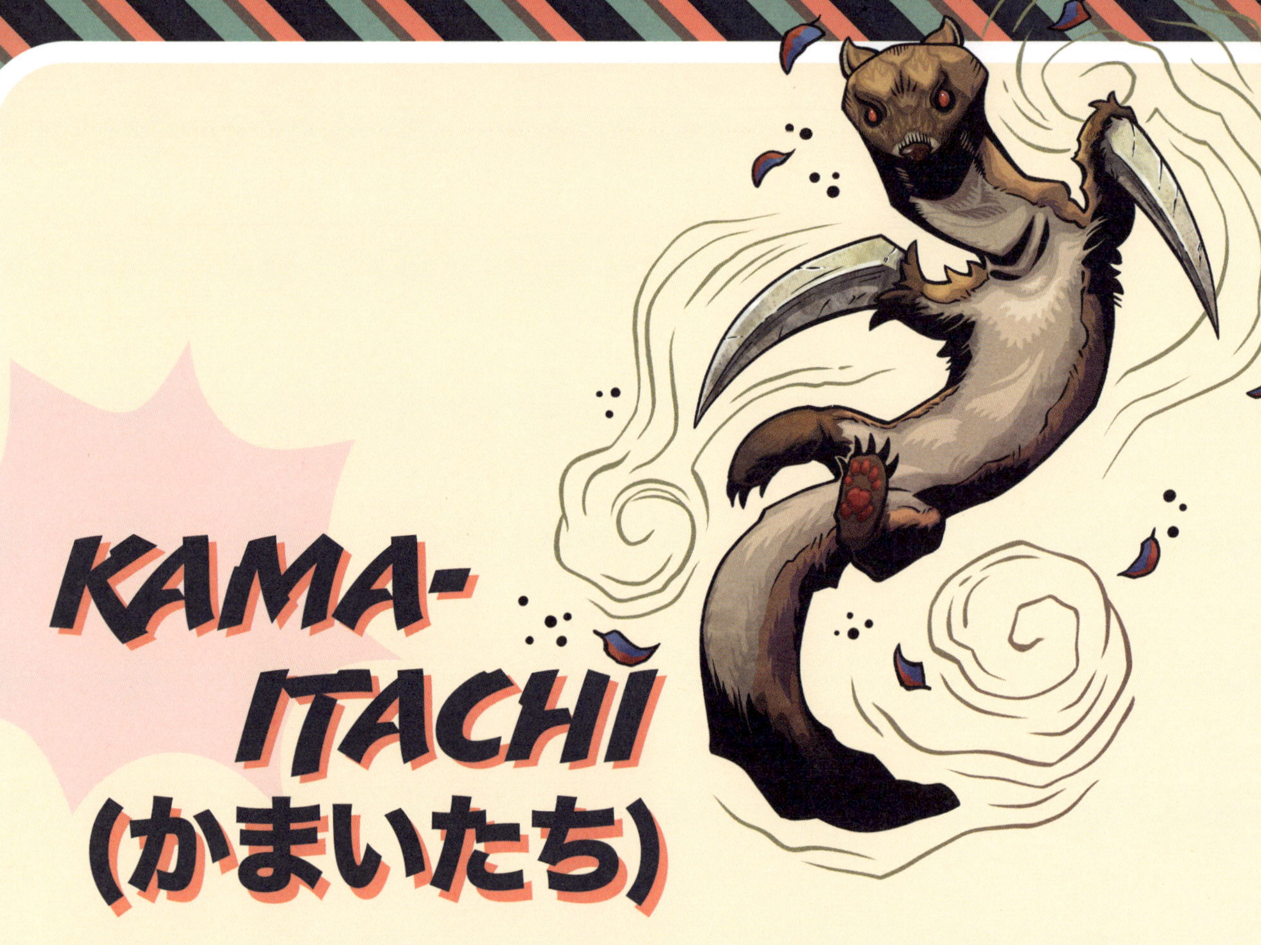

The kama-itachi was created to explain a phenomenon known throughout Japan: a sudden whirlwind kicks up, resulting in small cuts along the victims' legs and shins. This is the kama-itachi attacking. Visually, this yōkai is based on a real animal: the Japanese weasel. *Kama* means "sickle" (hence the large, sickle-like claws on their paws) and *itachi* means "weasel."

The kama-itachi are super quick and ride on powerful whirlwinds. When portrayed in art, they are usually shown in the center of these boisterous whirlwinds. In some regions, they are said to travel in groups of three. It is a very popular yōkai, especially in the entertainment and video-game industries; for example, the Pokémon Sneasel and its evolved form, Weavile, are believed to be inspired by this yōkai.

1

Start with a long, flowing line of action. Notice how it shifts direction at the base of the neck and tail. Draw a rounded, triangular head, and a long, bent oval for the body.

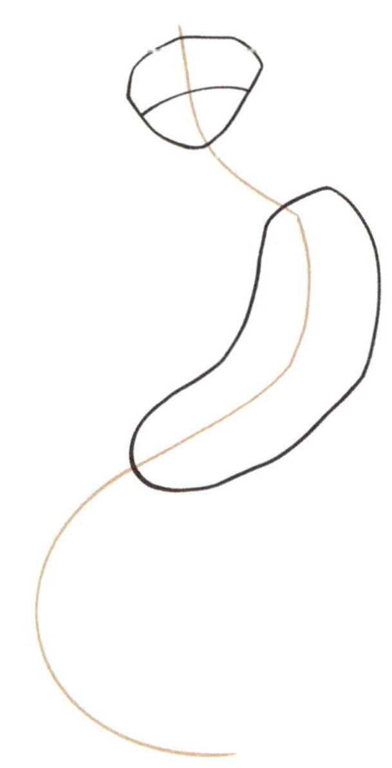

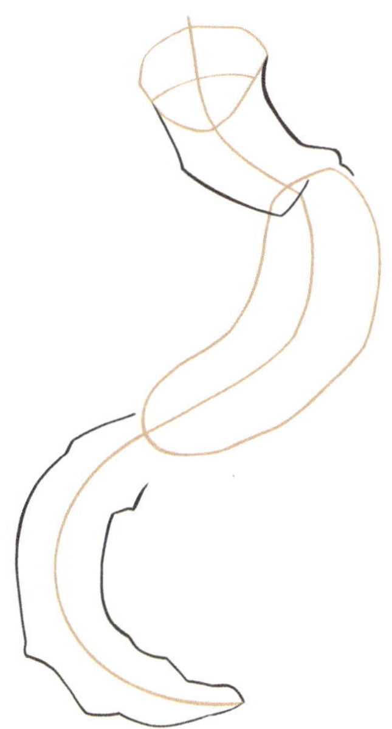

2

Following the line of action, draw the bent neck and the long, swooping tail.

3

Building off the body shape, add the upward curves of the arms, then the bent legs that follow the motion of the body.

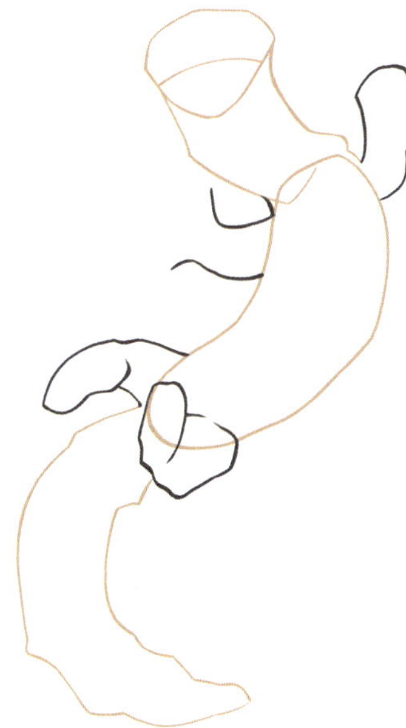

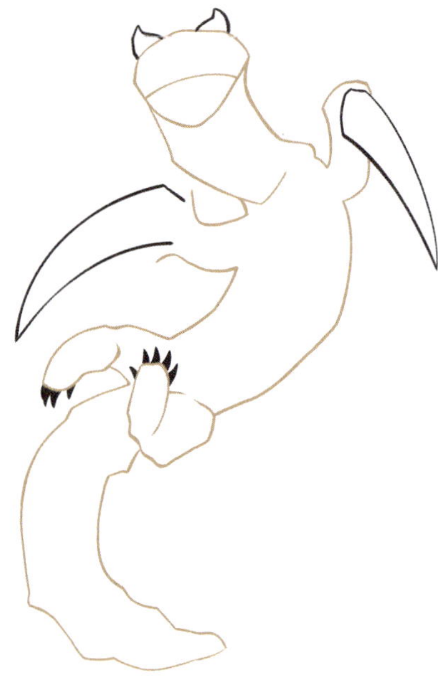

Use curved lines to draw the unique feature of this yōkai: the long, sharp sickle blades on its arms. Add the triangular ears and claws.

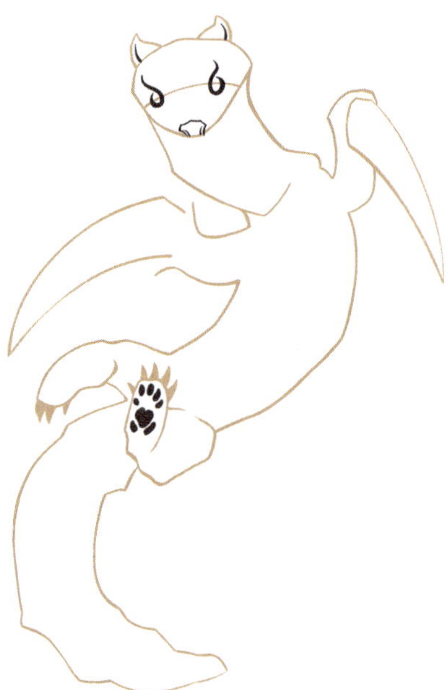

With the outer shape of the yōkai now established, move inside to add details: Draw the curves for the eyes and nose. Add the rounded toe beans to the kama-itachi's paw.

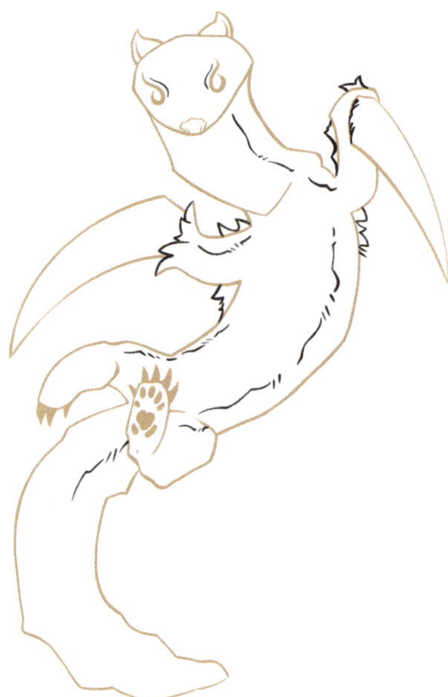

This step is all about fur. Refine the outline around the arms with triangular shapes to show its wild fur. Use broken lines inside the body shape to indicate the shorter fur along its belly and neck.

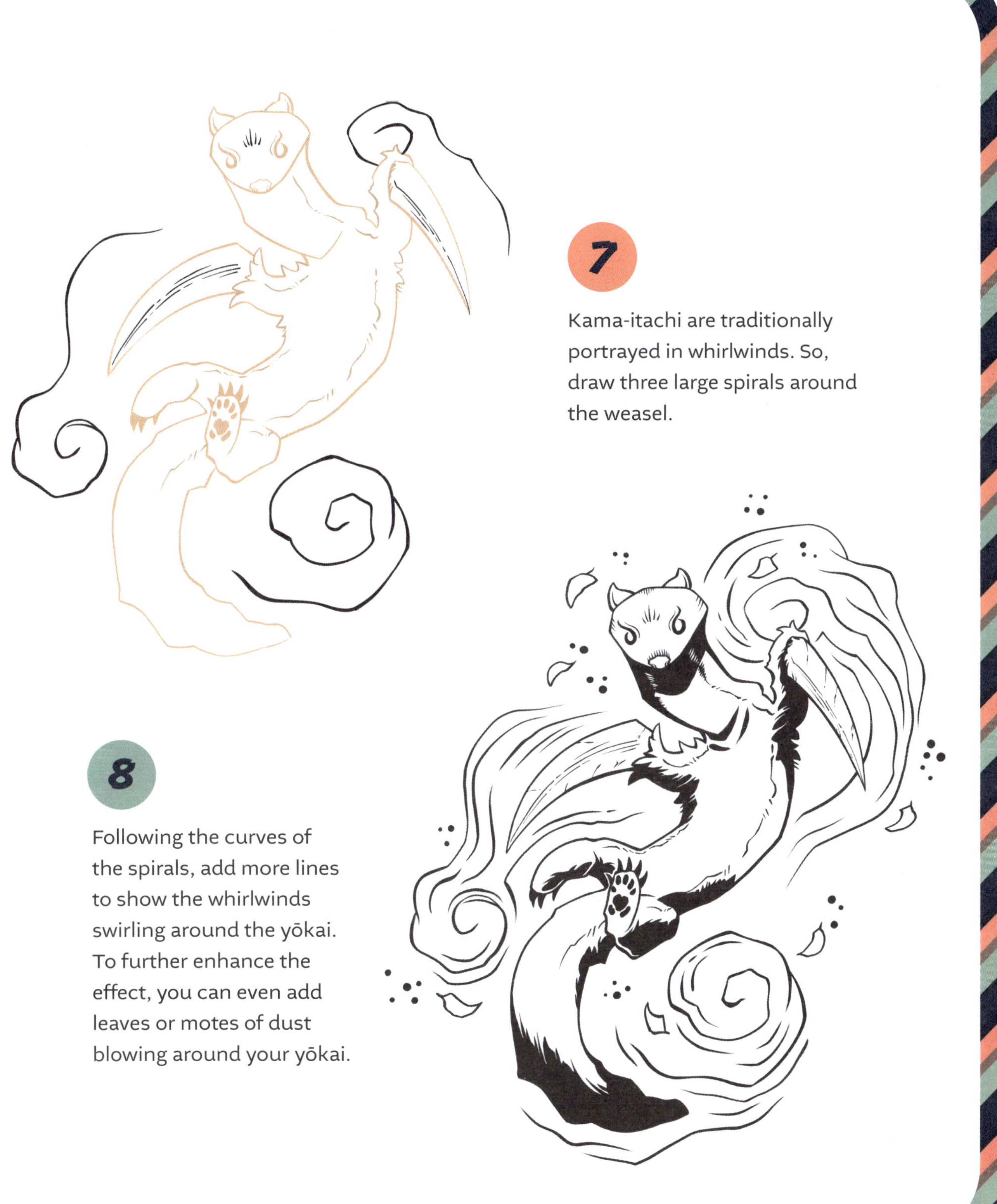

Kama-itachi are traditionally portrayed in whirlwinds. So, draw three large spirals around the weasel.

Following the curves of the spirals, add more lines to show the whirlwinds swirling around the yōkai. To further enhance the effect, you can even add leaves or motes of dust blowing around your yōkai.

NEKOMATA (ねこまた)

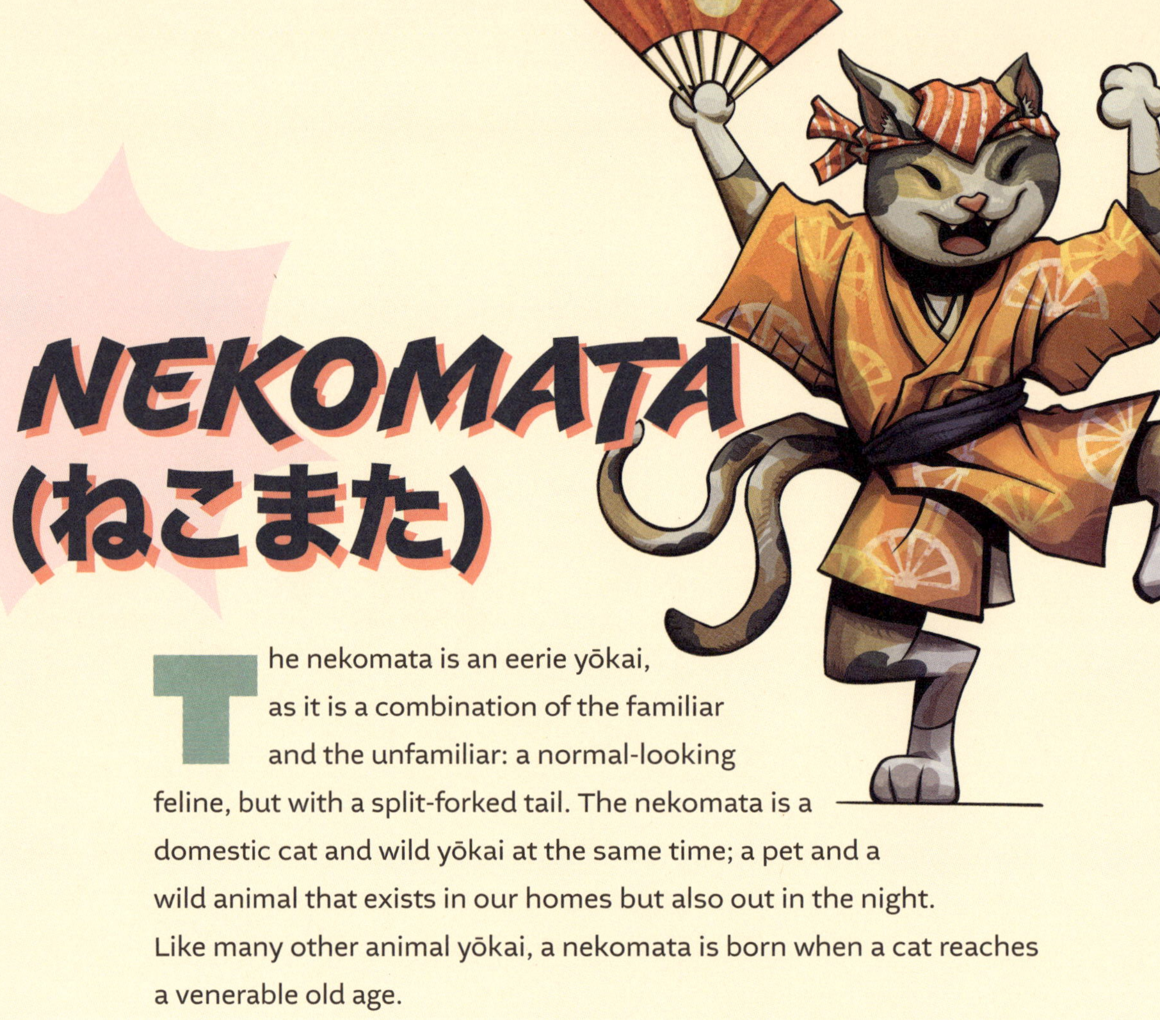

The nekomata is an eerie yōkai, as it is a combination of the familiar and the unfamiliar: a normal-looking feline, but with a split-forked tail. The nekomata is a domestic cat and wild yōkai at the same time; a pet and a wild animal that exists in our homes but also out in the night. Like many other animal yōkai, a nekomata is born when a cat reaches a venerable old age.

These feline yōkai can perform mischievous and even malicious acts, from using their shapeshifting abilities to trick people to killing their owner and controlling corpses. But in more lighthearted depictions (such as the one in this book), the nekomata can be seen dancing on two legs in yōkai night parades in Japanese picture scrolls called *hyakkiyagyō emaki*.

Since the nekomata is in a dancing pose, we will construct the nekomata using a process similar to the hitotsume-kozō (page 34).

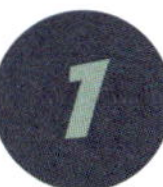

Start with a curved line of action. Draw an oval-like shape for the head. Then, use three curved rectangles to create the basic shape of the body: one following the line of action, and the other two shooting off to either side for the legs.

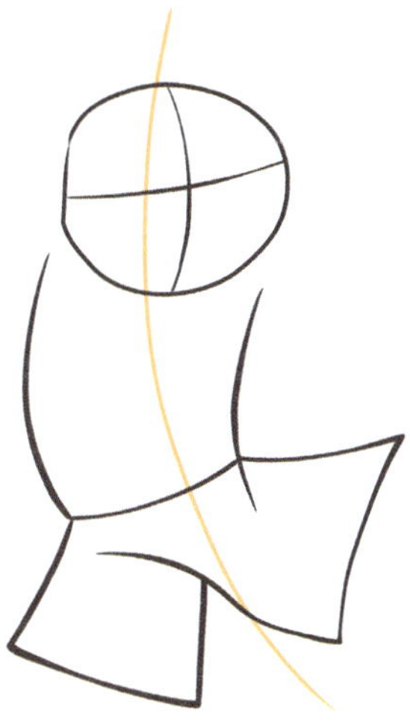

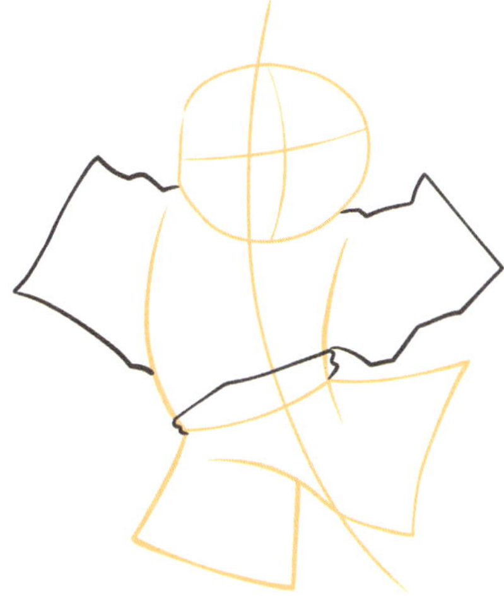

Draw the sleeve shapes on either side of the body. Add a line for the obi sash across the nekomata's waist.

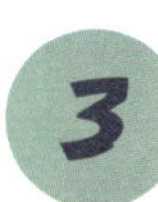

This step is all about tube shapes. Use these tube shapes to draw the arms and legs, as well as the nekomata's two long tails. Now we can start to see it dancing.

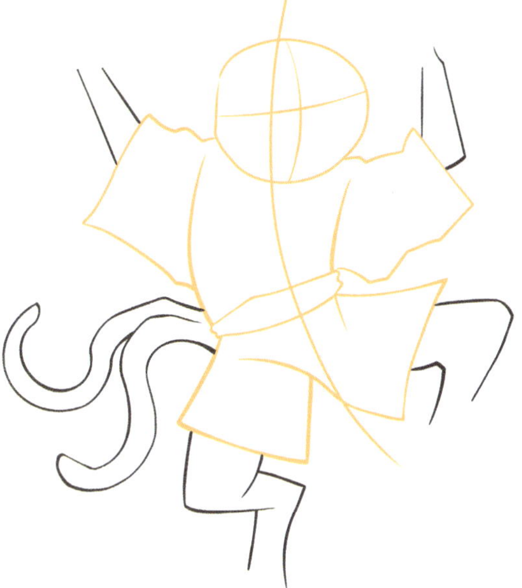

Draw rounded rectangles to create the feet and use a series of circles to draw the paws.

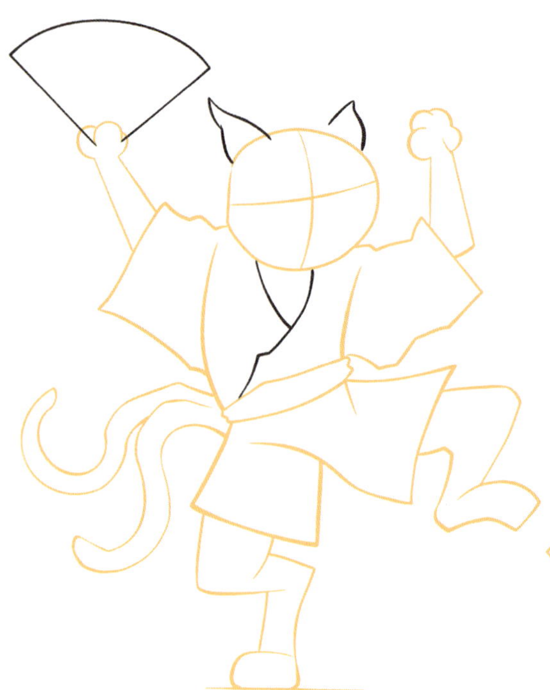

5

Use triangular shapes to refine the figure of this feline yōkai: its ears, fan, and, lastly, the collar of its kimono.

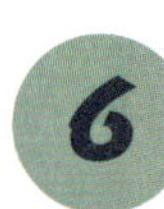

With all the major shapes established, we can add inner details. Start with curved dashes for the eyes and toes. Use angular shapes for its nose and handkerchief headwrap.

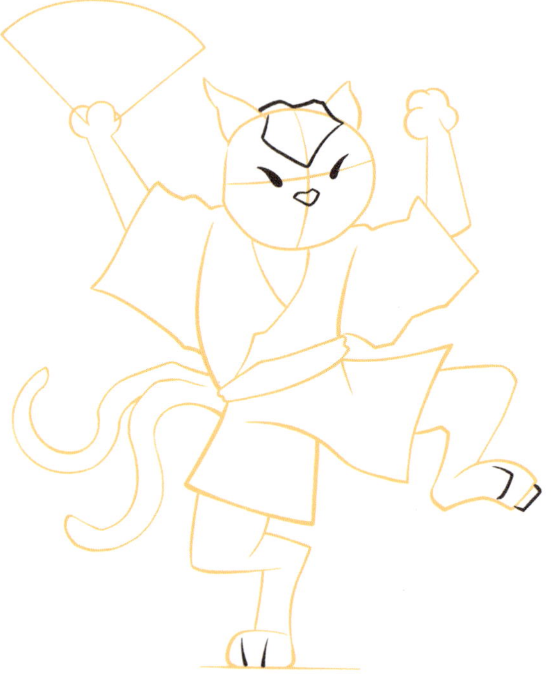

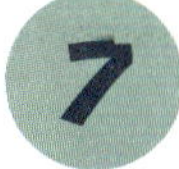

7

Complete the handkerchief around the head. Draw the mouth using a bouncy W line for the top lip and a U hanging open below. Add its teeth and tongue.

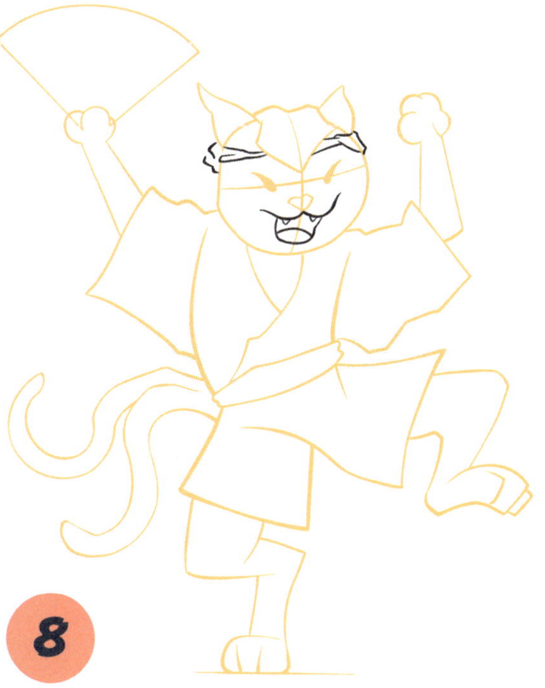

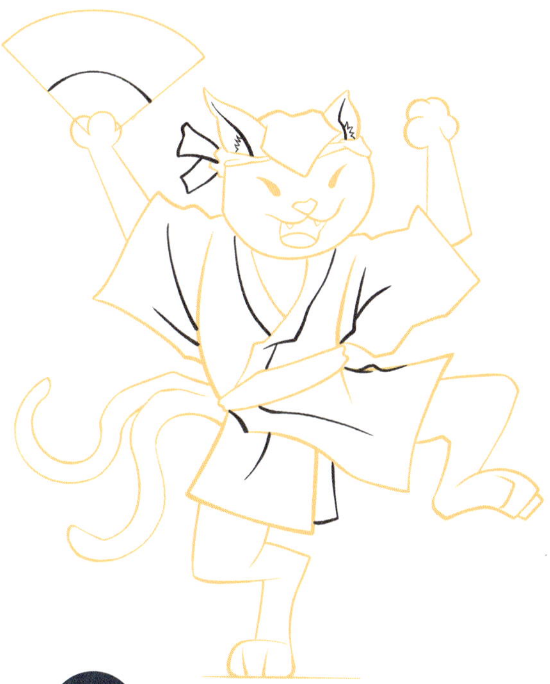

8

Continue to add details: wrinkles to the kimono, the little tufts of hair in the ears, the leaf of the fan, and the rectangular ends of the headwrap.

9

To finish, draw the ribs of the fan and whatever sort of decoration you would like on the fan. I used a simple circle design. Draw a round shadow under the head to help it stand out.

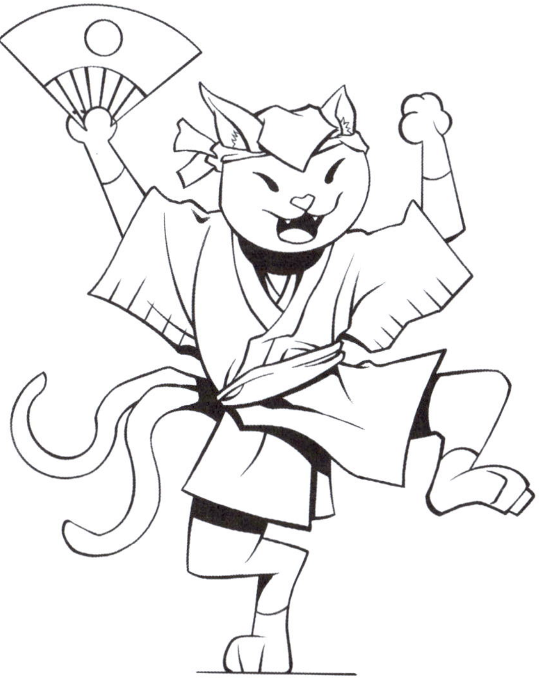

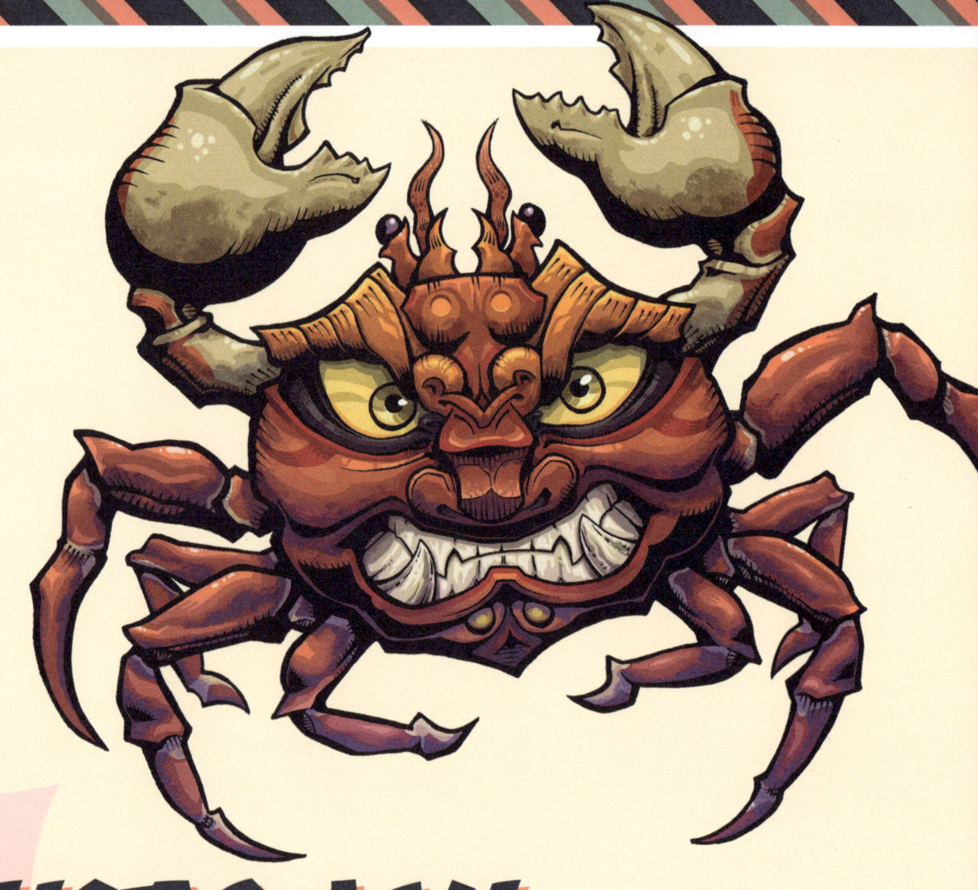

HEIKEGANI
(へいけがに)

Like the tanuki (page 18), this yōkai is based on an actual animal native to Japan. This species of crab has a shell that resembles a samurai's face. The fishermen of the area believe that these crabs are the reincarnations of warriors from the Heike clan, who were defeated in a land-ocean battle in the Seto Inland Sea. When looking at photos of the actual crabs, it's not hard to see why fishermen came to the conclusion that these crabs were possessed by the angry spirits of fallen samurai.

Draw a wide oval for the head and add the center lines. Draw lines of action for each of the crab's ten legs, extending from the body. Pay attention to where they bend and overlap.

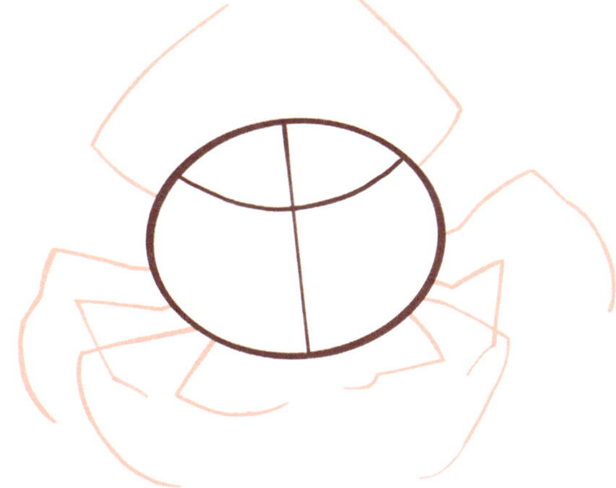

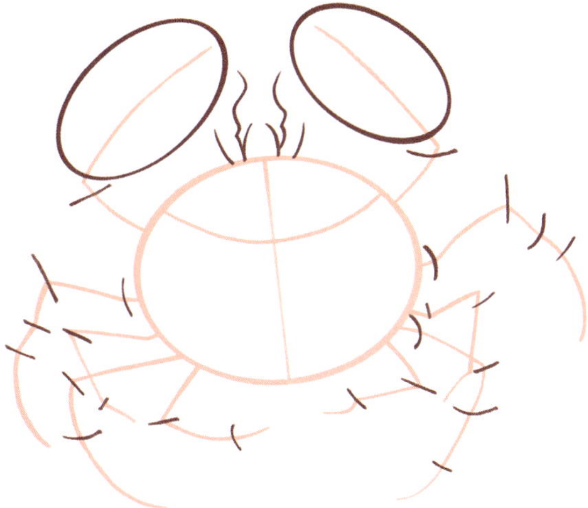

Draw large ovals for the claws. Add small line segments at each joint. Doing so will help you draw the legs. Draw curved lines coming out at the top of the heikegani's head. These are its antennae.

Using a series of scalloped lines, draw the outline of the crab's shell, paying attention to where the lines bend out and in. Add V shapes to create the claw openings. Use the center lines to help you draw the heikegani's mouth and the bottom of its nose.

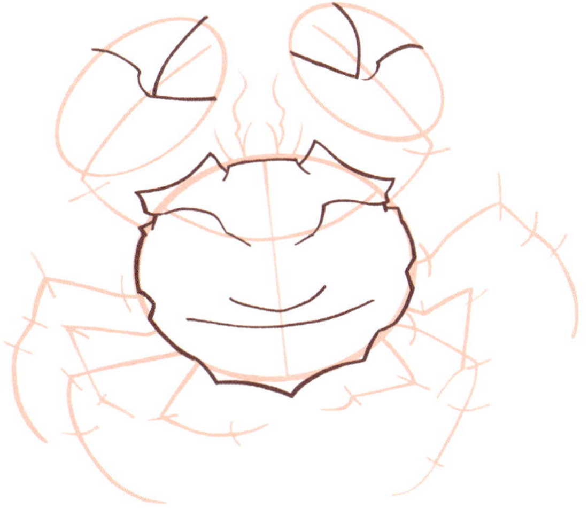

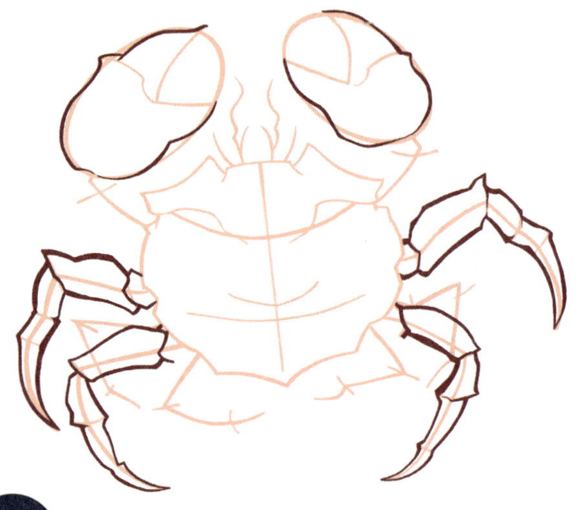

Using lines similar to those used to create the shell, draw the four larger legs of the crab. Each leg is made of the same shapes, so this is another example of repeating shapes. Use smooth, curved lines to draw the outline of the claws.

Repeating the leg shapes from step 4, draw the smaller legs in between the larger four, as well as the arms connecting the claws to the body. Draw an angry mouth shape using curved lines. Pay attention to how the lower lip spikes up and the upper lip curves down in the middle to create a ferocious expression.

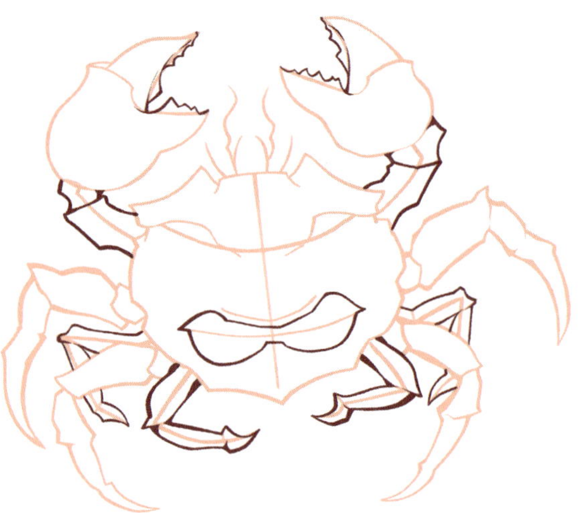

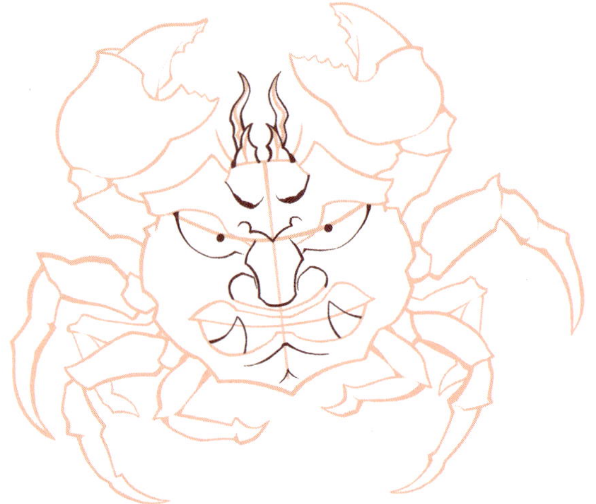

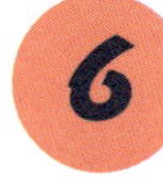

Begin to draw the symmetrical features of the face: its eyes, nose, and two fangs at the bottom of its mouth. Refine the antennae at the top of its head. This yōkai has a strong, angry expression, which is why most of the shapes we are drawing end in sharp points. This helps to accentuate that angry feeling.

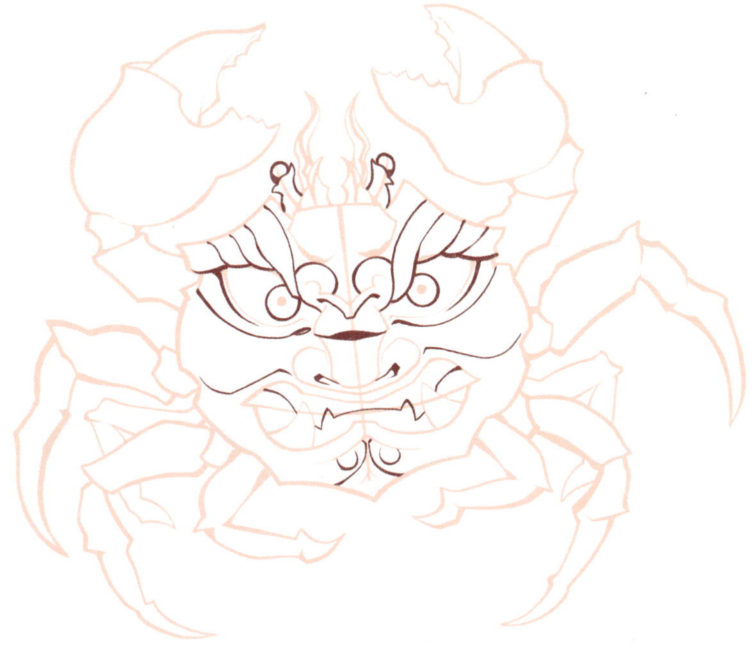

Use a series of repeating curves to create the heikegani's segmented eyebrows and the wrinkles under its eyes and cheeks.

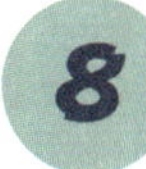

To finish, thicken the outlines of the crab's body and legs.

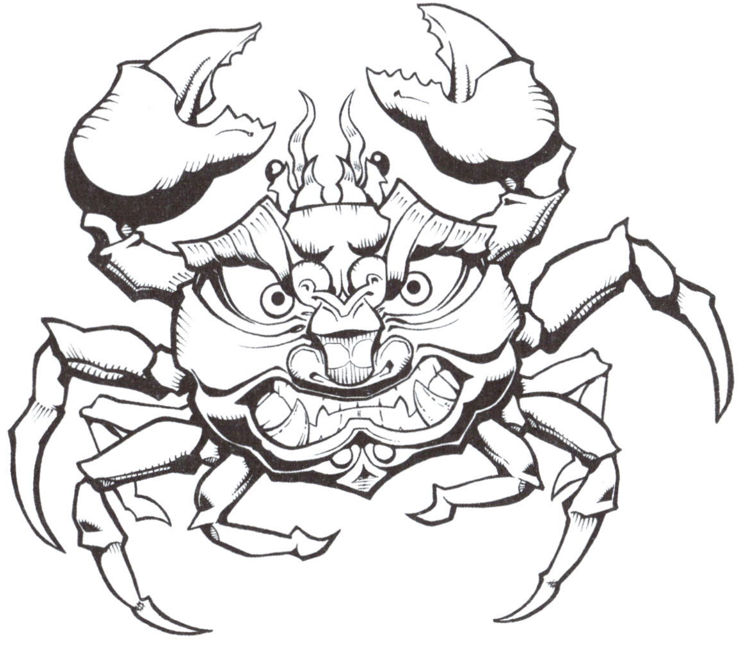

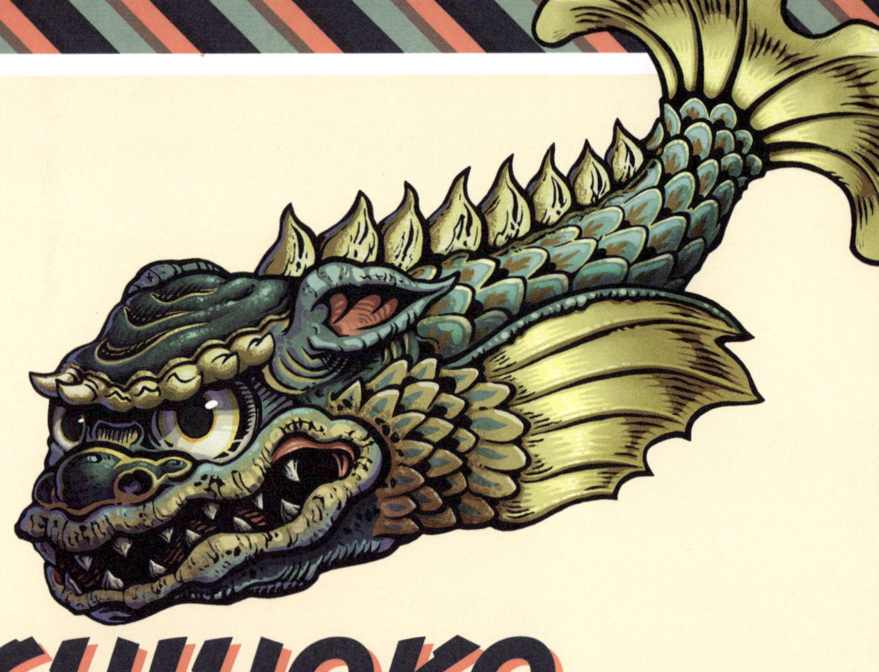

SHACHIHOKO
(しゃちほこ)

The shachihoko is a sea monster yōkai from Japanese folklore that looks like a creature with the head of a tiger and the body of a carp. They are believed to have the power to call forth rain, which is why there are often statues of these yōkai on the roofs of castles, temples, and other prominent buildings in Japan: They act as a ward against fire.

Like many aspects of culture, folklore and myth travel with people as they move and migrate to new countries. And so there are many mythological creatures that have been imported from neighboring countries like India or China and then evolved over time into unique Japanese yōkai. The shachihoko is one such yōkai. This is also why many variations of the same yōkai exist depending on the region of Japan you are in.

Lightly draw the basic shape of the yōkai. Create a circle for the head, along with center lines. Draw a long, curved tube for the body and a half-moon shape for the tail.

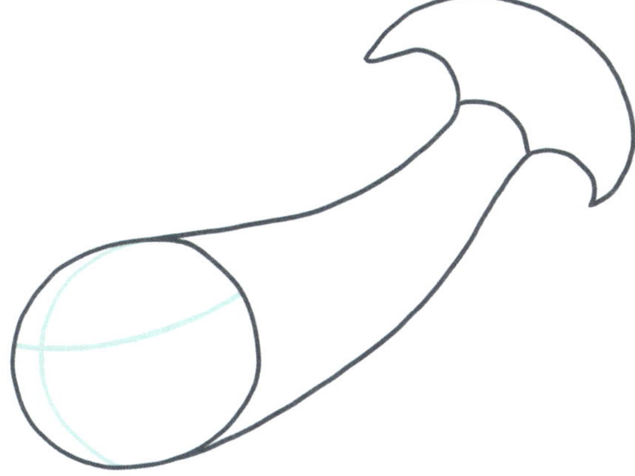

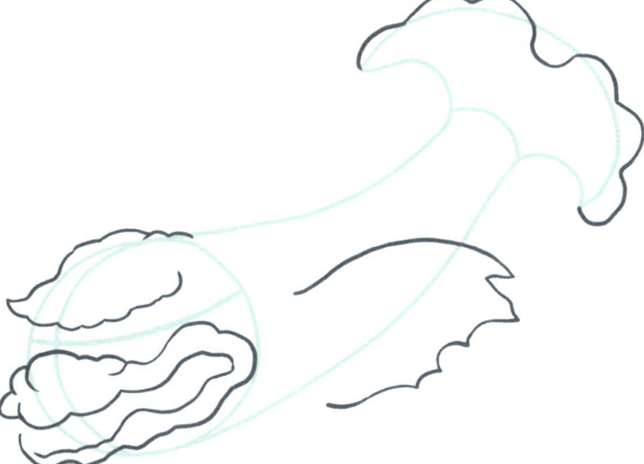

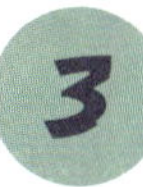

Use cloudlike shapes to draw the top of the head, the bulbous lips and nose, and the tail shape. Use a smooth curve for the top of the fin and a scalloped line for the fin's ragged edge.

Draw the ears and the bottom of the yōkai with more cloudlike lines.

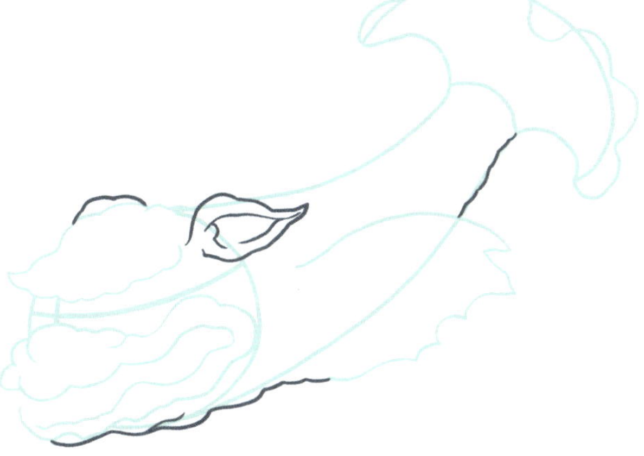

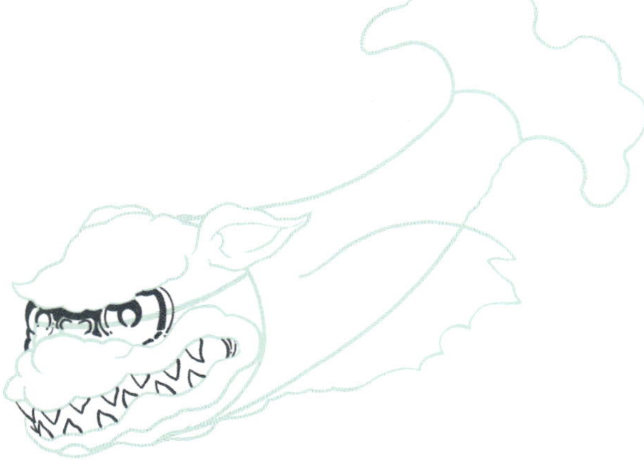

Draw curved triangles for the teeth. Draw two large circles for the eyes, then create the pupils using smaller circles.

Starting at the back of the head, draw the first spine-fin. Then, repeating the shape, work your way back toward the tail. Use similar curved shapes to add spikes along the shachihoko's brow.

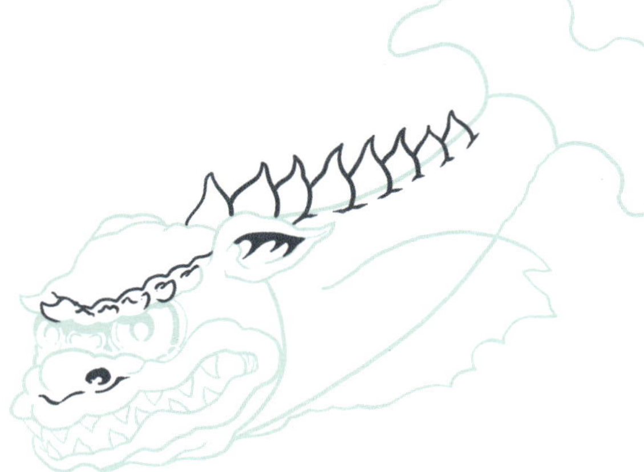

Use rounded triangles to draw the first row of scales near the mouth. Working backwards, draw the next row of scales. Note that each row of scales lines up with the apex of the previous row.

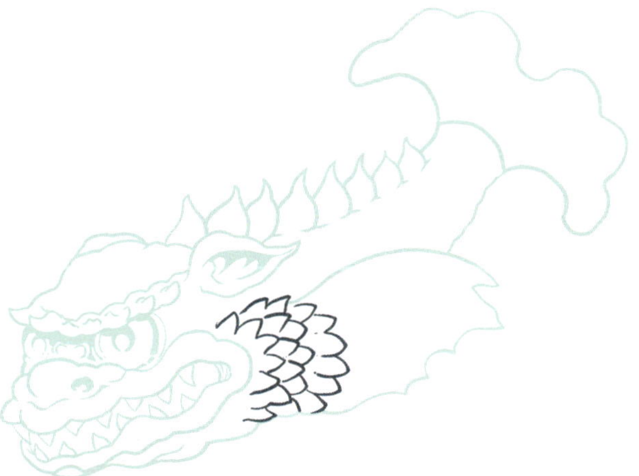

7

Continue adding scales to the body. This time, start at the back of the head and work back, toward the tail.

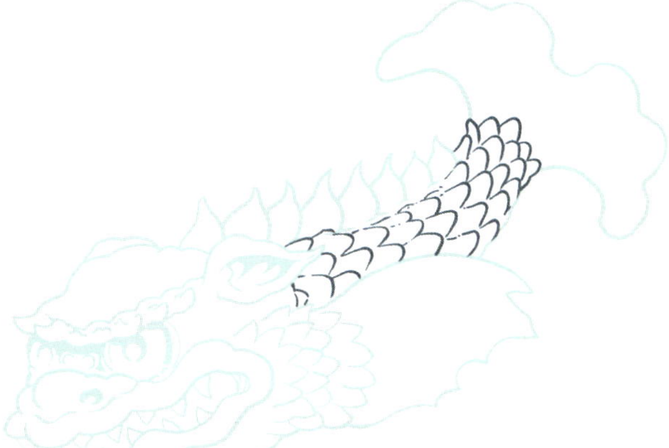

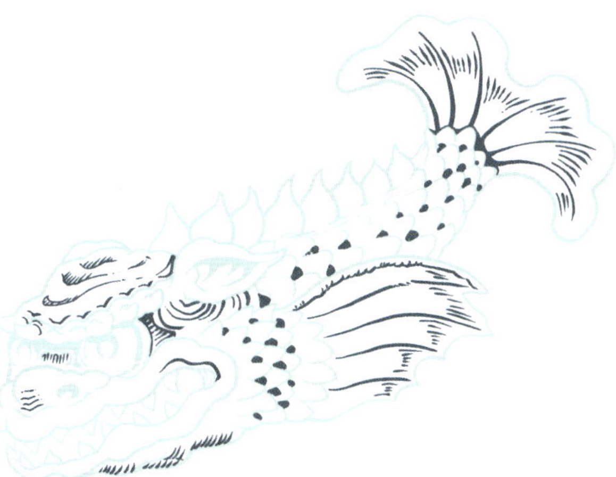

8

Add as many details as you would like. These could include the ridges in the fins, wrinkles around the ear and brow, or small shadows between the scales.

9

Thicken the outline along the bottom of the yōkai's belly and under its brow. Shade in the mouth.

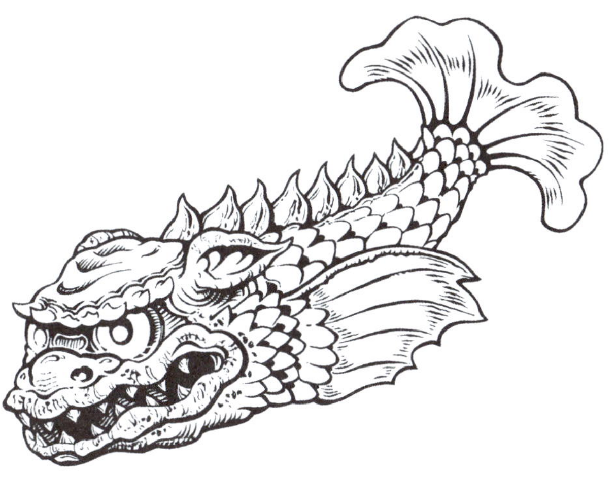

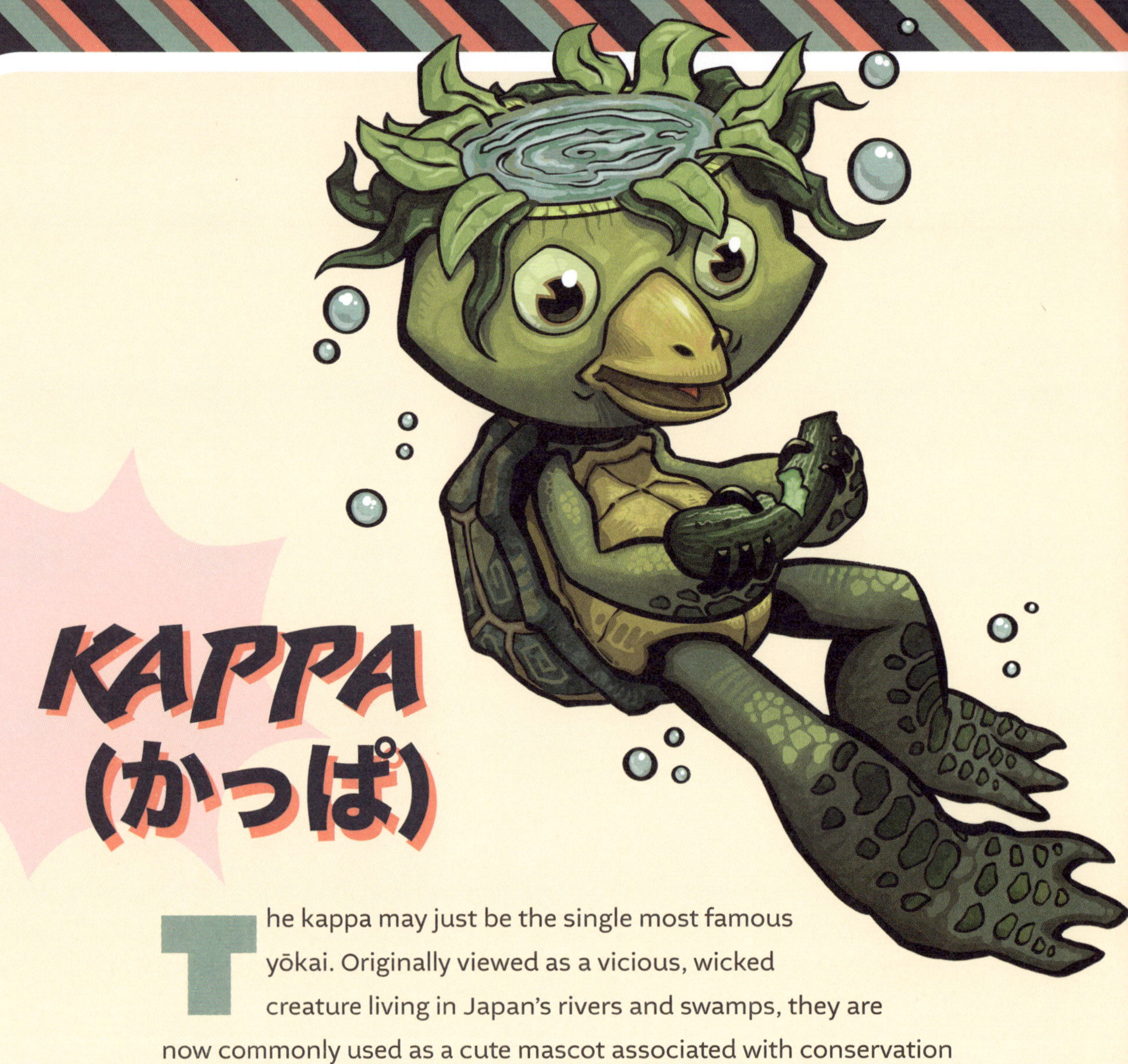

KAPPA （かっぱ）

The kappa may just be the single most famous yōkai. Originally viewed as a vicious, wicked creature living in Japan's rivers and swamps, they are now commonly used as a cute mascot associated with conservation efforts to protect the environment. They are often known as water goblins and water sprites, as the literal translation is "river child." They can be found in bodies of water such as rivers, lakes, or ponds.

They usually have a beak-like mouth, frog-like skin, a tortoise shell, and, most importantly, a bowl-like impression filled with water on their heads. Should the water fall out of this bowl, the kappa will be greatly weakened. Fun fact: Cucumbers are their favorite food, which is why the cucumber sushi roll is called a *kappa-maki*.

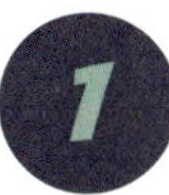

Start with a long sweeping line of action. Draw a large wide oval for the head and a bean shape for the body, showing the cute round belly.

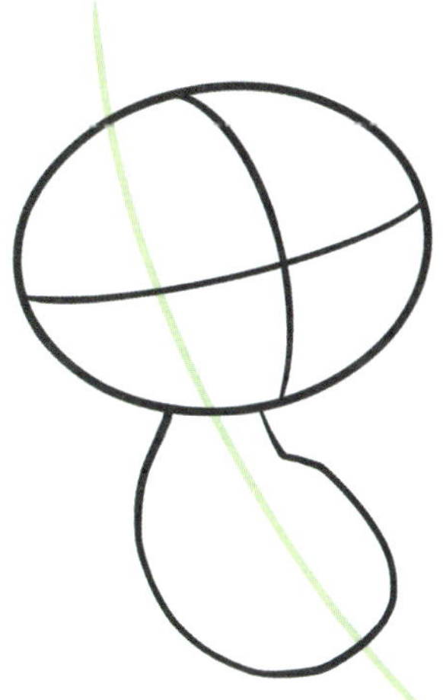

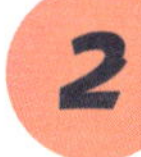

Draw tapered tube shapes to create the arms and legs: skinny where they meet the body, widening as they near the hands or feet. Pay attention to the bends in the joints.

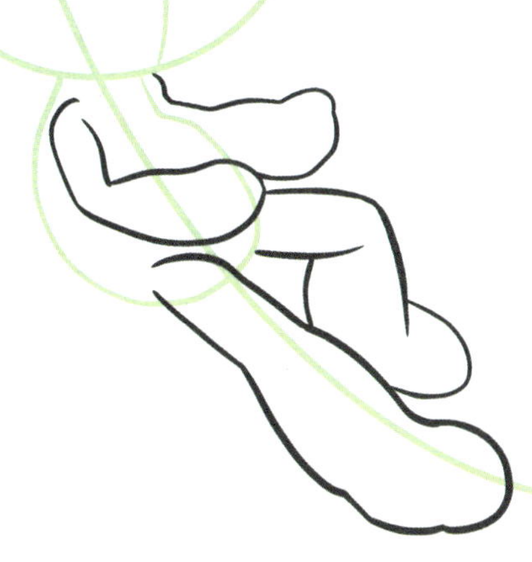

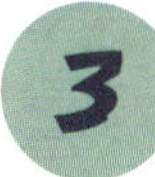

Draw two concentric circles on top of the head. These will be the rim of the bowl atop the kappa's head. Between its hands, draw a cucumber.

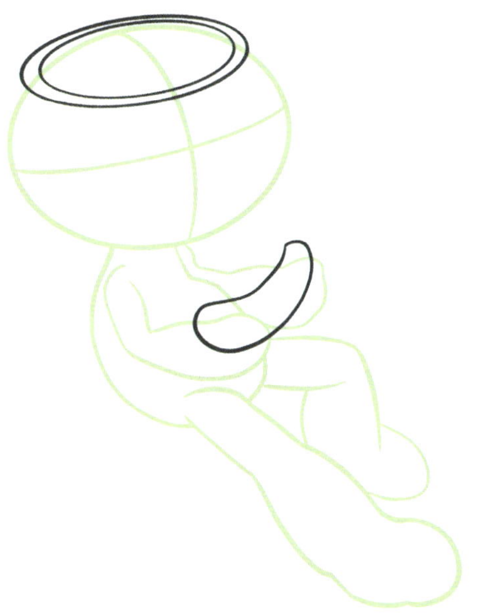

For the last major shape, draw the semicircular shape for the shell on its back, along with a rim where it meets the body.

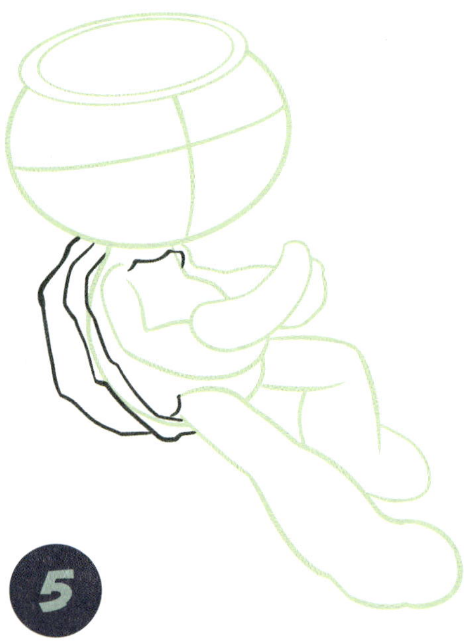

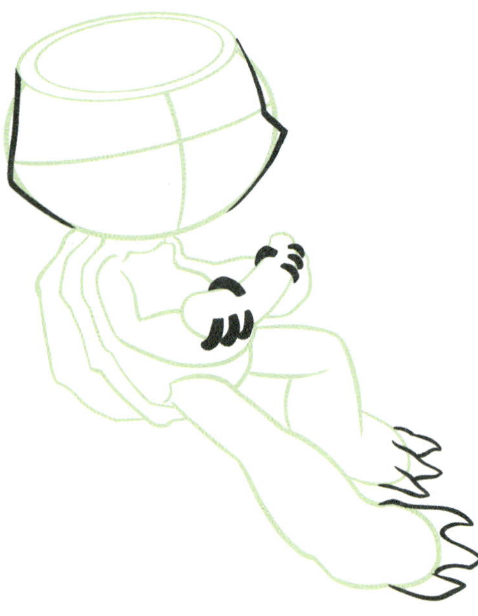

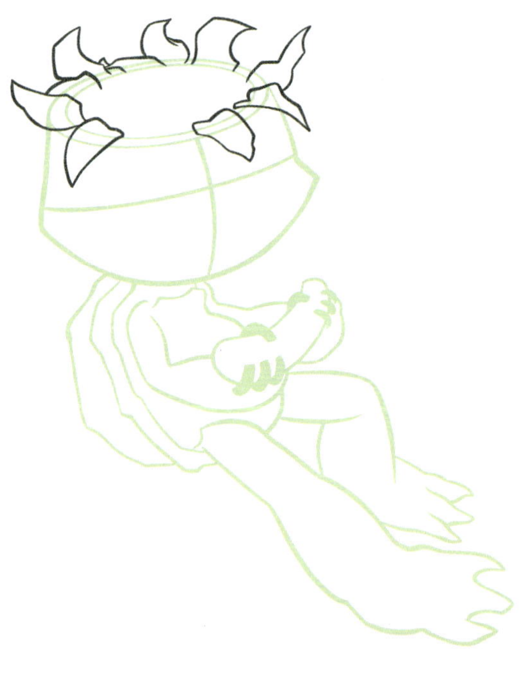

Refine the shape of the head, giving the kappa pointed cheeks. Add pointy toes and claws grasping the cucumber.

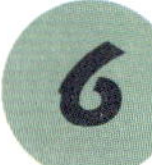

In place of hair, the kappa will have two rows of leaves around its head. Draw these with irregularly shaped triangles circling the rim.

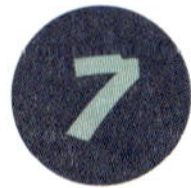

Draw the second row of leaves below the first. These leaves are longer, more akin to kelp than the tree leaves of the first row.

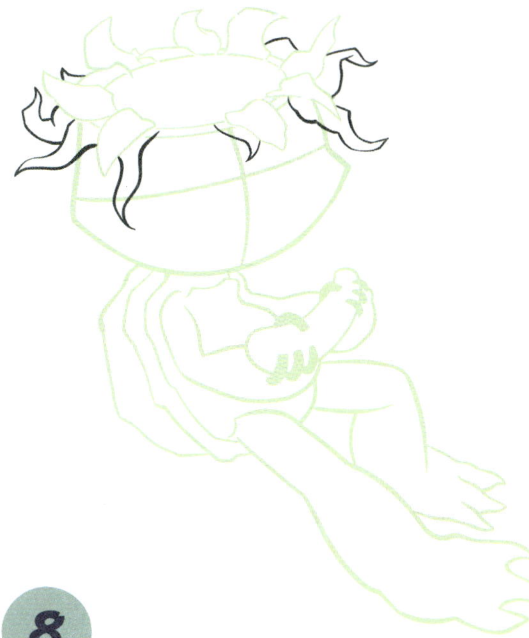

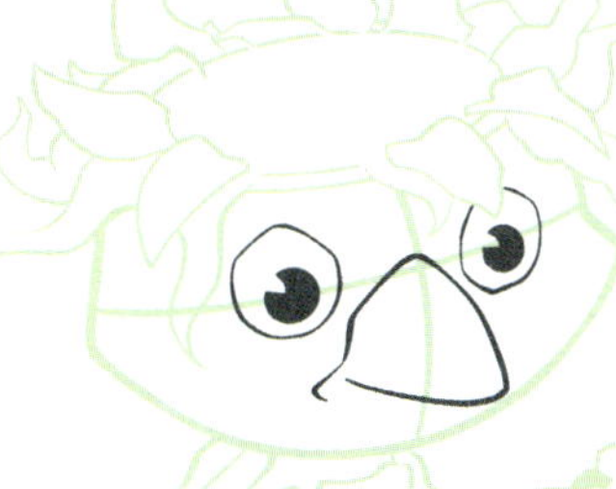

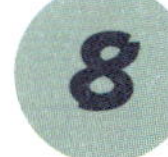

Draw the kappa's facial features, like its rounded eyes, followed by a rounded triangle for the top of its beak.

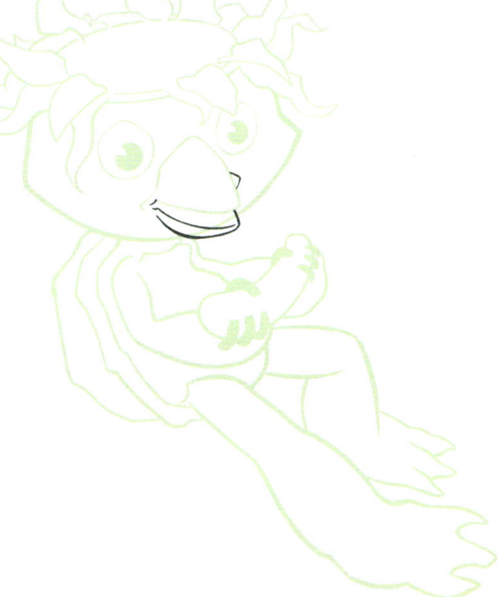

Draw the bottom half of the beak with sweeping curves.

10

The remaining steps all focus on detailing the kappa. Draw the center veins of the leaves, the kappa's small tongue, and its nostrils.

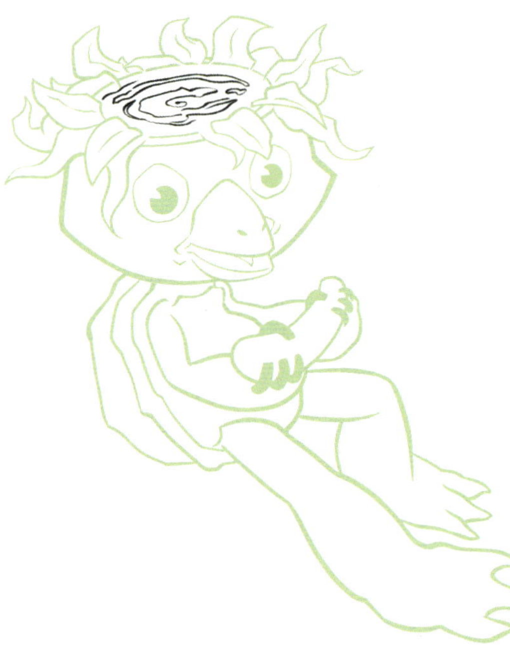

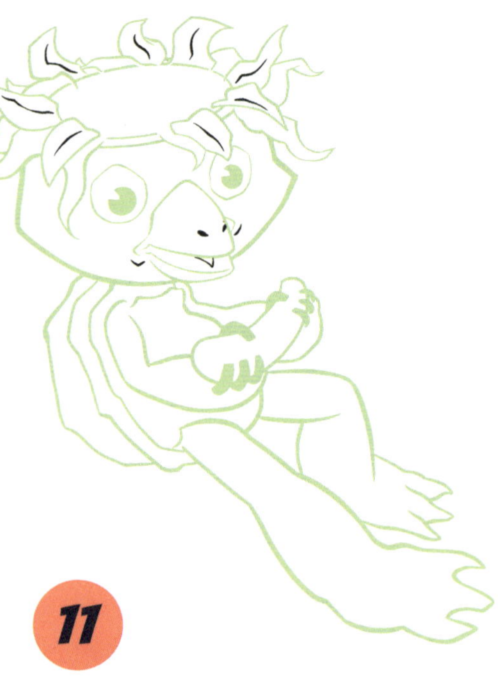

11

The bowl on its head is filled with water. To show this, draw swirling lines, starting in the center, that mimic ripples in water.

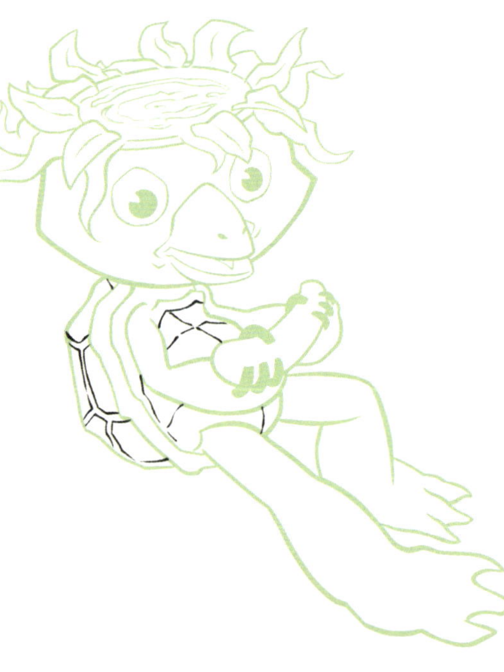

12

Draw the pattern on the turtle shell, including both parts of the shell, the piece on its back and then on its belly.

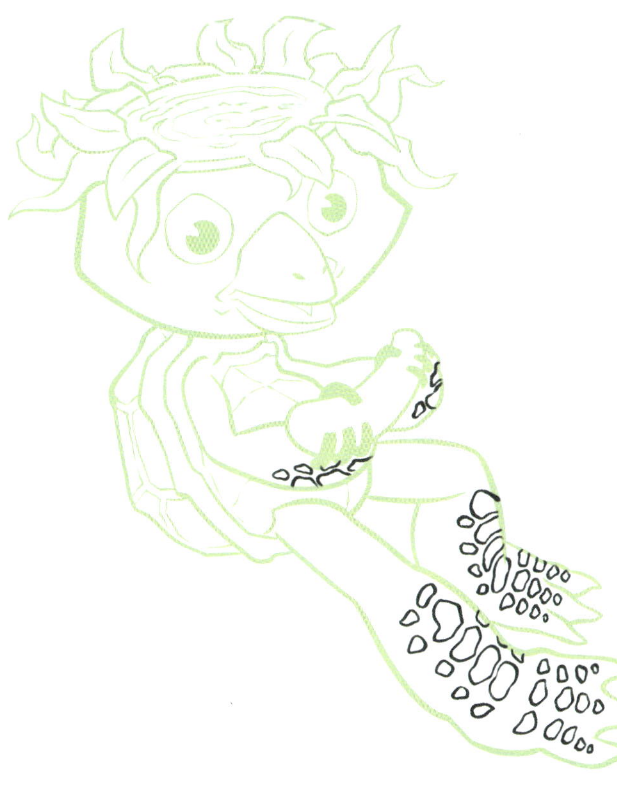

Use repeating shapes to draw the mottled scale pattern on its forearms, shins, and feet. Notice how the shapes in the middle are larger and the shapes on the outside are smaller.

To finish the kappa, draw circular bubbles since it's swimming underwater. Draw a bite mark in the middle of the cucumber, showing the kappa enjoying its favorite snack.

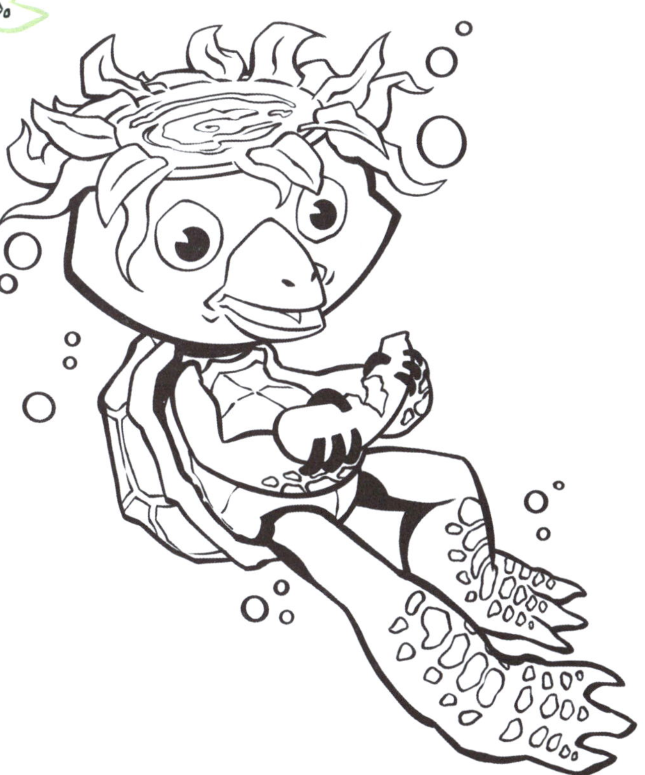

NINGYO (にんぎょ)

A mermaid-like yōkai of the sea, the literal translation of ningyo is "human-fish." The traditional design of a ningyo is of a mer-creature, with the head of a person and the body of a fish. It has also been portrayed as a small, beast-like creature with a top half resembling a small monkey and the bottom half of a fish. In more modern versions, taking inspiration from depictions of mermaids in the West, they are beautiful in appearance, with the top half of a human's body and the bottom half of a fish.

There are many unique legends around ningyo. Eating a ningyo could bring long life or immortality, and they could be interpreted as signs of prosperity. However, catching a ningyo could bring great catastrophe. In some stories, catching one could bring great disaster upon the village of the fisherman who caught it.

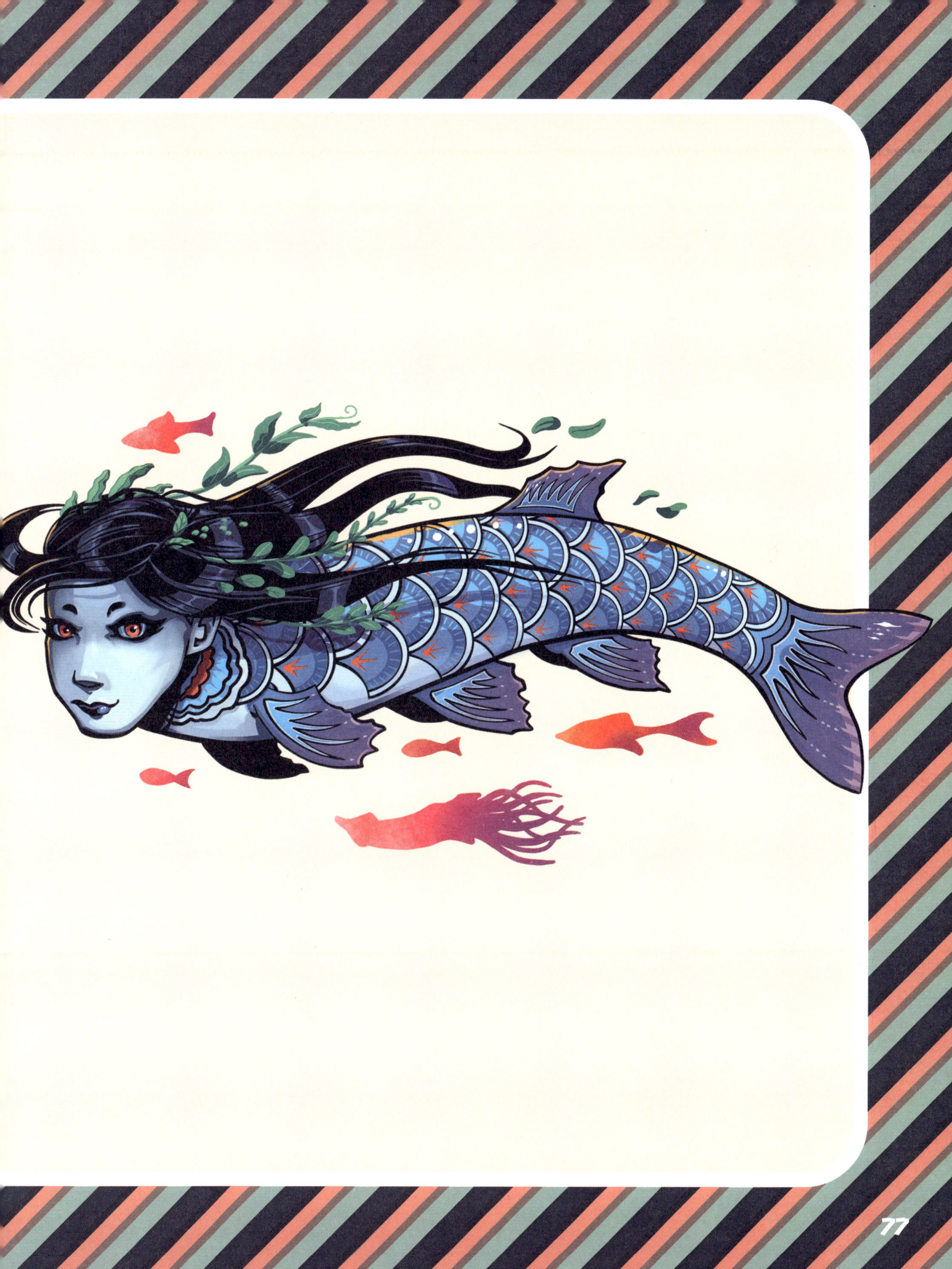

1

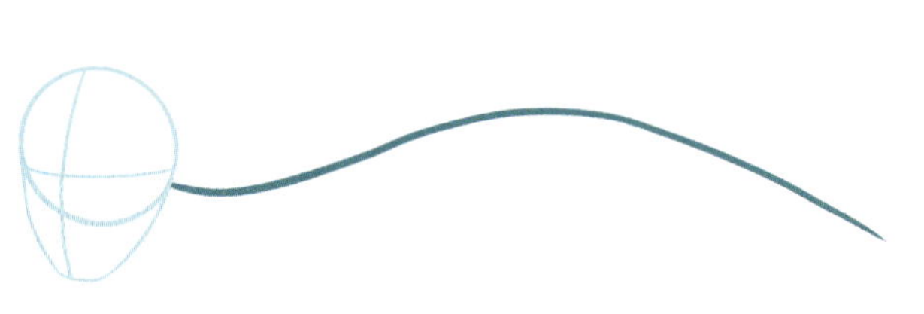

Draw the basic head shape, consisting of a circle with a U shape for the chin. Draw the center lines. From the head, have the flowing line of action extending outward.

2

Draw a flowing tube shape for the body, following the line of action.

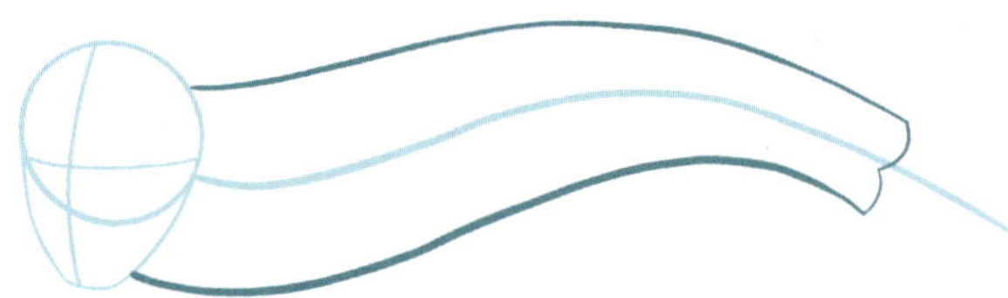

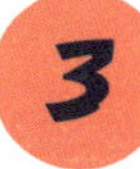

3

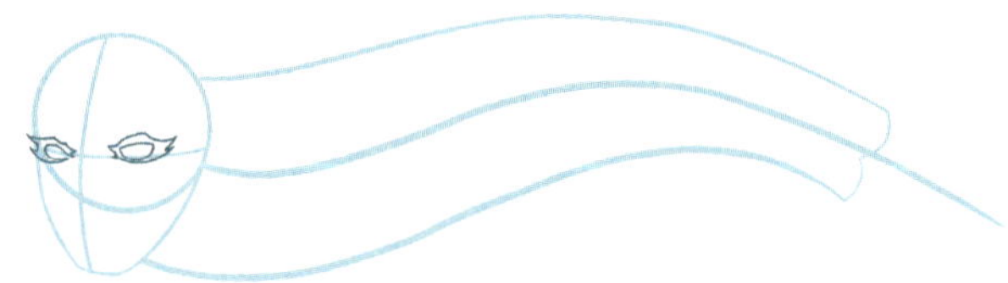

Use angled ovals to draw round eyes. Then, draw the shape of the lashes around the eyes.

4

Draw the nose using angled lines just below where the circle of the head meets the center line. Beneath the nose, draw the mouth. Connect the ends of the tube body shape with the tail.

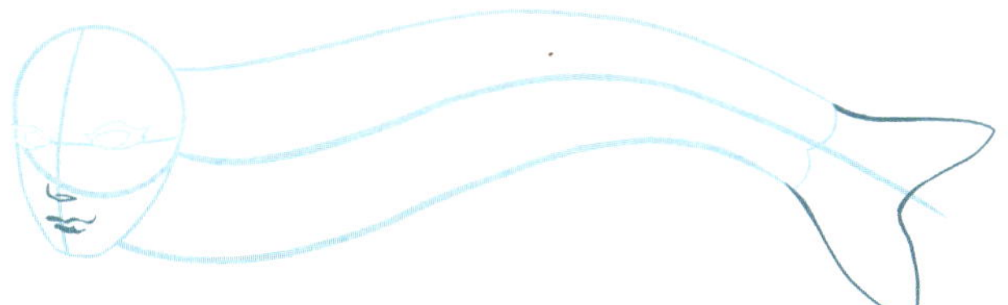

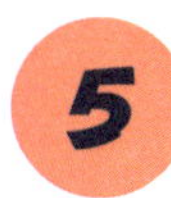

5

Refine the outline of the face by accentuating the cheeks and chin. Draw the ear using angled lines.

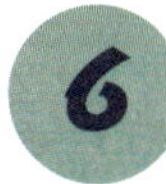

6

Create the fins by drawing a smooth curve for the leading edge, then an uneven scalloped line for the backside.

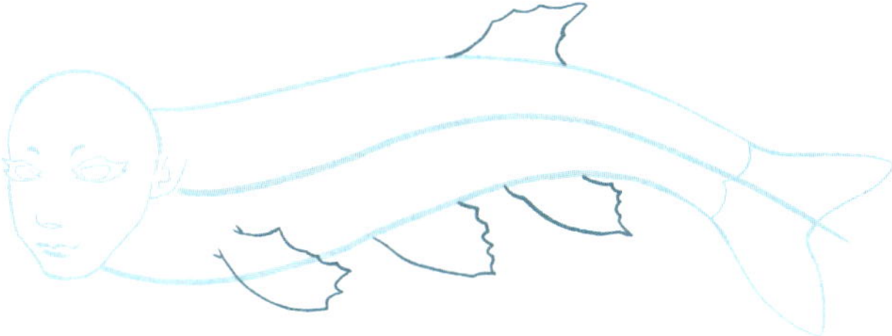

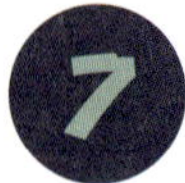

Use flowing curves to draw the hair in masses, starting at the forehead. Work toward the back of the head, layering one mass atop the other. The hair should flow back along the body. Add three curves to show the fins on the backside.

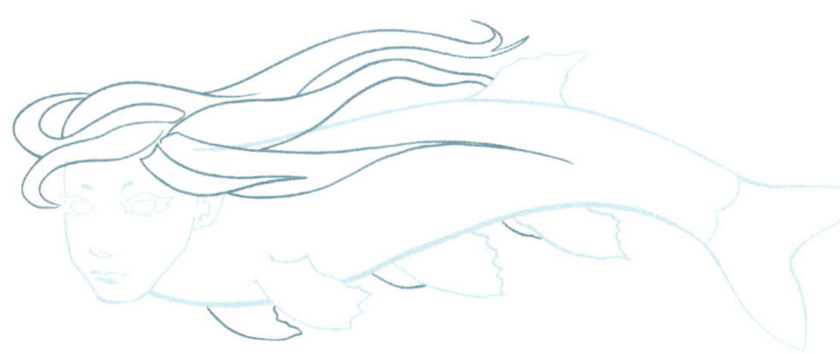

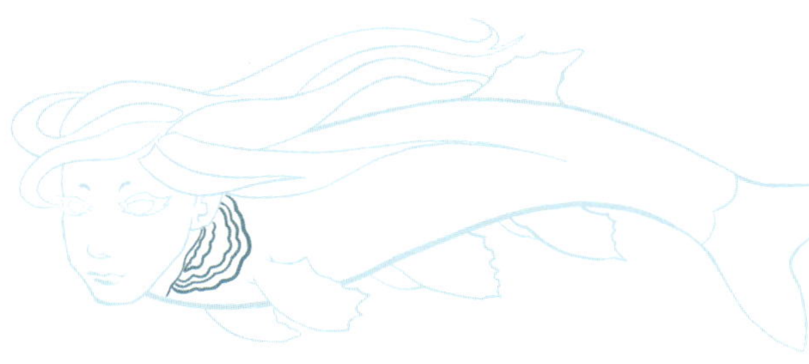

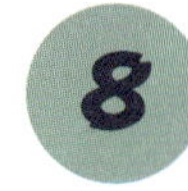

Draw the gills using repeating, cloudlike shapes.

Draw the details of the inner fins, using the same spike-shaped curve to match the flow of each fin.

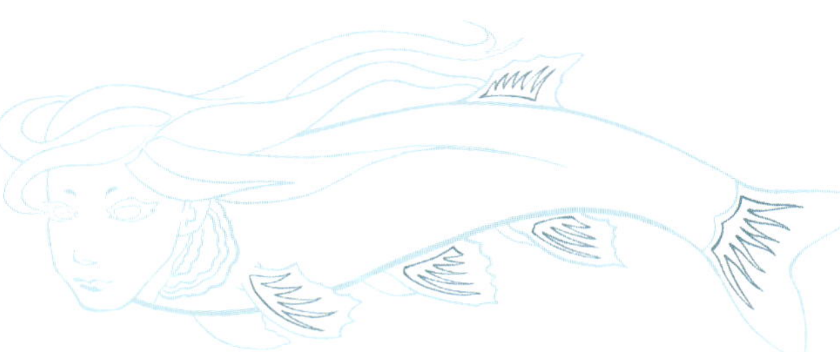

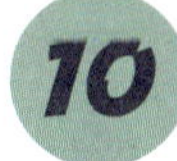

10

Draw semicircles for the scales, starting at the head and working toward the tail. For added detail, draw a thin semicircular line inside each scale.

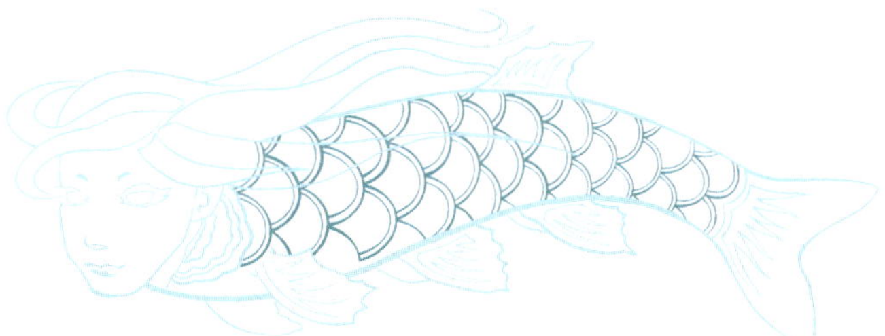

TO DRAW SIMPLE SCALES

1. **Draw a row of semicircles; keep the shapes even in size.**
2. **Draw the next row of semicircles starting at the apex of the last row.**
3. **Repeat.**

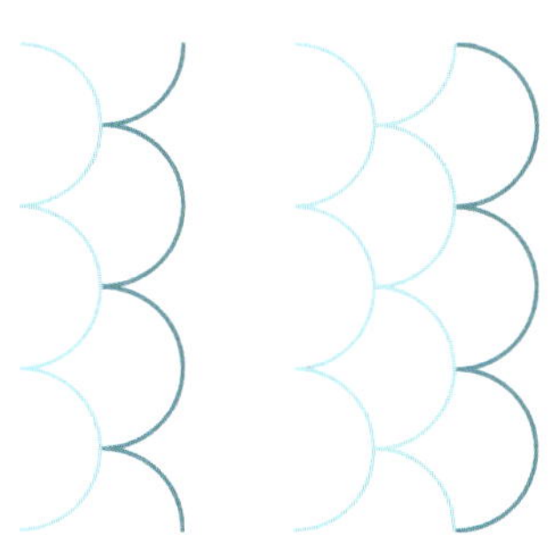

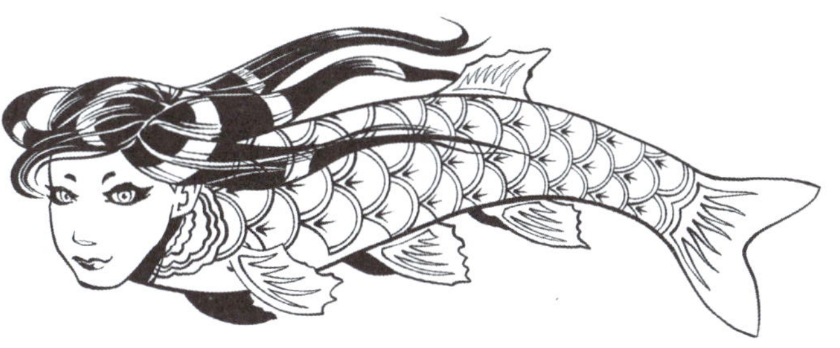

11

Use repeating shapes to draw the small, arrow-like shapes inside each scale. For an extra touch of depth, shade in the hair and the fins on the backside of the body.

HOUSEHOLD & EVERYDAY YŌKAI

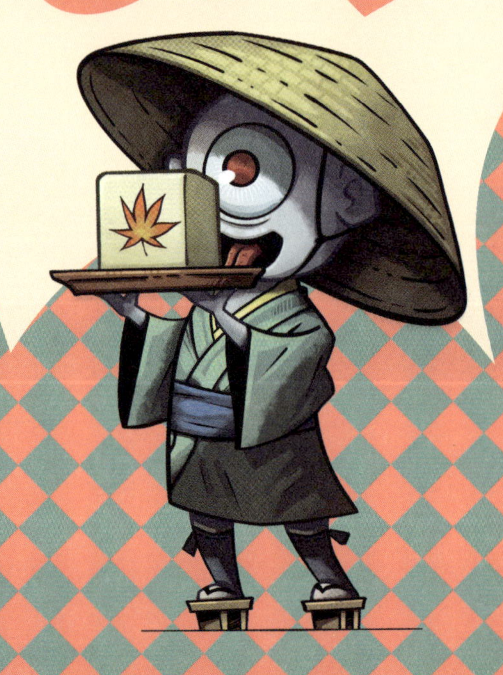

In this section, we dive into yōkai connected to everyday life, past and present. Many of these yōkai can be encountered inside the home, while others can be encountered as a person goes about their daily life in Japan. Yōkai come in a wide variety of shapes and forms, which is why they are so much fun to draw. They can be born from wooden buckets, kettles, teacups, instruments, and gongs, or even from normal people suffering under a curse or malediction.

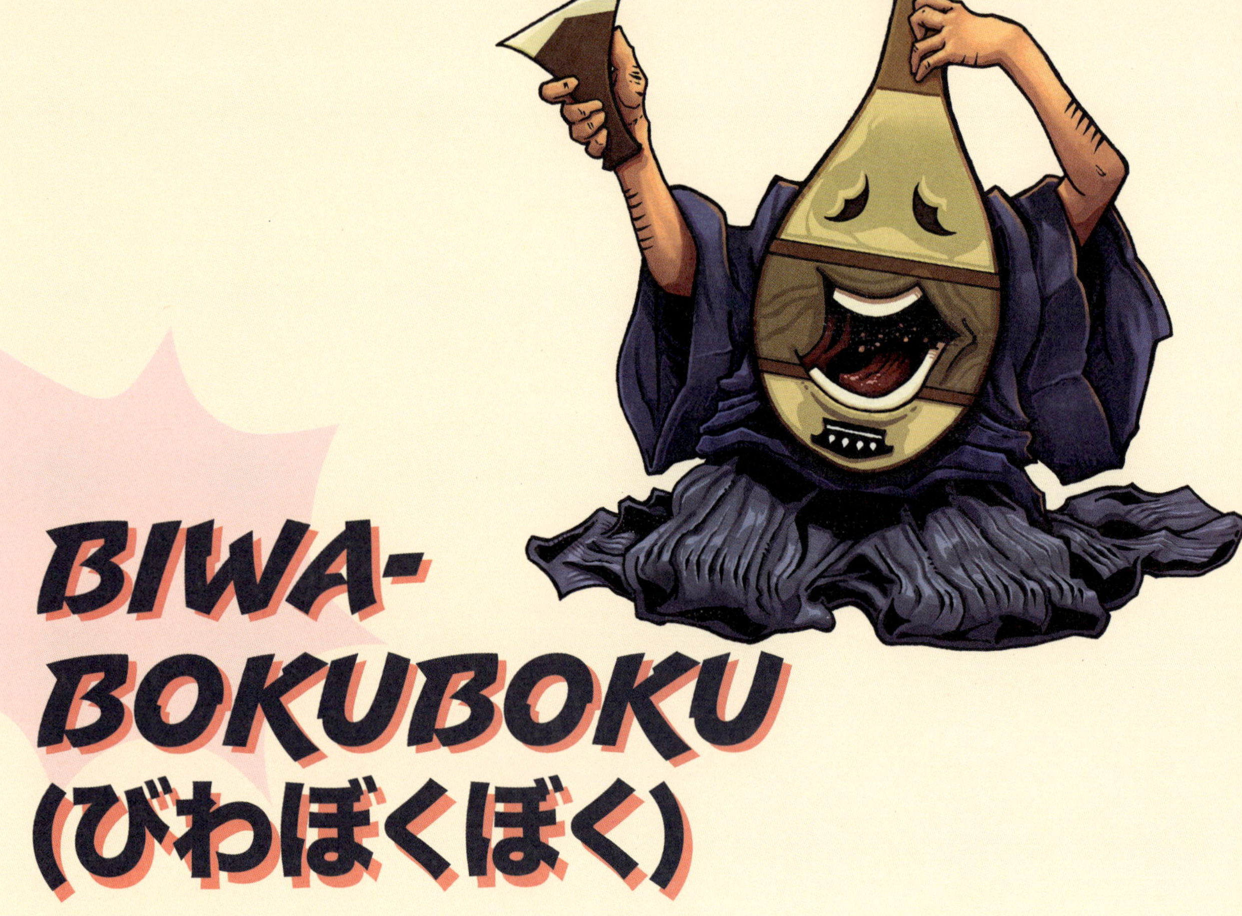

BIWA-BOKUBOKU (びわぼくぼく)

The biwa-bokuboku is a tsukumogami (page 22) born from a traditional Japanese lute called a *biwa*. Made of wood, the biwa has a short neck and is played using a plectrum called a *bachi*. This playful yōkai can often be seen dancing in Japanese art prints, wearing *mino*, a traditional Japanese straw raincoat, and pulling along the *koto-furunushi*, a koto instrument come to life as a yōkai. (The koto is a zither instrument and the national instrument of Japan.)

If you are not familiar with the biwa, or any subject matter you are drawing, it is good practice to do some research before beginning so that you are familiar with the instrument upon which this yōkai is based.

Draw a diagonal line of action and an oval, which will be the head of the biwa.

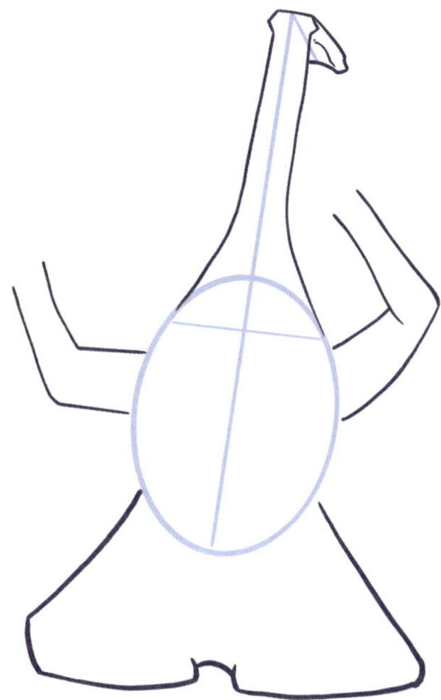

Draw straight and curved tubelike shapes for the arms and neck. The biwa-bokuboku will be kneeling on the ground in a kimono. To begin showing this pose, draw the rounded, triangular-shaped lower body.

Use rounded shapes to draw the hands. Draw the obi sash going around the waist, paying attention to how it rises over each leg. Add the side pieces of the kimono resting on the ground on either side of the biwa-bokuboku's knees.

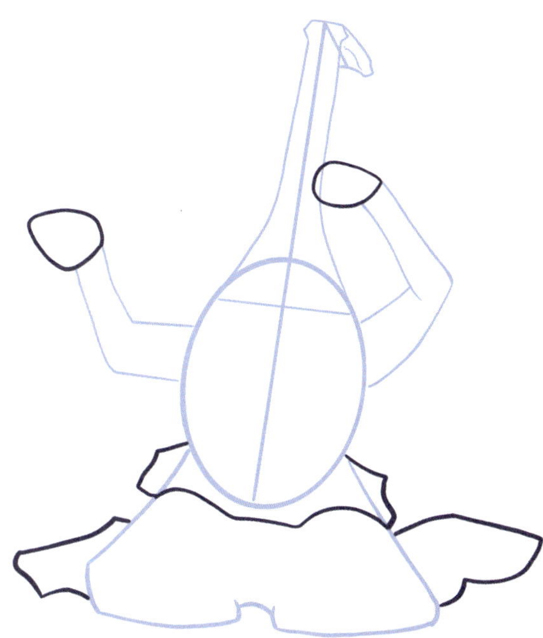

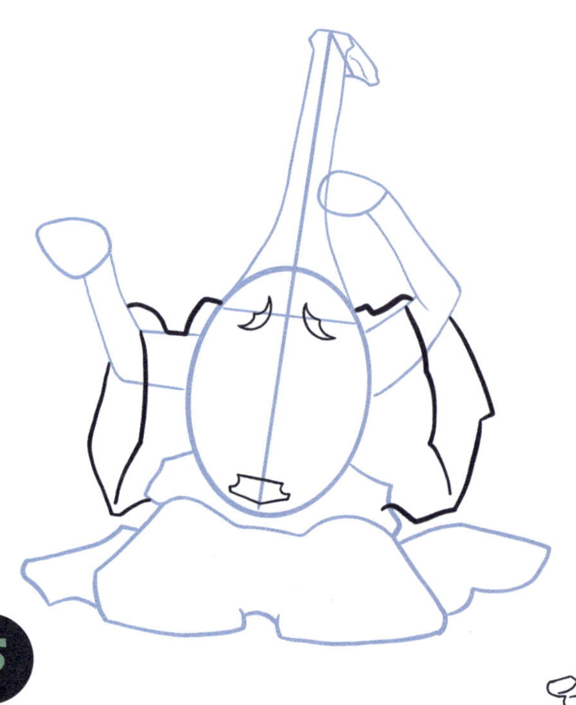

Draw the kimono, with its long open sleeves hanging down from the arms. Use angled, half-moon shapes to draw the eyes. Draw the bridge piece (called a *fukuju*) at the base of its head.

Complete the hands by drawing the bent fingers, paying attention to the position of each finger. Use two downward curves for the top and bottom of the mouth. Connect these curves with two more inward curves, forming the sides of the mouth.

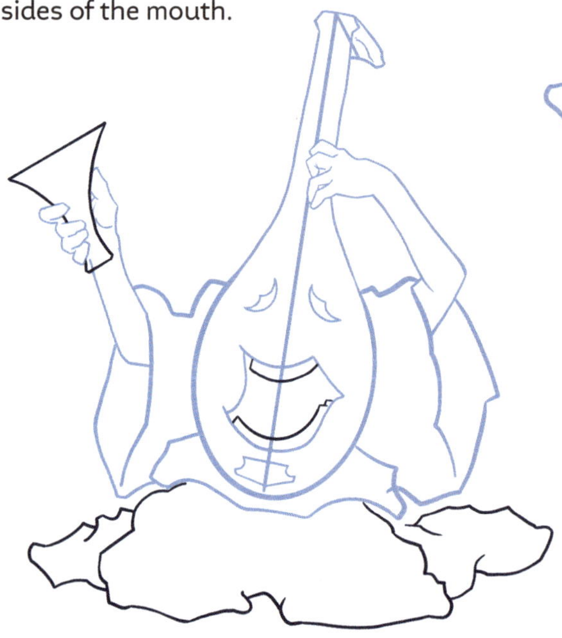
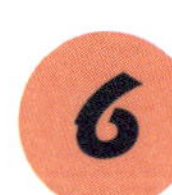

Refine the shape of the kimono around the knees. Draw the bachi with its triangular top and narrow curved handle. Draw the teeth following the upturned curves of the mouth.

7

Since the yōkai is sitting, the kimono will be very wrinkled. Draw these wrinkles in the obi and a few around the sleeves. Add the tongue and tuning pegs.

8

For final details, add more inner wrinkles to the knee area and two horizontal decorative stripes going across the face of the instrument.

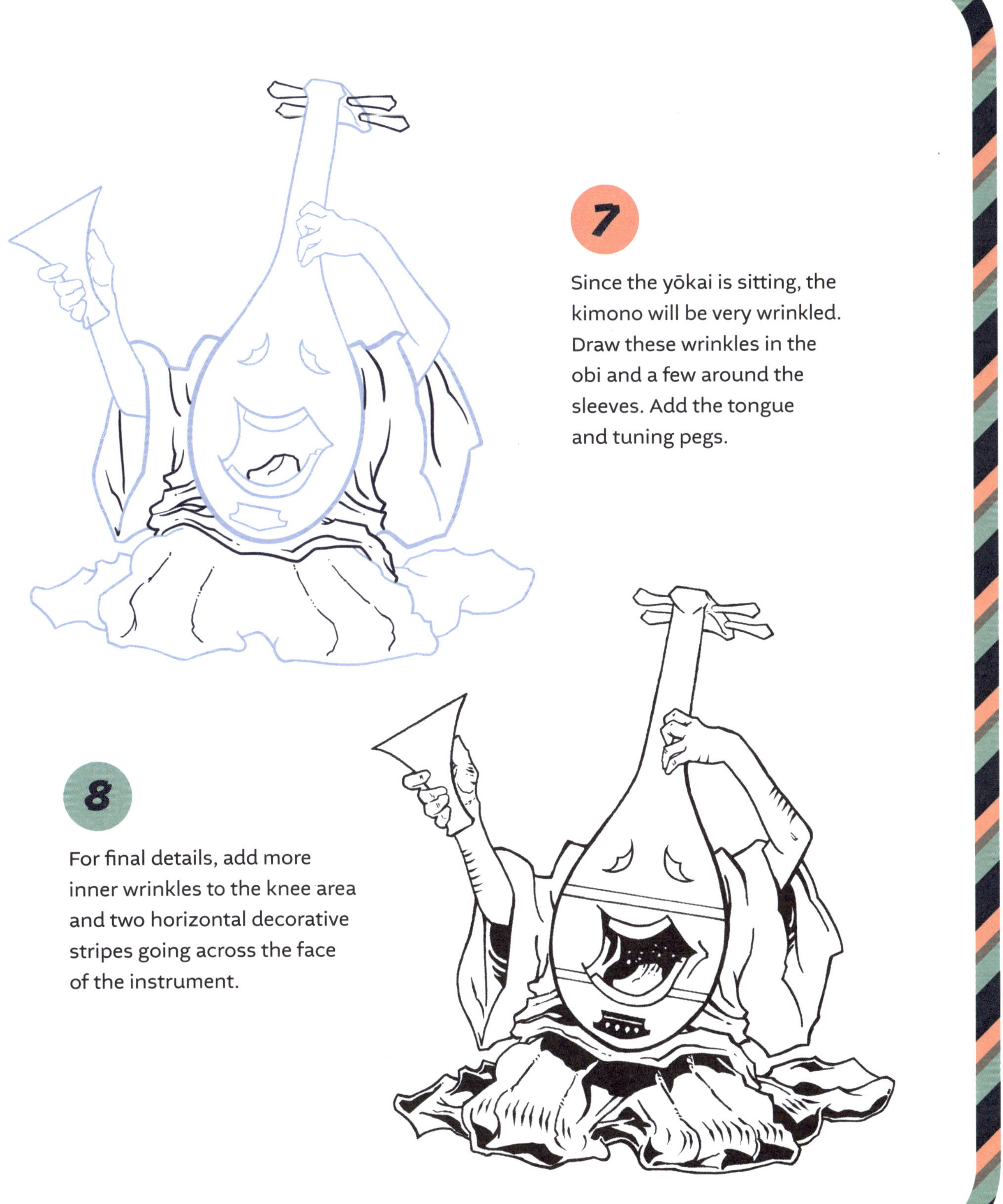

SHAMI-CHŌRŌ (しゃみちょうろう)

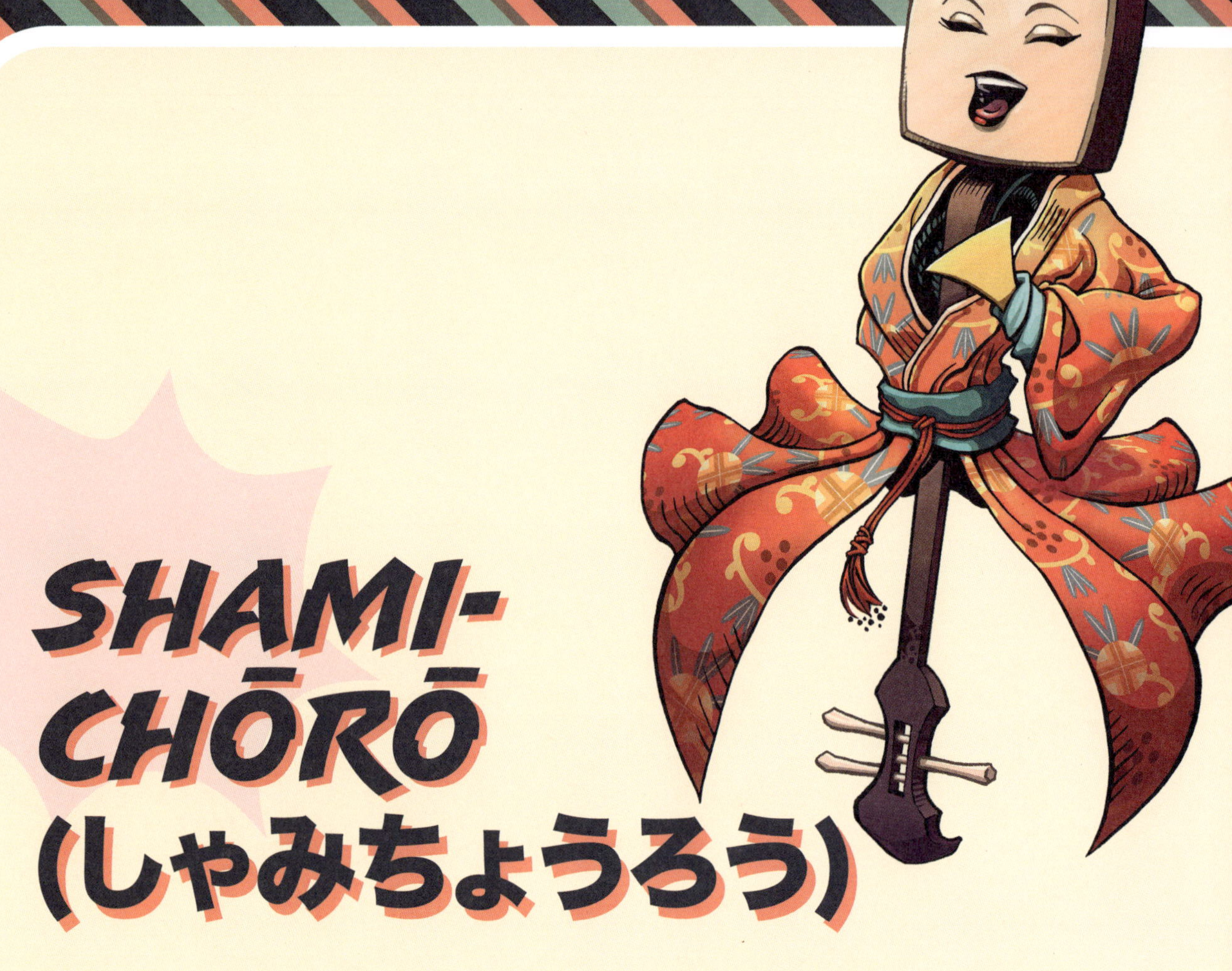

The shami-chōrō is another musical tsukumogami yōkai like the biwa-bokuboku (page 84). This yōkai is born from a shamisen instrument said to be possessed by the spirit of a shamisen maestro. The three-stringed shamisen is a traditional Japanese instrument with a distinct sound and is also played with a bachi plectrum.

The kimono pattern in this drawing is based on the pattern seen in the original shami-chōrō illustration created by Toriyama Sekien for his yōkai encyclopedias. During the Edo period, these yōkai encyclopedias were instrumental in popularizing yōkai and taking them from being the creatures of nightmares to fun entertainment.

Begin with a straight, diagonal line of action. At the top, draw a rounded cube, which will serve as the head of our yōkai. Draw the center lines on the head and the center line for the spine of the shamisen. Notice that it curves away as it approaches the head and then again as it nears the end.

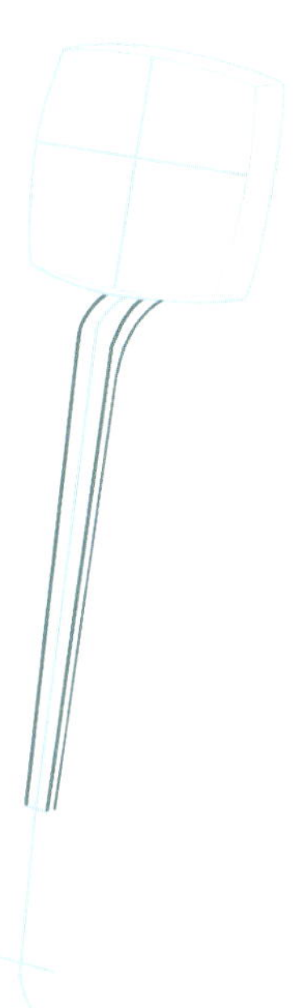

Draw the sides of the shamisen forming the *sao*, which is the neck of the instrument, and taper the shape as you move away from the head. Use a ruler for straight lines like these.

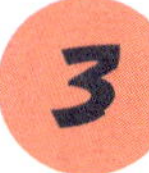

Begin to draw in the form of the *tenjin*, which is normally the top of the instrument, but in this case serves as the foot of the yōkai.

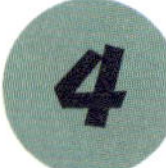

The shami-chōrō is wearing a flowing kimono. Begin the kimono by drawing the obi sash around the waist.

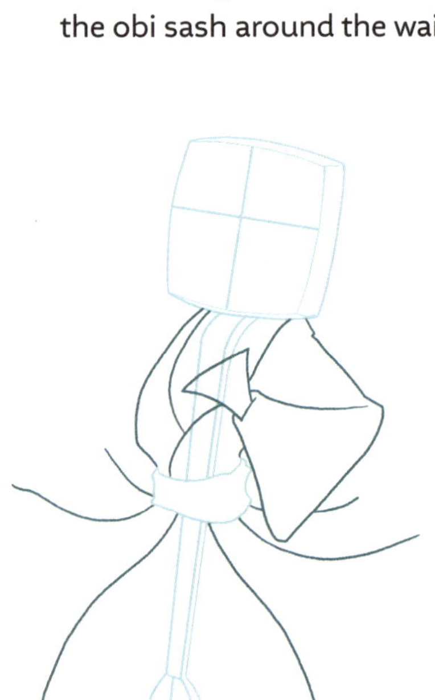

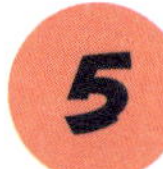

Draw the basic shapes of the kimono. For the chest area, use a series of curves to connect the obi to the head. Notice the triangle shapes for the bachi and the sleeve. Splay out lines from the bottom of the obi to show the kimono billowing out.

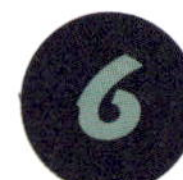

Continue to create the kimono by connecting the lines that are billowing out at the bottom. Add the collar of the kimono, called the *eri*, and the shapes of the sleeve wrapping around the bachi.

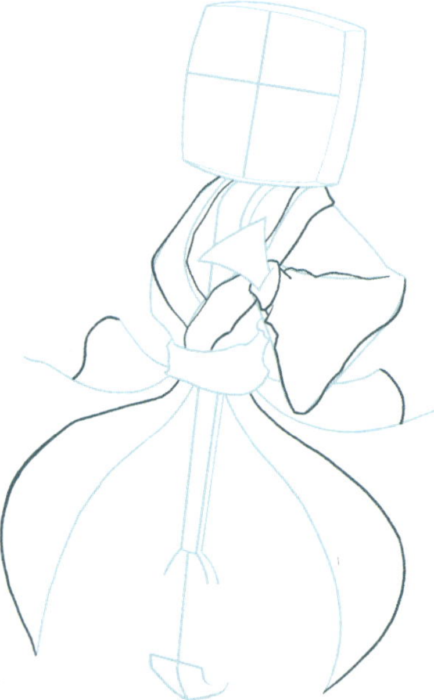

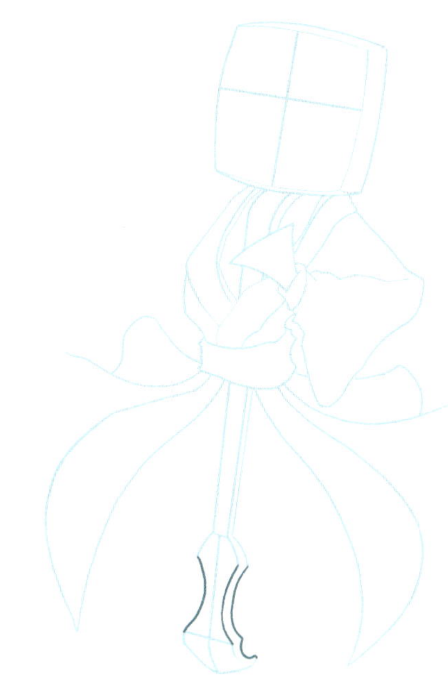

7

Add the curved sides of the tenjin.

8

Refine the character more by adding layers to the kimono and tuning pegs to the tenjin.

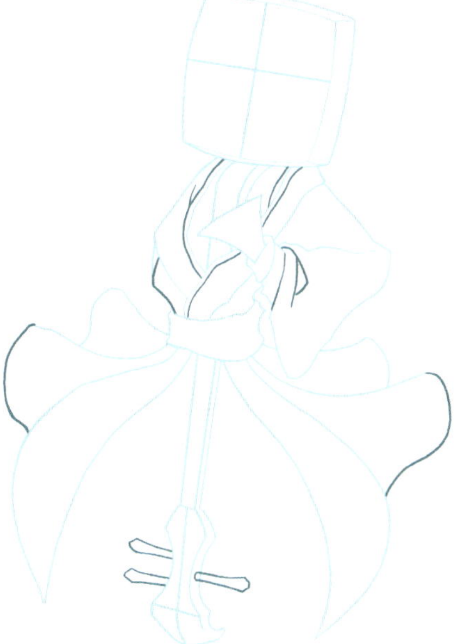

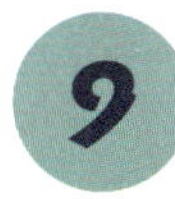

9

Using swoosh shapes, draw the eyelashes and upper mouth. Add a ridge going around the head.

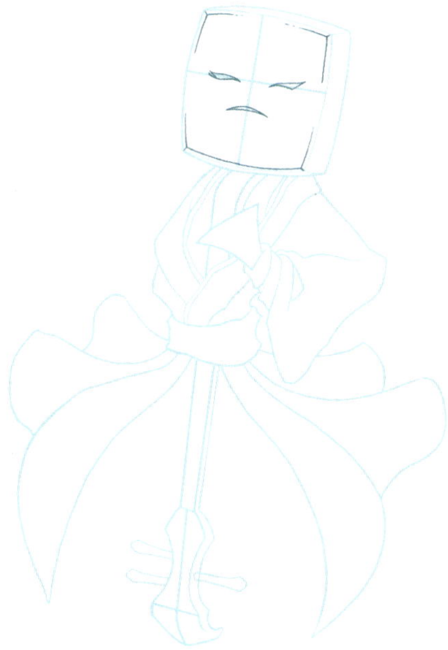

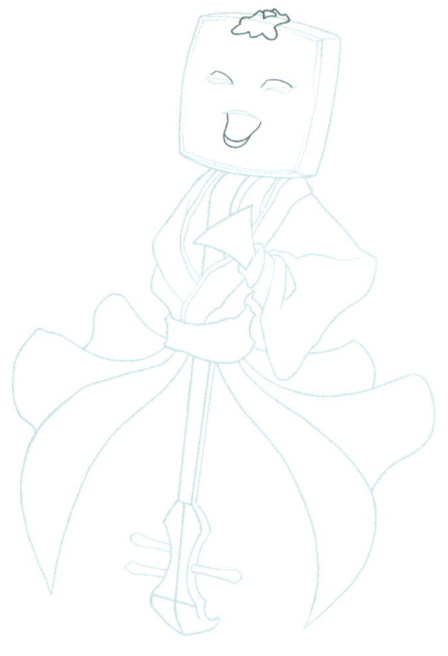

10

Draw the shape of the *neo*, which are the cords knotted at the top of the head to which the strings of the instrument would be tied. Continue with the facial features.

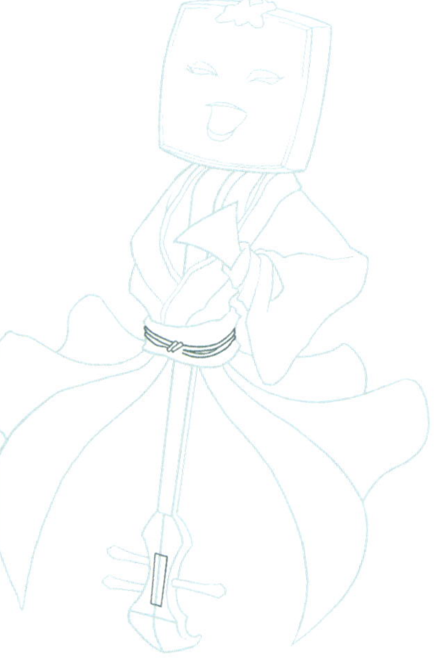

11

Add the *obijime*, which is the braided cord tied around the obi.

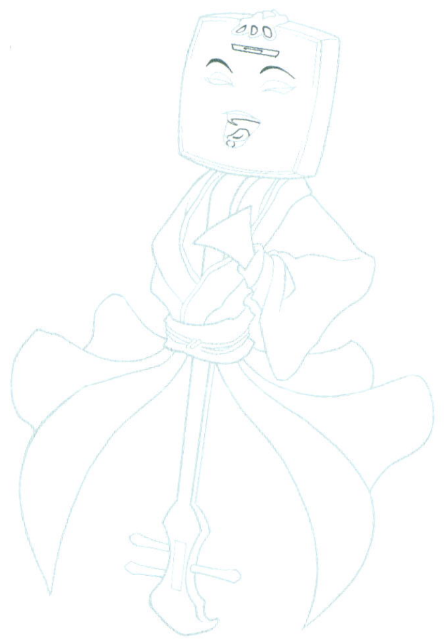

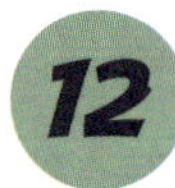

12

Draw the arched eyebrows, teeth, tongue, and *koma* (the straight bridge piece above the eyes), completing the singing expression.

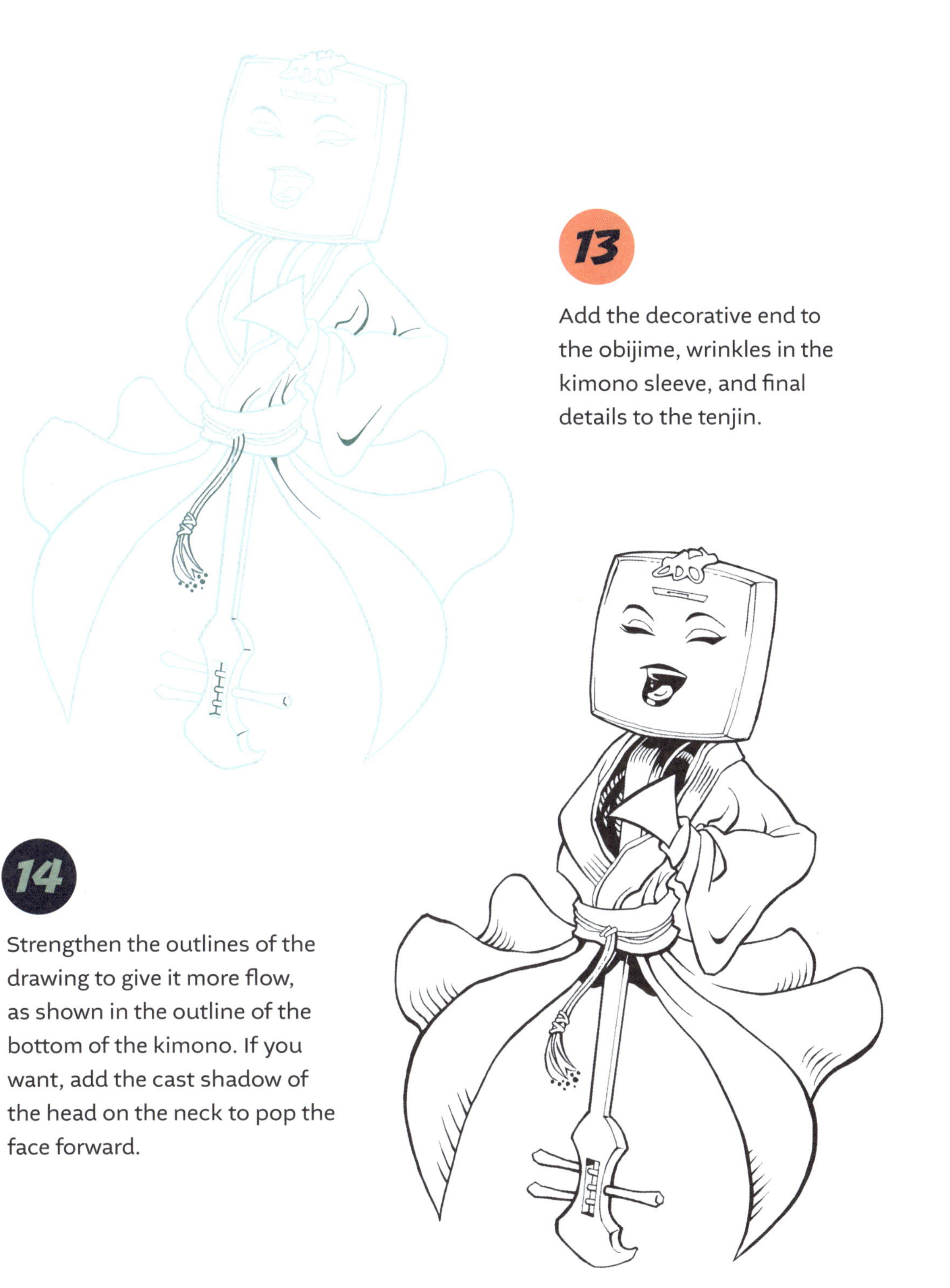

13

Add the decorative end to the obijime, wrinkles in the kimono sleeve, and final details to the tenjin.

14

Strengthen the outlines of the drawing to give it more flow, as shown in the outline of the bottom of the kimono. If you want, add the cast shadow of the head on the neck to pop the face forward.

AMABIE (あまびえ)

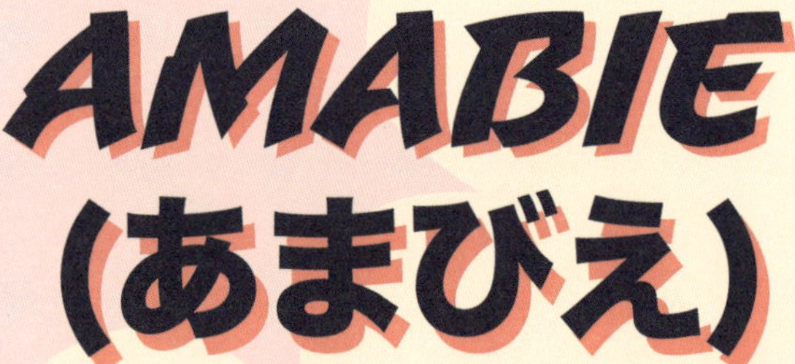

An amabie is a legendary mermaid-like yōkai, with three fins/legs and a beak. In Japanese mythology, the amabie is said to be prophetic and protect people from sicknesses. It was first reported in 1846, when sicknesses were spreading throughout Japan. At that time, an amabie appeared from the sea and told a local official to spread pictures of it, telling him that anyone who saw a picture of the amabie would be protected from ill health, or healed if they were already sick. Amabie were also believed to bring messages of good fortune, like abundant harvests.

This is not a yōkai that would normally be in the household category or even everyday life, but during the COVID-19 pandemic the amabie saw a resurgence in popularity within yōkai and Japanese culture. Artists throughout Japan and the world, thanks to the internet, illustrated and shared pictures of the amabie on social media hoping to halt the pandemic, like in 1846.

1

Start with the line of action, as always. Add a circle for the head, an oval for the body, and three additional lines of action indicating the center of each of the three fins.

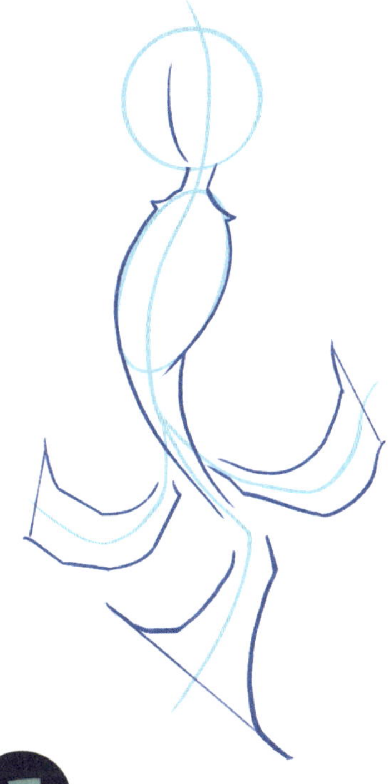

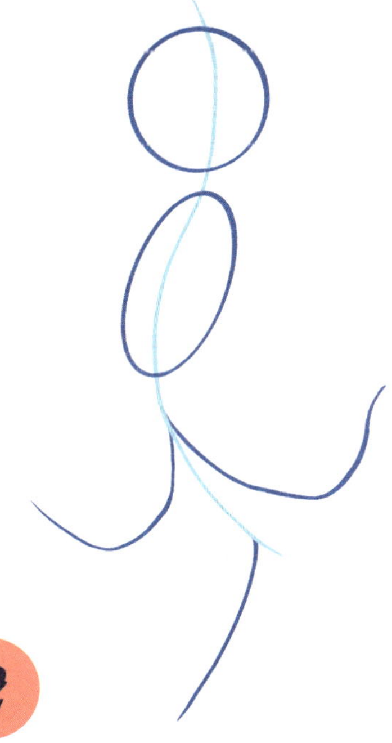

2

Sketch the center line of the face, following the curve of the circle. Use the oval as a guide to draw the sides of the body, tapering as you approach the tail fins, which are curved triangles.

3

Imagining the hair as if it were floating underwater, draw the wavy outline of the hair. Place tufts of hair on top of her head.

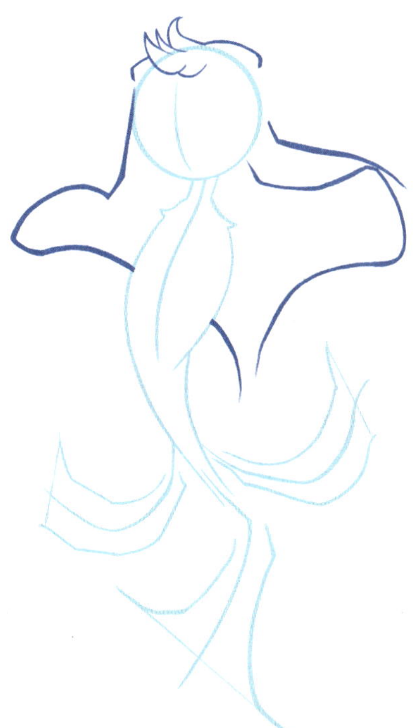

4

Add two circles for her eyes. Draw
the curves of the beak, as well as the
curves of her fin-like ears. Using similar
shapes to the ears, draw the ends of
each fin.

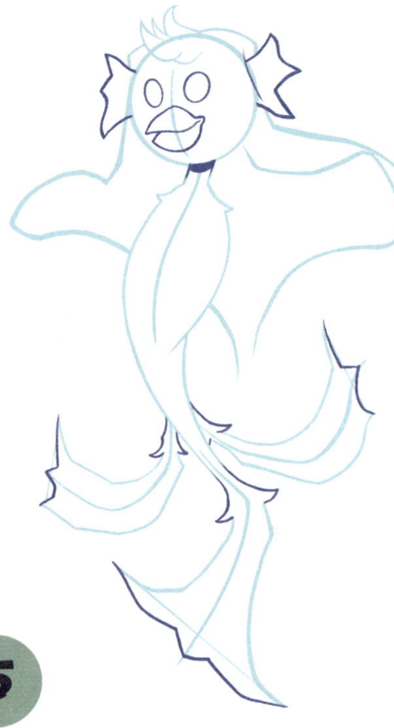

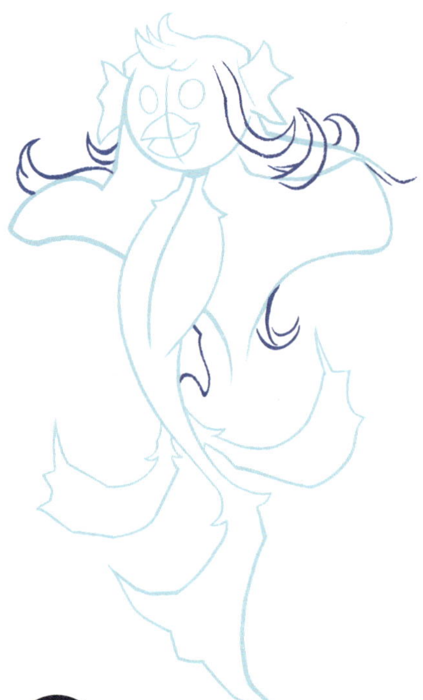

5

Now that the major hair shapes have been
established, use them as a guide to draw
wavy masses of hair. Add a small wavy fin
to her back.

6

Draw lashes to enhance the eyes.
Add a downward curve in the beak
to create the mouth and draw the
pointed tongue inside. In preparation
for the next step, lightly draw curved
guidelines across the body, showing
that the body is round.

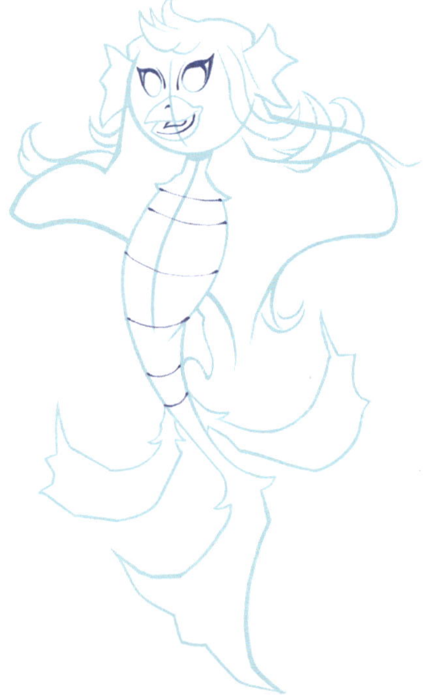

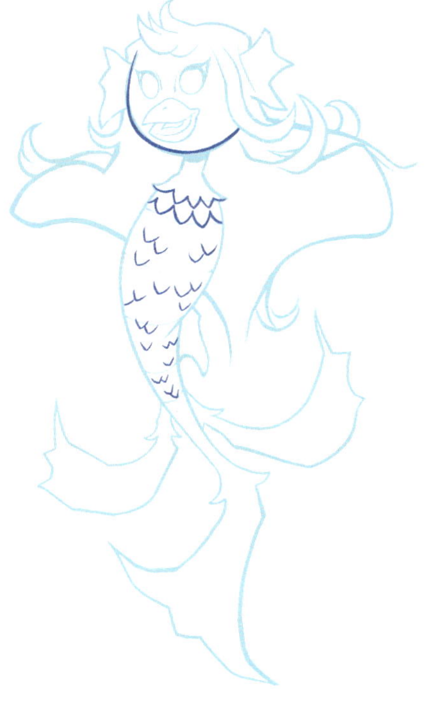

7

Using the guidelines as reference, add scales to the body with curved triangles. There is no need to draw every scale—just enough to give the impression of a scale-covered body. Use a large curve to bulge the cheeks slightly. This gives the yōkai a cuter appearance.

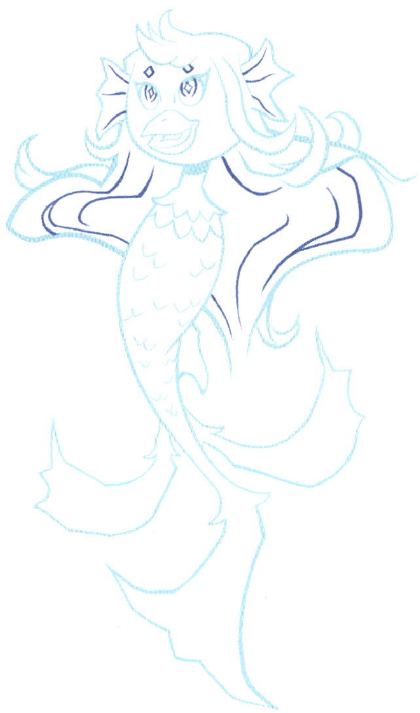

8

Continue to add in lines showing the flowing hair. Draw additional details, such as the diamond-shaped pupils and the ridges in the amabie's ears.

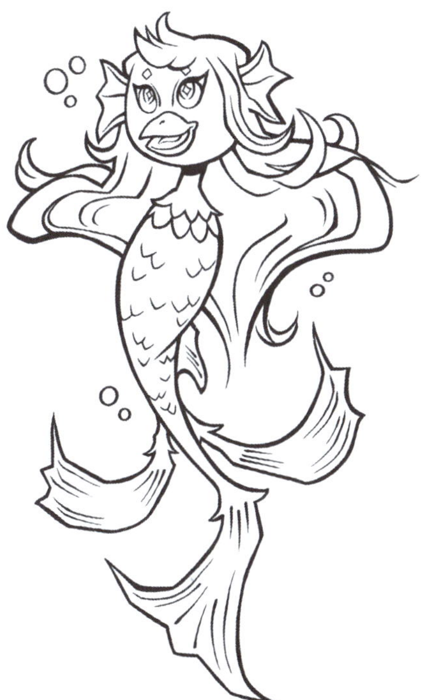

9

To finish the drawing, thicken the outline of the figure. Add bubbles around the amabie to show that she is underwater.

TŌFU-KOZŌ (とうふこぞう)

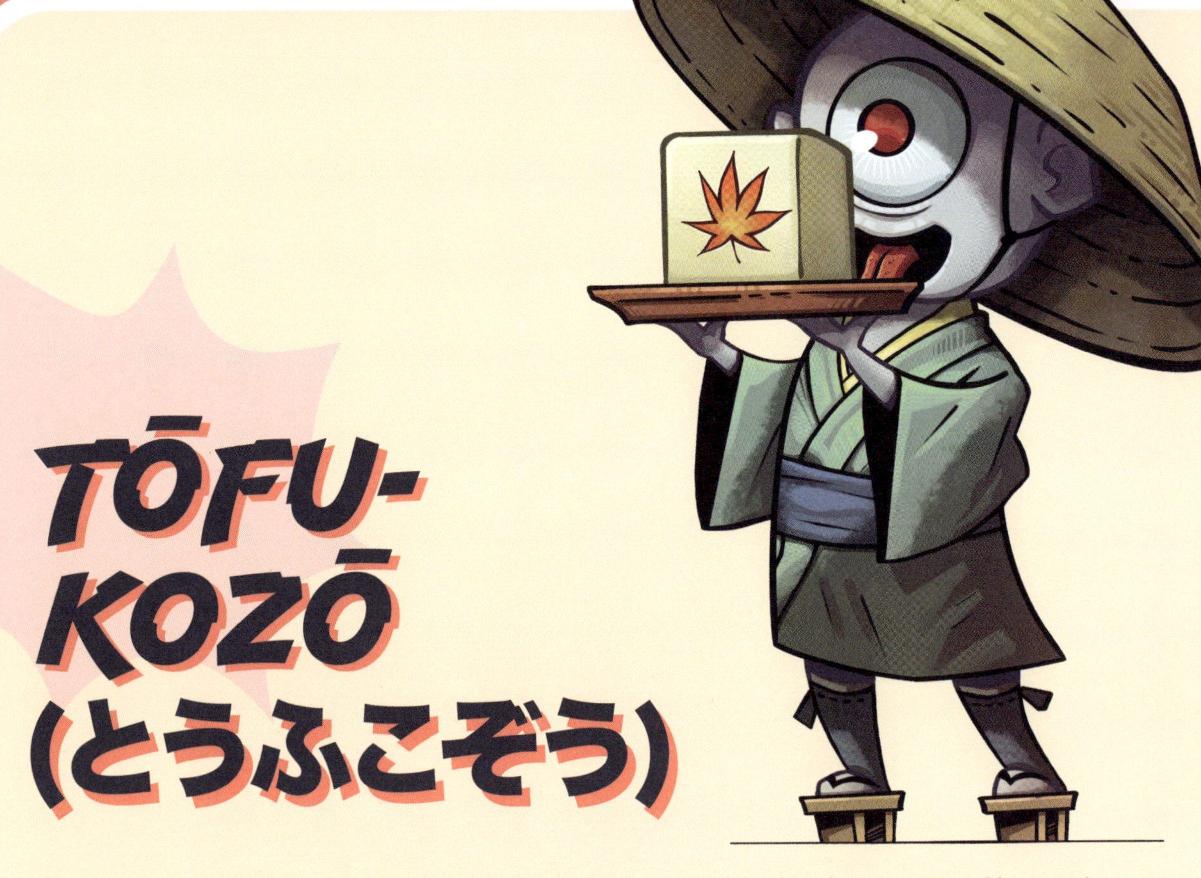

The tōfu-kozō—the tofu-boy—holds the distinction of being the first modern yōkai born of urban life during the Edo period. During that time it became a widely popular character, appearing in children's books, as toys, and even in advertisements for tofu.

As a yōkai of modern origin, there are no traditional tales or stories of the tōfu-kozō, but it is considered a generally harmless yōkai with no unique powers. It is a childlike, timid, bald figure dressed in a bamboo hat, wearing a child's kimono, and carrying a large tray. On this tray sits a block of tofu embossed with a maple-leaf design that he might offer to travelers on the road at night. In tales and artwork the tōfu-kozō often overlaps with the hitotsume-kozō (page 34), another childlike yōkai, and so is sometimes portrayed with one large eye and a long, abnormal tongue.

1

Start with a curved line of action, horizontal ground plane, and an oval head shape.

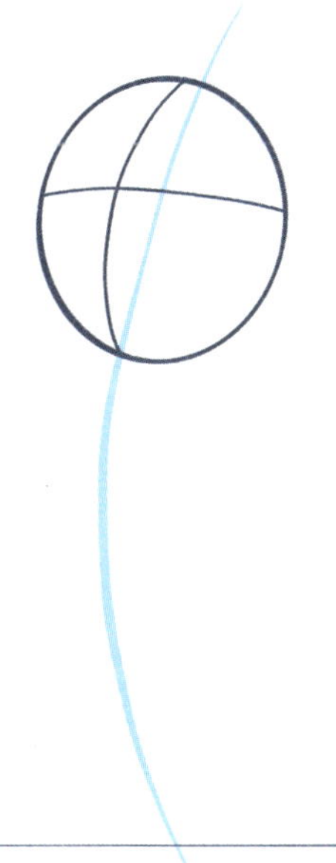

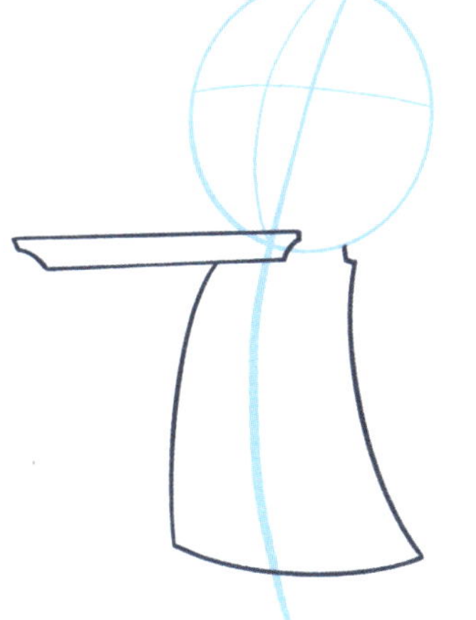

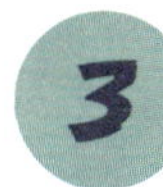

2

Draw a curved box for the body, following the flow of the line of action. Add the flat tray where the tofu will be placed.

3

Draw the rounded block of tofu. Use swooping, curved lines to create the sleeves. Draw curved tubes for the tōfu-kozō's legs.

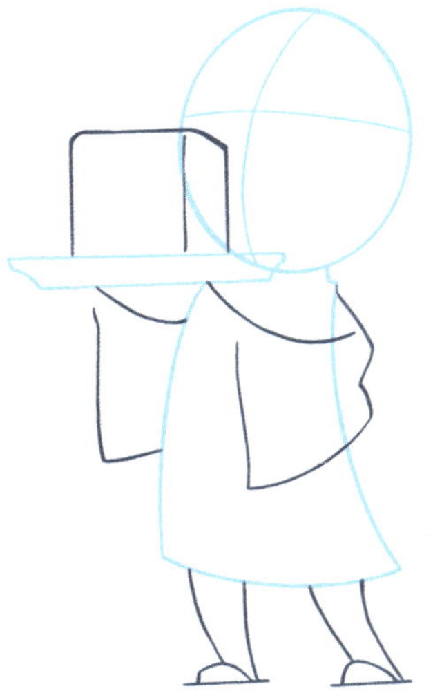

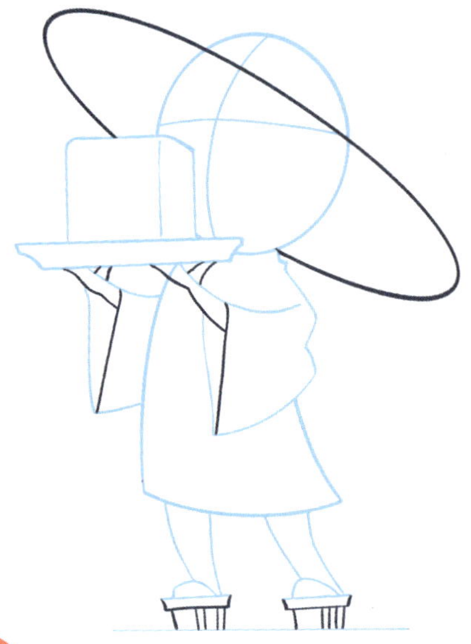

Draw a wide oval for the sugegasa hat. Complete the hand and arm shapes by following the curves of the sleeves. Draw his geta sandals.

Add facial details. Start by drawing circles for the eye. Follow up with a bean shape to create a wide-open grin. Draw the large top curve of the sugegasa.

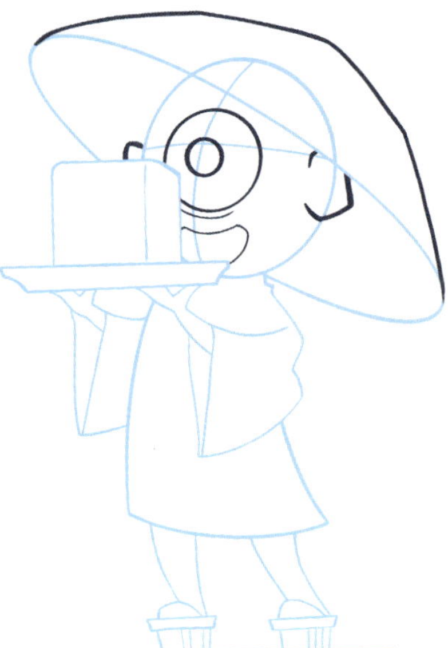

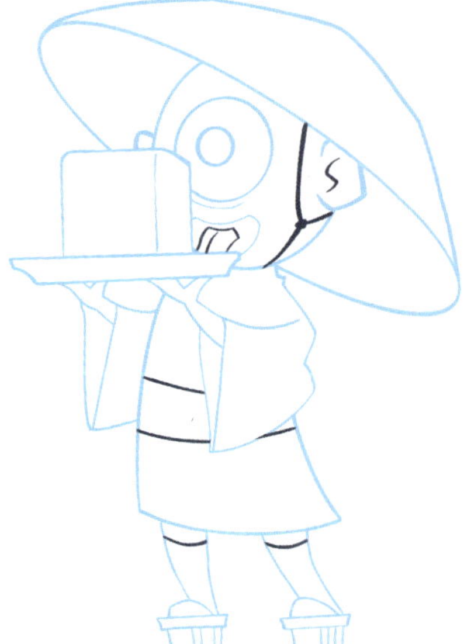

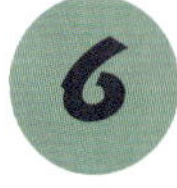

Start the final details of the drawing. Use shallow curves to create his obi sash and leg wraps. Draw the string that secures the hat on his head and the S shape of the inner ear. Don't forget his tongue hanging out.

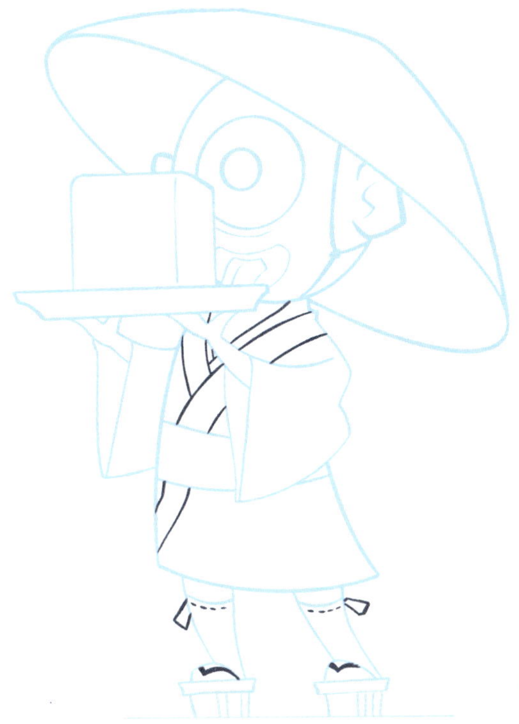

Finish the details of his kimono. Draw the curved collar of the kimono inside the body shape. Add smaller details, such as the straps of his geta and the stitching of his leg wraps.

The tofu that this yōkai carries is traditionally shown embossed with a Japanese maple leaf design. Add texture to the sugegasa hat by using broken lines that follow the form of the hat.

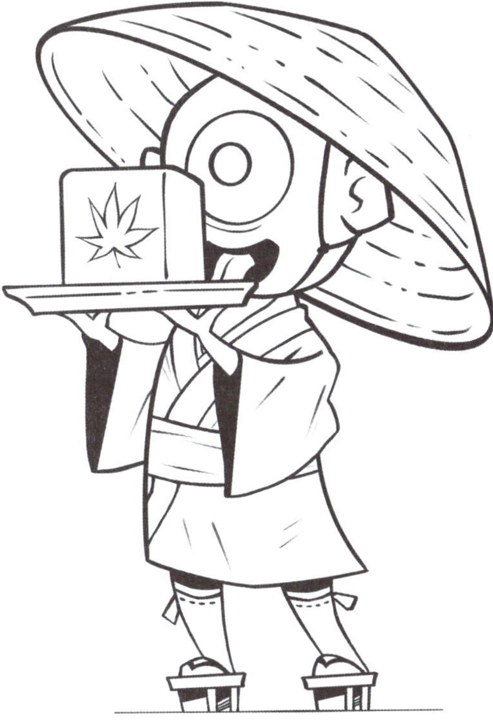

ROKUROKUBI
(ろくろくび)

The rokurokubi was originally a human who has been cursed. What makes this yōkai especially scary is that the cursed victim might not even know she is a rokurokubi, as she is completely normal during the day. But when night falls and she sleeps, the curse awakens and her head moves around on its own, stretching out on a long, entangling neck to seek sustenance. Rokurokubi have been known to feed on bugs, insects, and lamp oil, but they prefer to feed on qi, the vitality of human beings. However, rokurokubi are not necessarily directly harmful to people.

Since the head shapes of the rokurokubi are so distant from the rest of the body, we will work on both parts concurrently. Doing so is how artists normally work on characters: developing the whole drawing with each step.

Draw the pointed oval of the head with center lines. Draw a long, curving line of action for the neck. Below the neck, draw the triangle shape of the body.

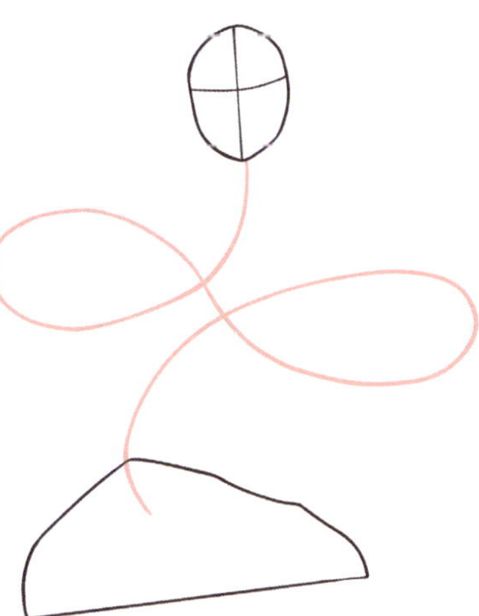

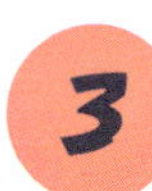

Draw the other major forms of the figure. To the head, add a heart-shaped bun of hair on top and a bun on either side. Draw the long shape of the blanket and bent cylinder of the pillow the rokurokubi is resting on.

Continue to add hair buns to the head. Following the line of action, draw the long, curved neck.

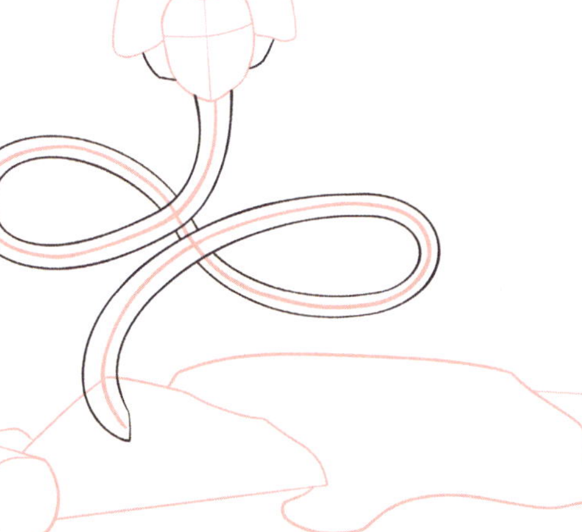

Draw the eyes and the angled baseline of the nose. Draw the rokurokubi's bent arm, which she is using to prop herself up. As you draw, pay attention to the sharp angle of the elbow and the curves of the cloth.

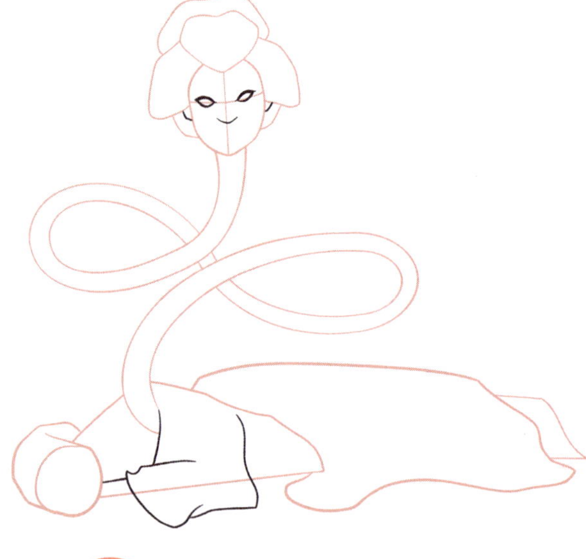

Refine the shape of the blanket by drawing wrinkles where it is bunched up, having been pushed down off her back. Continue to draw the rokurokubi's face. Add her smiling mouth and arched eyebrows.

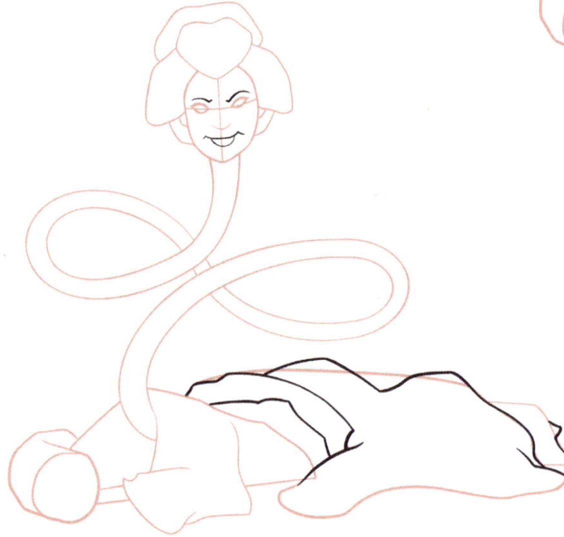

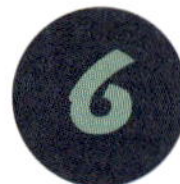

Draw a line for her smiling teeth and add lines to the hair that follow the curve of each bun. Draw the eri collar of her kimono, as well as the trim on the blanket and pillow.

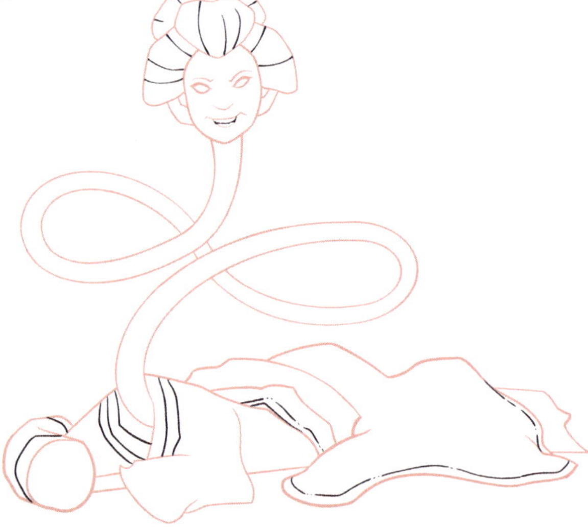

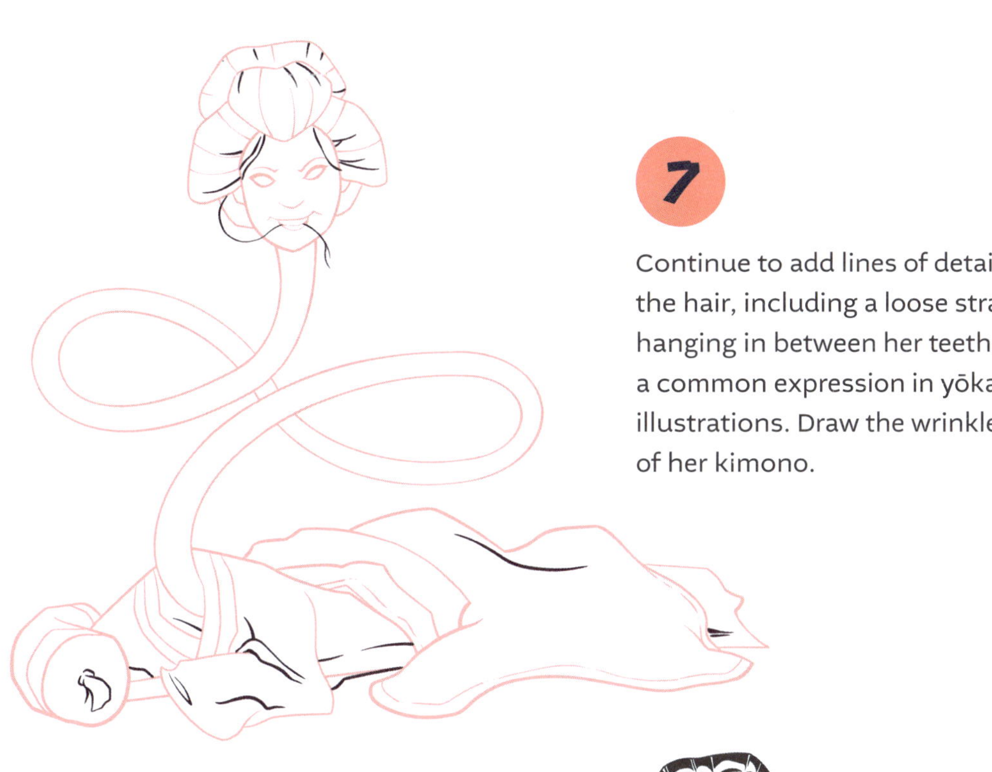

Continue to add lines of detail to the hair, including a loose strand hanging in between her teeth: a common expression in yōkai illustrations. Draw the wrinkles of her kimono.

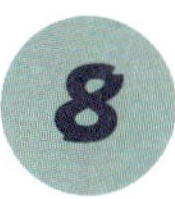

Use broken lines to add texture to the blanket, indicating seams. Finally, add a few loose strands of hair hanging down to give her a slightly disheveled look.

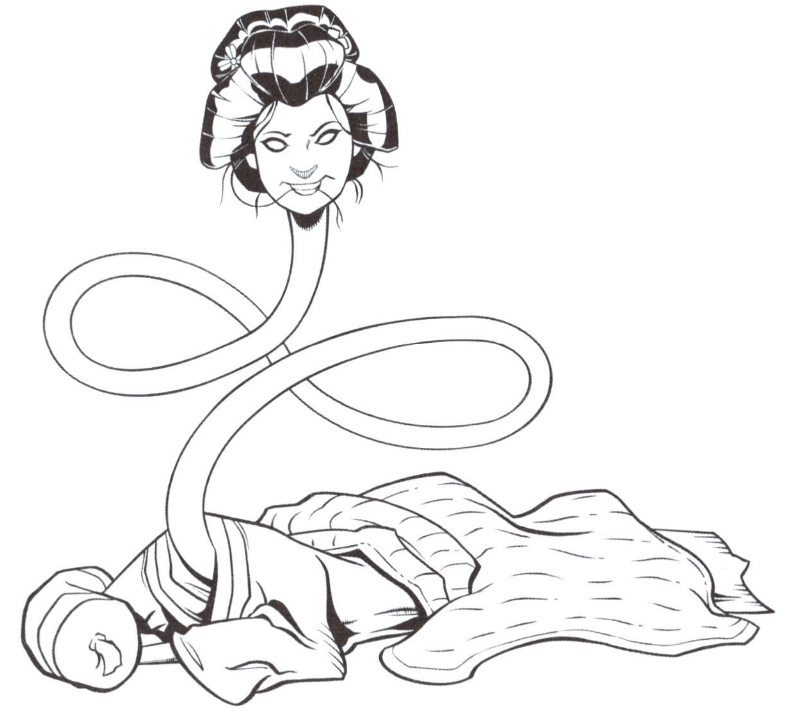

FUTAKUCHI-ONNA
（ふたくちおんな）

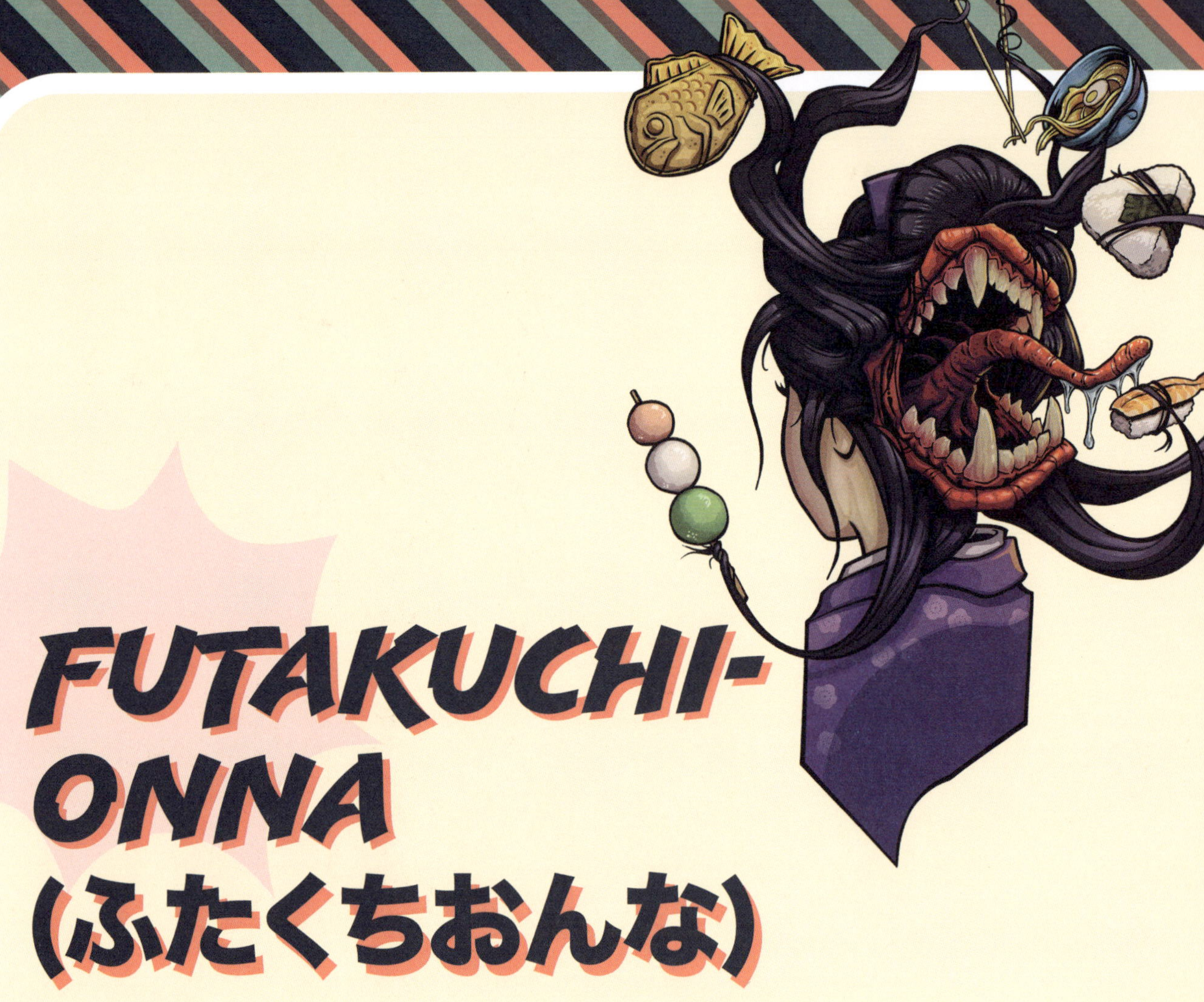

The futakuchi-onna is an eerie and unsettling yōkai, whose name translates as "two-mouthed woman." The key distinct feature of this yōkai is that on the back of her head, concealed behind cascading, long, dark hair, is a second large, grotesque mouth. This second mouth possesses a ravenous appetite and a mind of its own. It can even manipulate hair like appendages, reaching out and grabbing food to eat and quench its voracious hunger. A sign that a futakuchi-onna might be in the house is if there is a guest who barely eats, but food supplies keep disappearing. Like the rokurokubi (page 102), in Japanese lore the futakuchi-onna has been cursed either for her own misdeeds or for the misdeeds of her spouse or family.

Steps 1 to 4 will focus on laying out all the major shapes of the futakuchi-onna.

Draw a circle for the head. Below the head, block in the shape of the upper body.

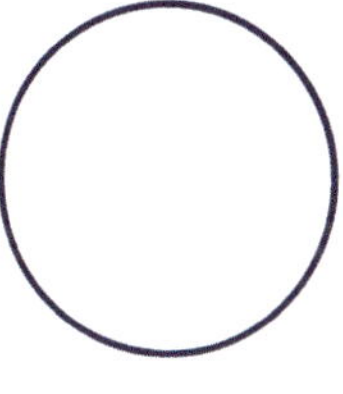

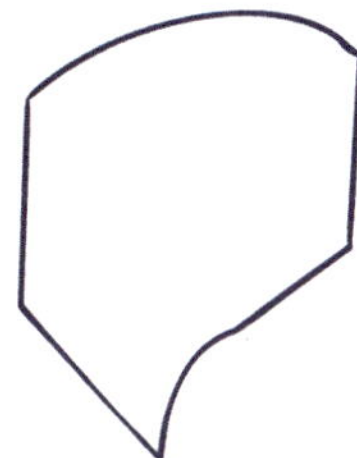

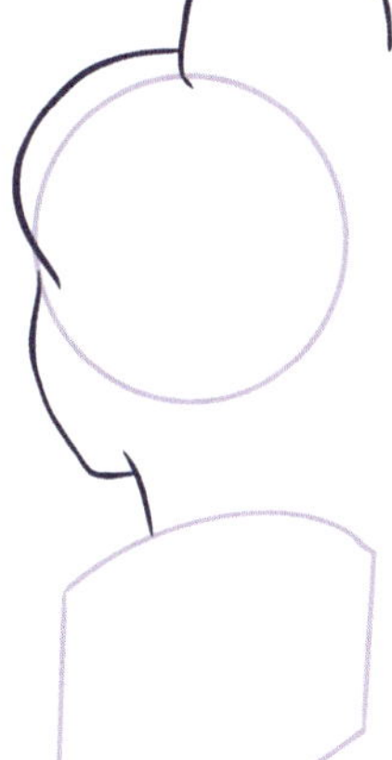

Connect the head to the body by drawing the side of her face and neck. Begin to sketch the hair-bun shapes on the top of her head.

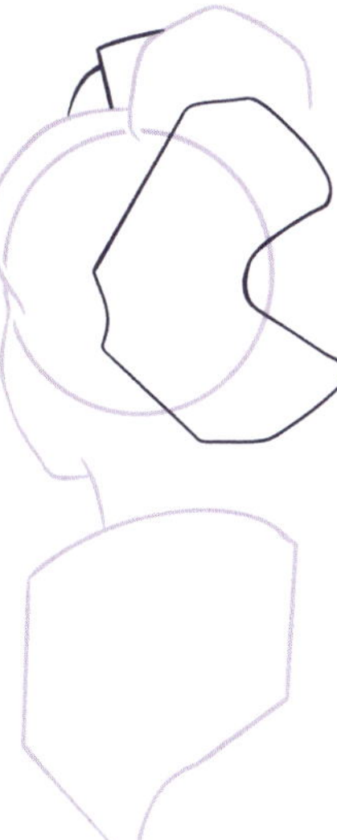

Draw the basic outline of the gaping maw of a mouth on the back of her head and continue to build up the hair shapes.

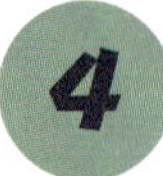

4

Surrounding the head, draw the basic shape of the various iconic Japanese food items that the futakuchi-onna is eating. Starting on the bottom left, draw circles to create dango, then the fish-shaped taiyaki, a bowl and chopsticks for the ramen, a triangle for the onigiri, and a block for the nigiri.

With the major shapes blocked in, the next set of steps will focus on refining these forms.

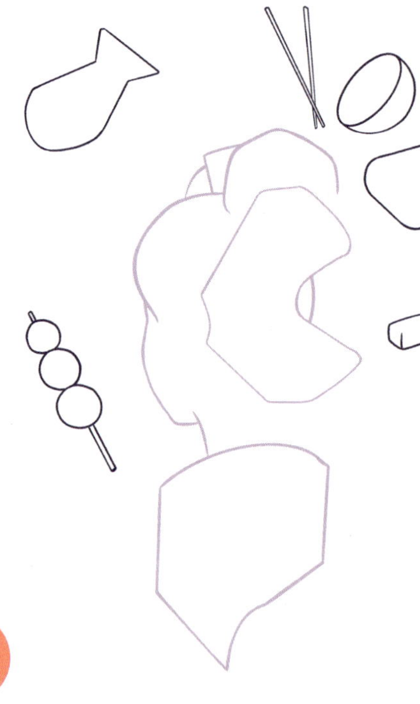

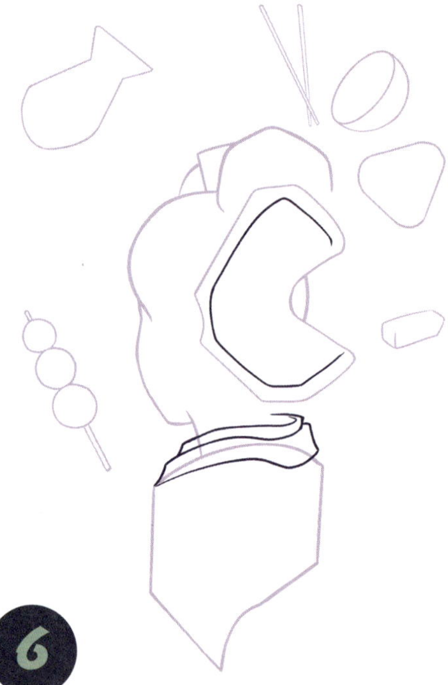

5

Draw the curve of the lips. Add the layered collar to the kimono.

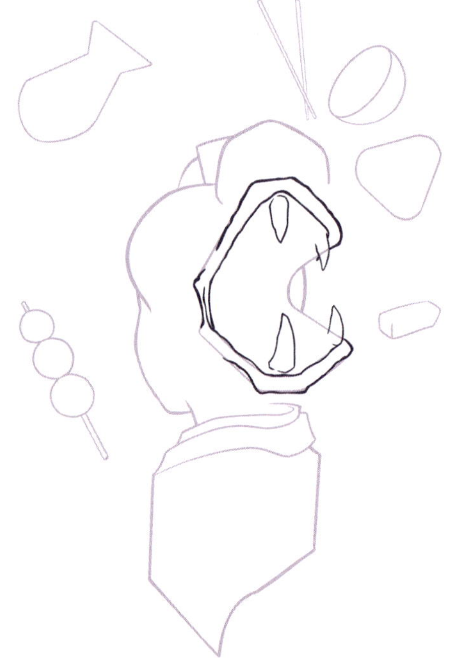

6

Refine the outline of the lips by drawing an uneven, bumpy edge to give them a more "monster-like" texture. Draw large fangs in the four corners of the mouth.

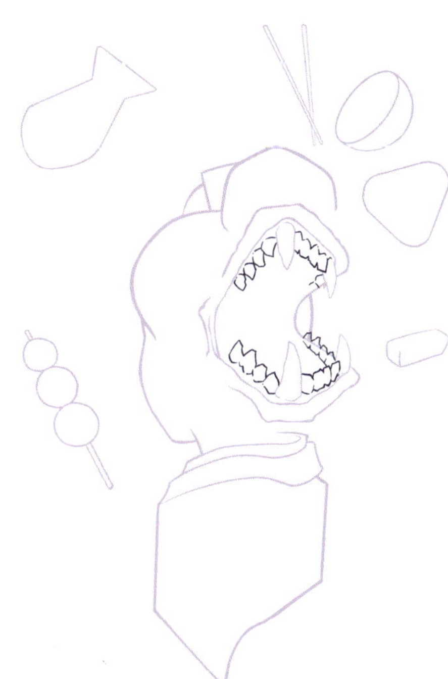

7

Use scalloped triangles to draw four sharp teeth on each side of the fangs.

8

Draw the long, repugnant tongue.

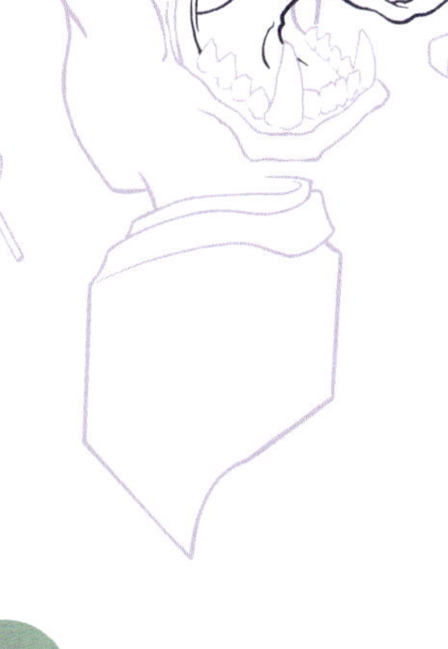
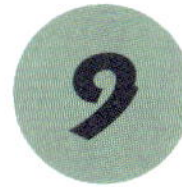

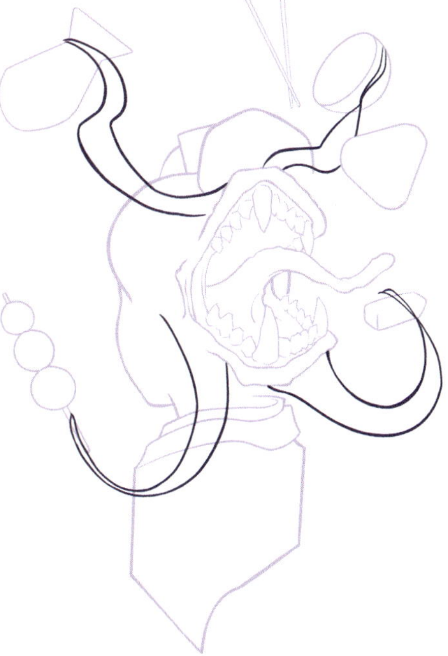

9

The futakuchi-onna uses her hair like hands. Draw the long curves of these hair tendrils, connecting the head to the food all around it.

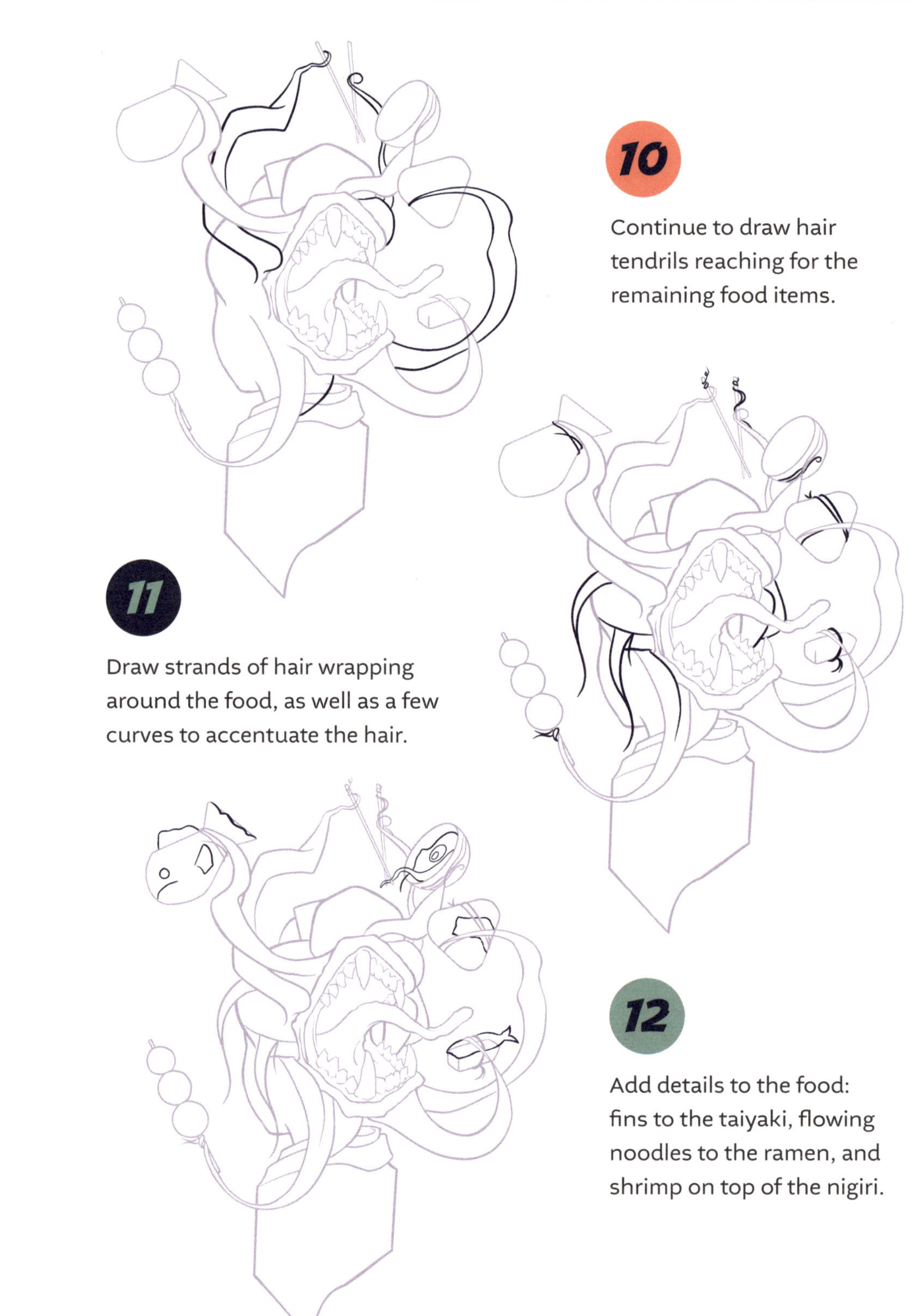

10

Continue to draw hair tendrils reaching for the remaining food items.

11

Draw strands of hair wrapping around the food, as well as a few curves to accentuate the hair.

12

Add details to the food: fins to the taiyaki, flowing noodles to the ramen, and shrimp on top of the nigiri.

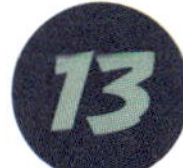

13

Continue to add details to the food like ridges to the taiyaki and bumps to the outlines of the onigiri and nigiri, showing that they are made of rice.

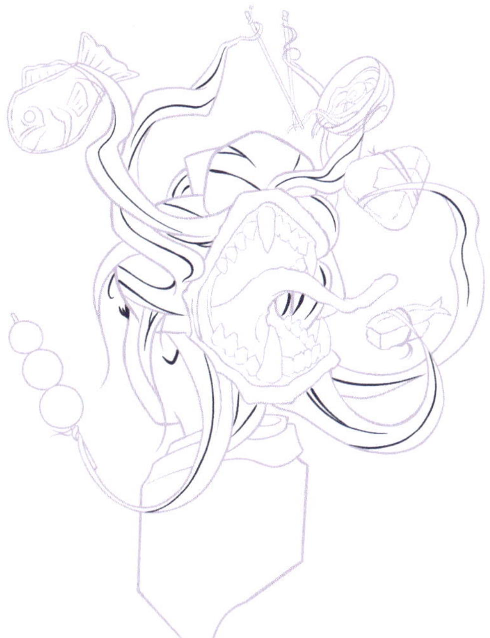

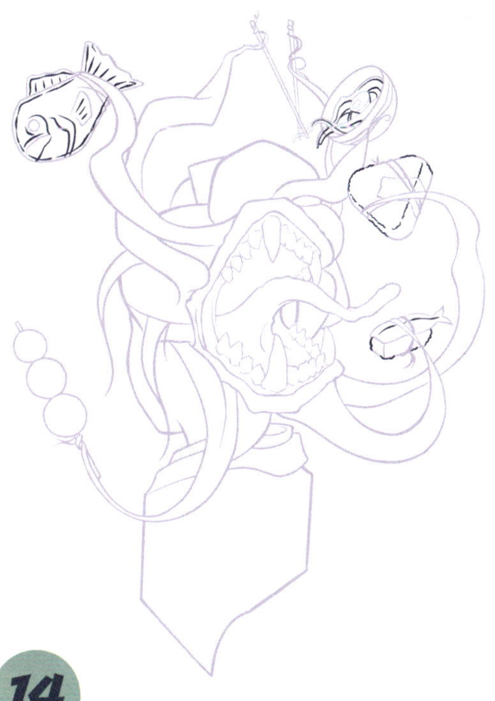

14

Draw long, sweeping curves inside the hair tendrils and buns, which add detail and complexity.

15

Add more sweeping curves to the hair. To show the voracious hunger of the futakuchi-onna, draw drool hanging from the long tongue.

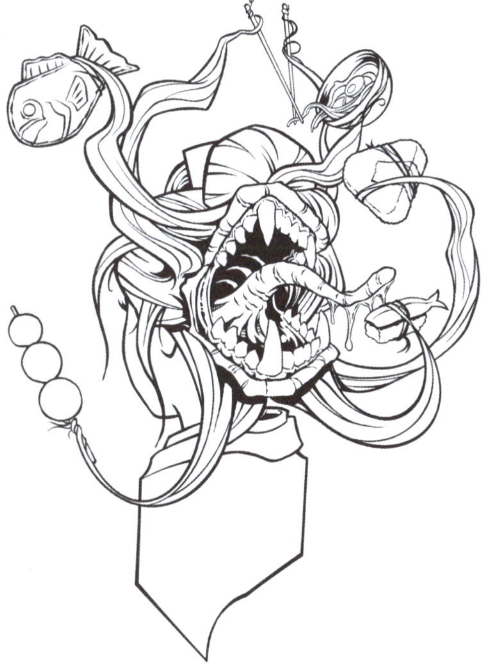

FRIGHTFUL
SPIRITS
YŌKAI

Centuries before yōkai inspired anime and manga characters, they were the nightmares of the Japanese people. Yōkai were the spirits stalking the wilderness, bringing death in their wake. Demons whispered about and warded against. The monsters lurking in the dark that parents warned their children about.

In this section, we delve into the horror side of yōkai, in which malicious ghouls roam the night and wicked spirits prowl in the shadows seeking vengeance on the living. Here you'll find ghostly whales haunting distant shores, spirit fires in a variety of forms flitting about the night sky, and malevolent yūrei with a deadly grudge.

HAKA-NO-HI (はかのひ)

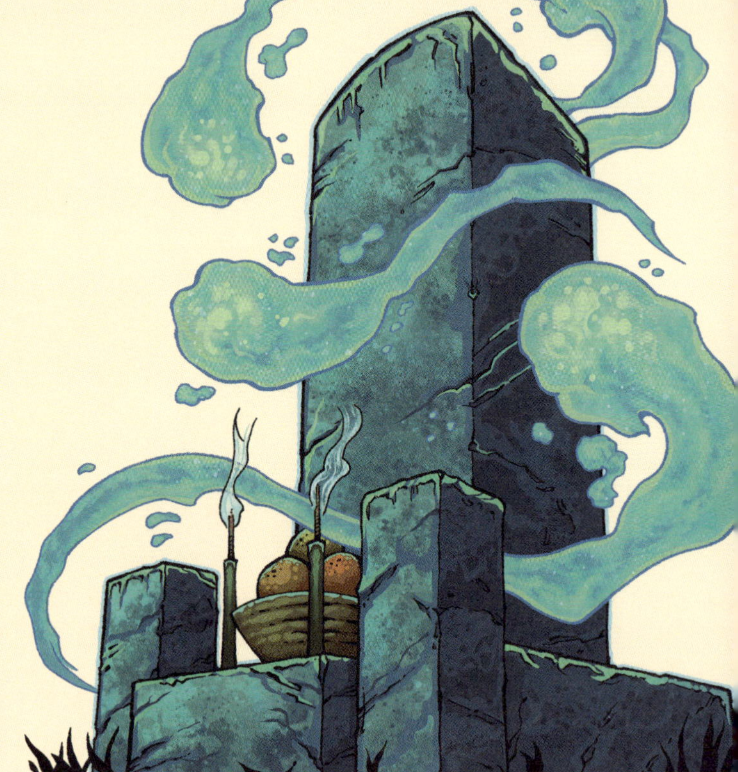

This grave-fire yōkai is one of the many various types of magical fireball yōkai spirits. The haka-no-hi is a mystical fire that can be observed lingering around ancient graves. In Toriyama Sekien's book *The Illustrated Demon Horde from Past and Present, Volume II*, he said that this yōkai is a "sign of the tenacity of the human soul."

Closely connected to this yōkai is another spirit-fire yōkai called the *hitodama*, which is one of the more common yōkai spirits. These yōkai are glowing fires that fly through graveyards, forests, and villages at night. They are the souls of the recently departed and most often portrayed as blue flames with long fiery tails. Both the haka-no-hi and hitodama are harmless.

In steps 1 to 3, we will begin by drawing a stack of various blocks to form a traditional Japanese grave.

1

Lightly draw a line for the ground with a ruler and a standing block in the center.

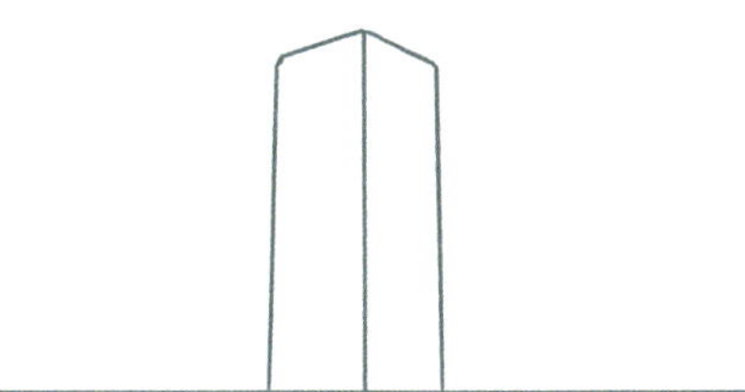

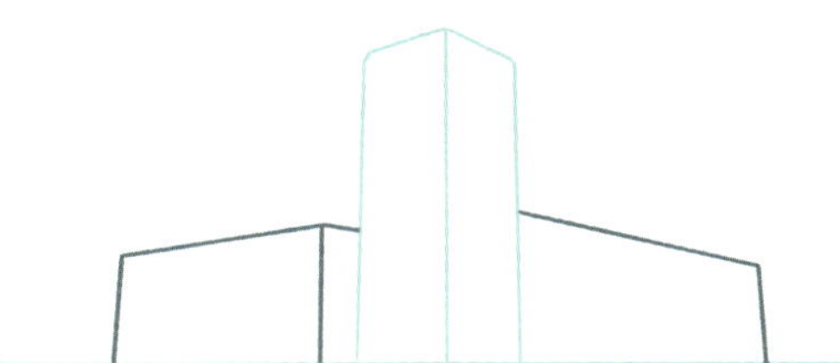

2

Draw the foundation stones: a larger stone on the right and a smaller block to the left of the first block.

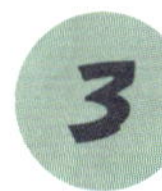

3

Draw the main stone monument, centered on the grave, with a slightly curved top line and a smaller block on the far left.

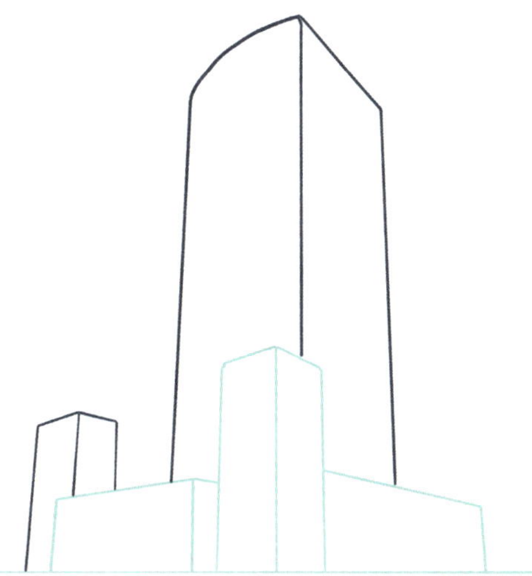

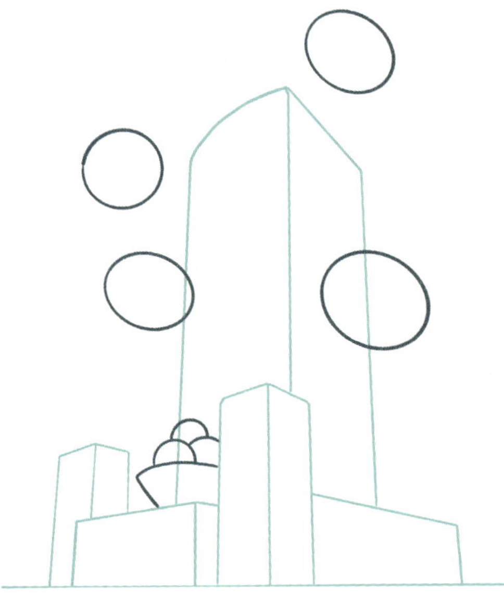

The front area of the grave is where loved ones leave food offerings as well as sake for the deceased. Add a bowl filled with fruit in front of the main gravestone. Draw four ovals in the air surrounding this grave; these will eventually become fireballs.

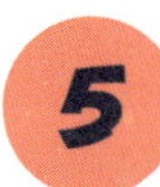

In the front area of the grave, draw two thin cylinders flanking the bowl with thin, sticklike lines emerging from the top. These holders are where incense is placed and burned. Add lines of action to each oval, showing the direction of the tails of each fireball.

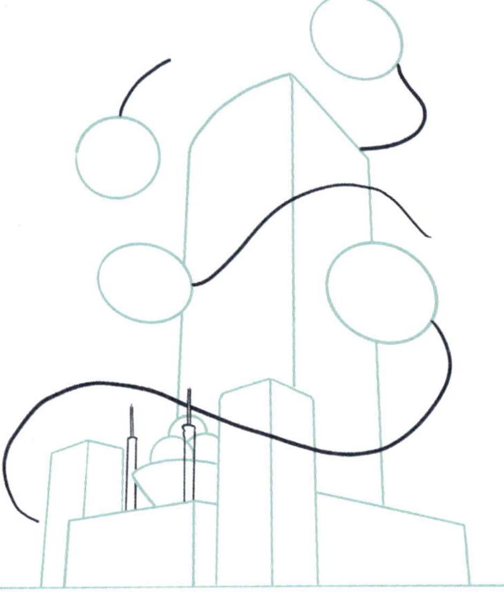

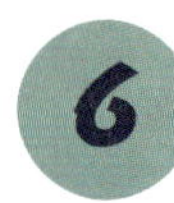

Starting at the top, draw the fire shapes. Since these are spirit fires, use flowing lines as opposed to the jagged lines used to draw natural fire. Start adding small details like wisps of incense smoke and blades of grass.

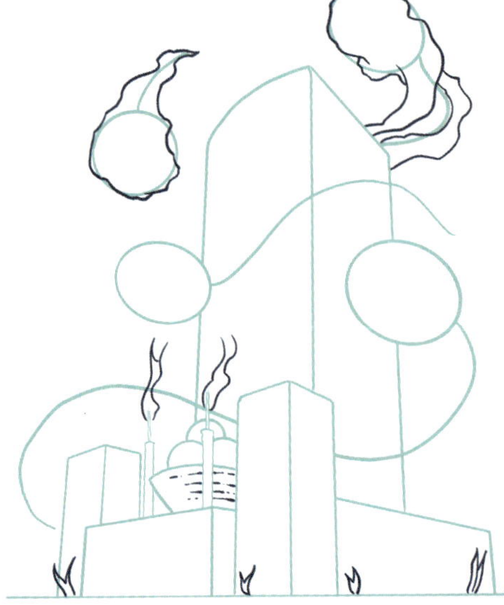

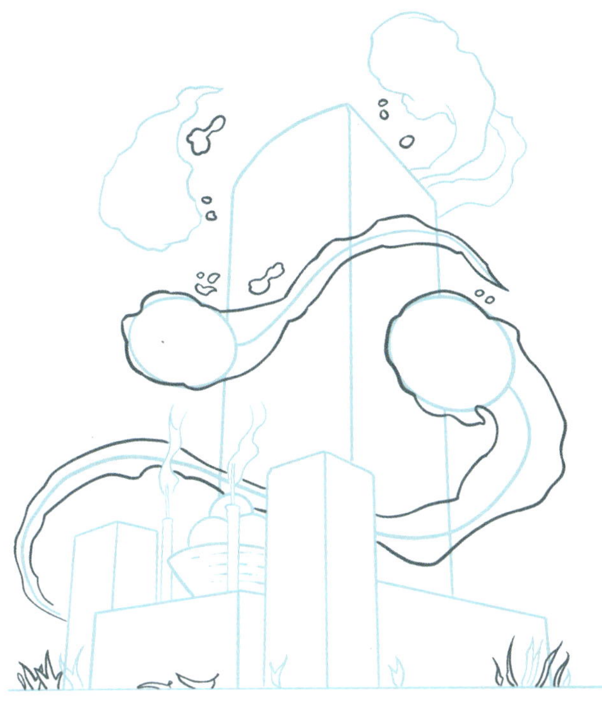

Continue drawing the spirit fires. See how the bottom one weaves between the grave. Add the smaller embers floating around the haka-no-hi and continue adding grass.

To finish, continue adding floating embers around the bottom two haka-no-hi. Draw small cracks on the grave to give it texture and make it look old and weathered.

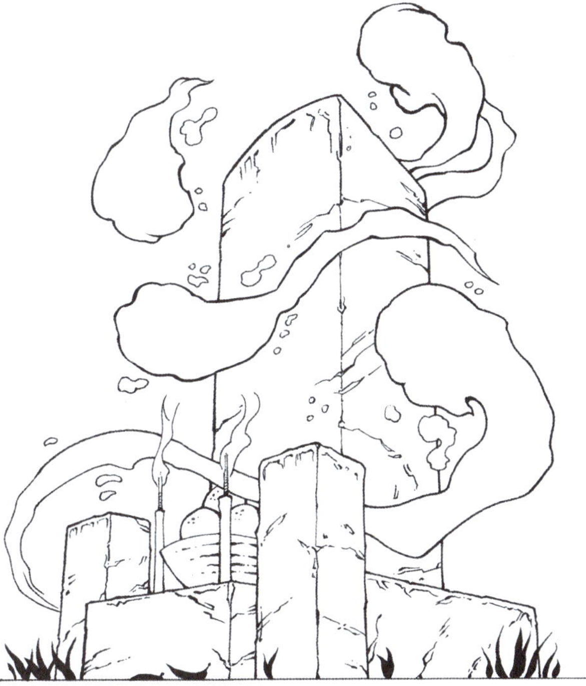

BAKEKUJIRA (ばけくじら)

The bakekujira is the ghost of a dead whale coming back for vengeance. These yōkai are seen as harbingers of destruction; stories say that just the sight of this strange apparition would bring famine, plague, or destruction upon villages. This is the opposite of what the sighting of a living whale would bring to a village, which, when caught, would yield food and materials lasting months. When seen floating over the ocean waves, this yōkai is often accompanied by ghastly birds and nightmarish fish.

Japan has a history of whale shrines along the coast that originate from the country's ancient whale cults. Shrines dedicated to Ebisu, the Japanese god of fishing and luck, viewed the whale as an incarnation of Ebisu, since they brought so much prosperity to villages. As an island nation with a long history of fishing, there are many whale graveyards and whale mounds throughout Japan as offerings of thanksgiving for the bounty that whales have brought to the people.

This yōkai may look complicated with its many tiny pieces, but it is a good exercise in using simple repeating shapes to create the look of complexity. Be sure to take your time and observe the shapes closely.

Draw the curved line of action. Flowing in the same direction, draw a deep, curved line for the underbelly of the whale and a more shallow curve for the top.

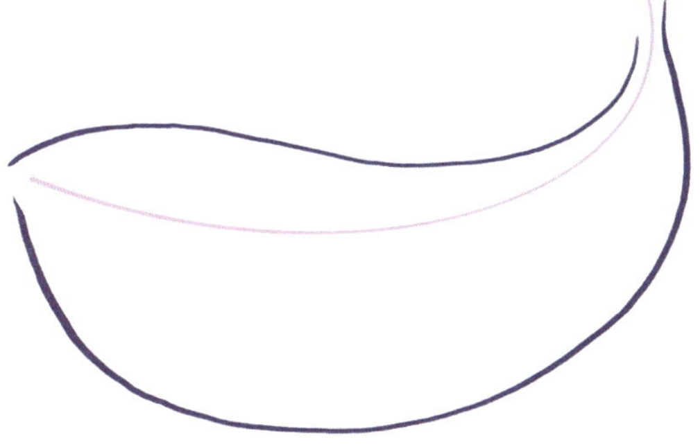

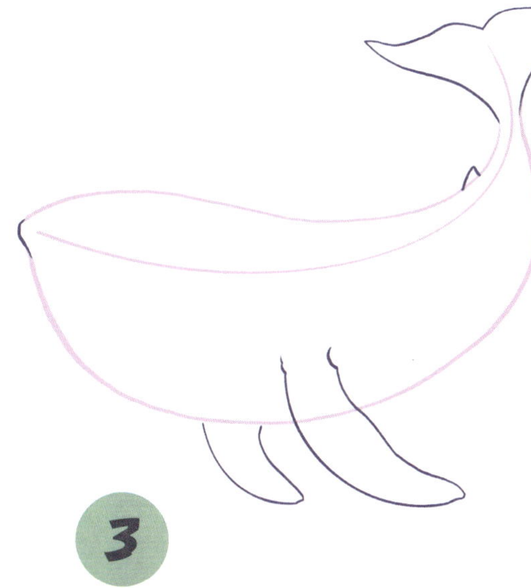

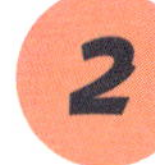

With swooping curves, draw two long pectoral fins. Add a wide triangular tail fin. Pay special attention to the curved top edge of the tail fin to capture the signature look of a whale's tail. On its back, add a small triangular fin just before the tail.

Draw the long, thin shape of the whale's skull and scapula. Take your time and carefully observe the edges of each shape and how they fit together. Include a small curve line where the whale's eye will be. From the skull, draw a curved tube for the spine.

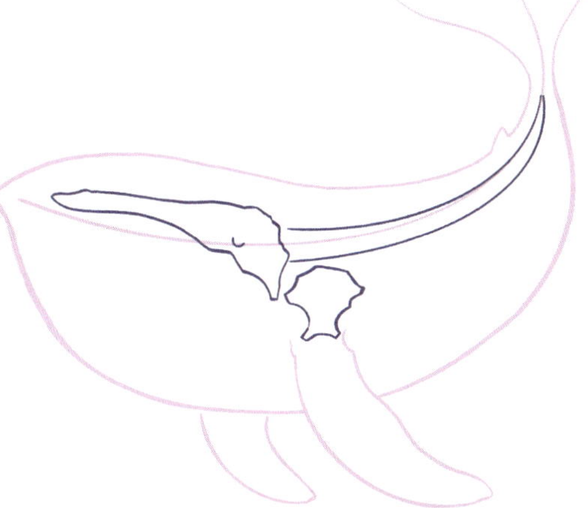

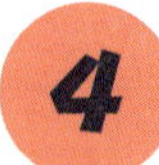

Draw the lower jaw using three long, shallow curves. Starting at the scapula, add bones to the pectoral fin. These bones are just tube shapes that narrow in the middle. Make sure to note their different sizes and shapes. Add two light lines at the top of the whale's skull to add more definition.

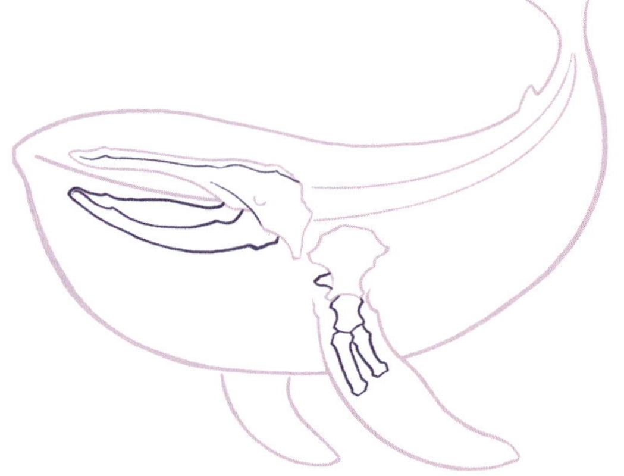

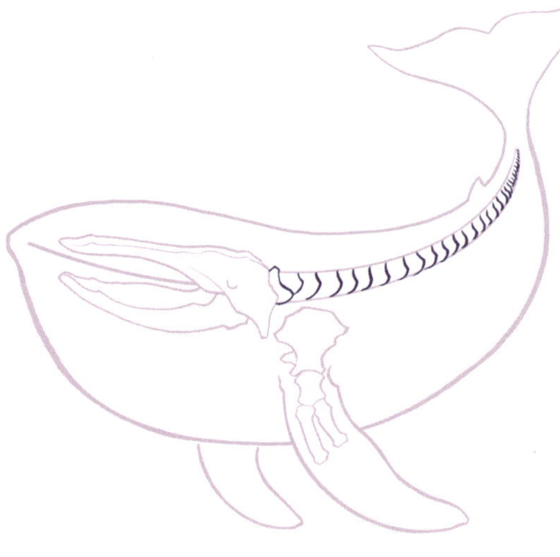

Starting at the skull, draw the individual bones of the whale's vertebrae. Each is the same curved line layered one after the other. As you near the tail, they become smaller and closer together.

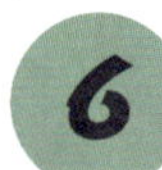

Finish the spine by drawing in the tops of the vertebrae shapes. As before, start at the skull and repeat the same shape as you work toward the tail. Using long, curved tubes, draw the ribs of the whale. The ribs, too, are a repeating shape.

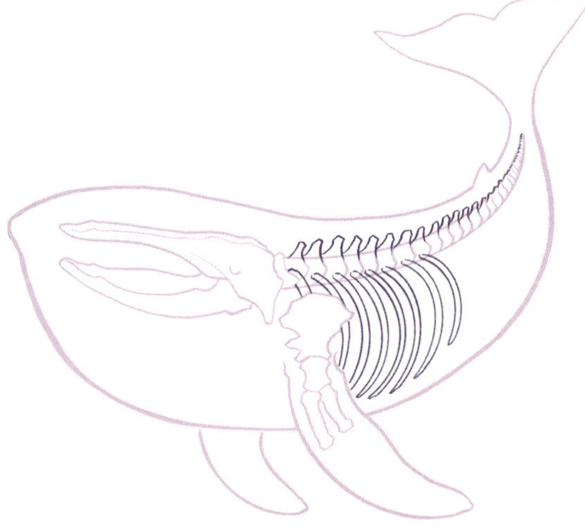

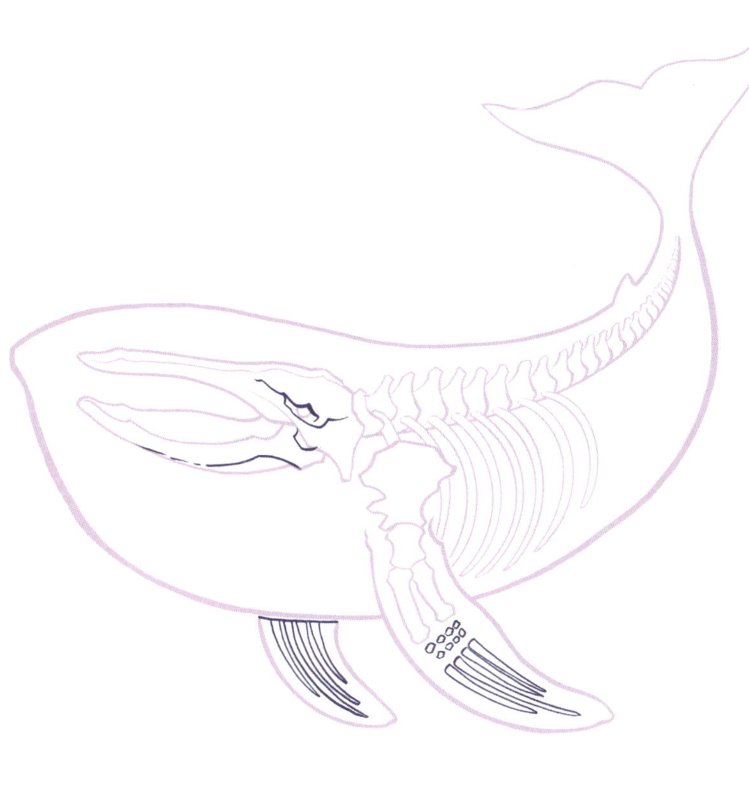

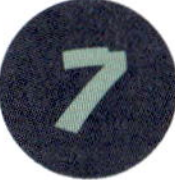

Draw the lower bones of the whale's pectoral fins. Similar to the ribs, use long, curved, tapered tubes. Add details to the skull, like the ridges around the eye, cheek, and along the lower jaw.

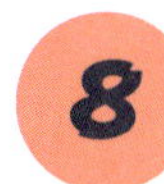

Divide the long pectoral fin bones into smaller segments. To finish, color in the body shape, leaving the bones white so that they pop.

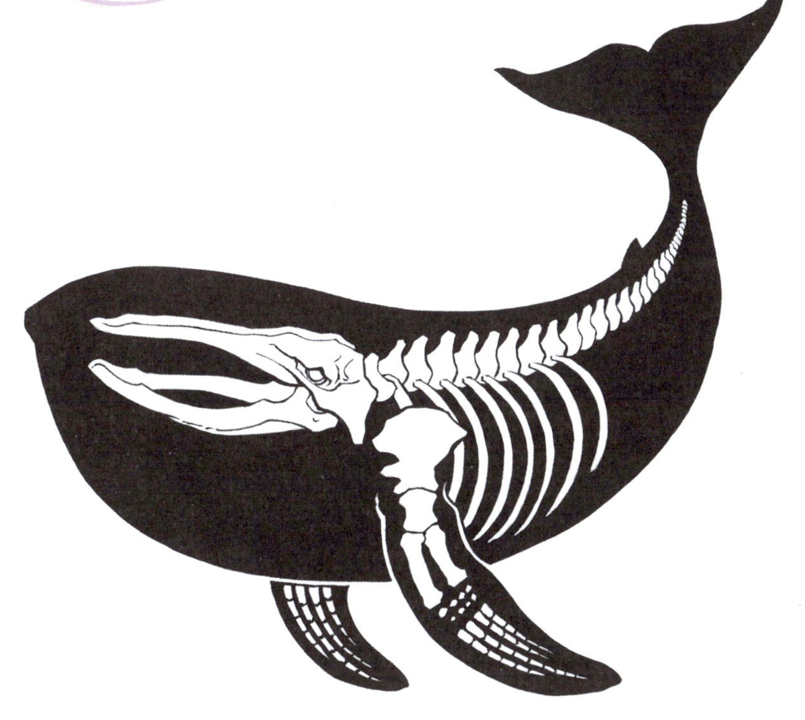

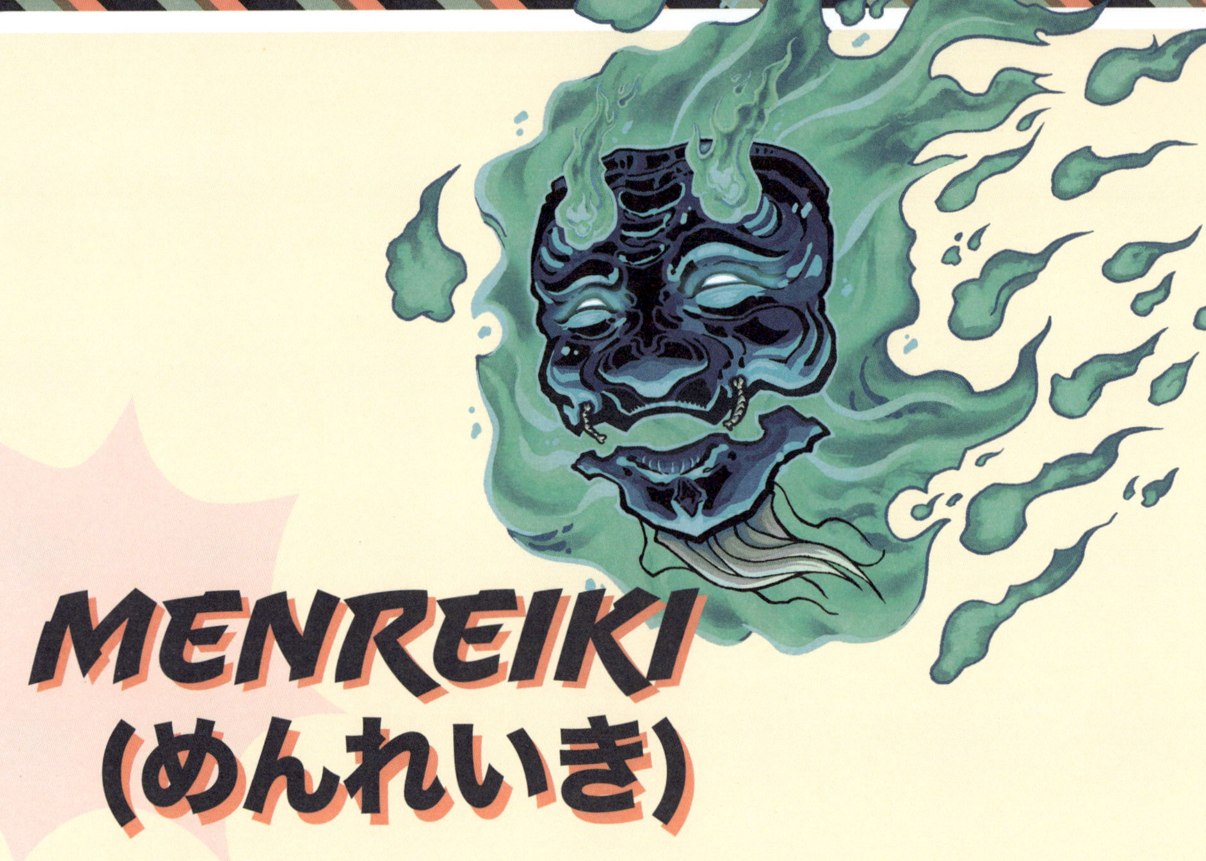

MENREIKI
(めんれいき)

The menreiki is a tsukumogami yōkai (page 22) that was created when Toriyama Sekien gazed upon finely crafted Noh theater masks and dreamed that they had come to life. Noh theater is an ancient Japanese performing art that dates back over six hundred years. In Noh theater there are a wide variety of wonderful masks used to portray various types of characters from nobles to courtesans to demons. When a performer dons a mask it is a special act called *kakeru* (or *tsukeru*), which implies much more than simply putting on a prop. This act involves transforming into the mask character, becoming the mask, and embodying the character and emotions of the mask.

This menreiki is a possessed Okina mask, which is one of the oldest and most sacred Noh masks, depicting an old man or, at times, the embodiment of a god.

Draw the roughly triangular shape of the mask. Add the center lines. Lightly draw the major fire shape around the mask with flowing lines.

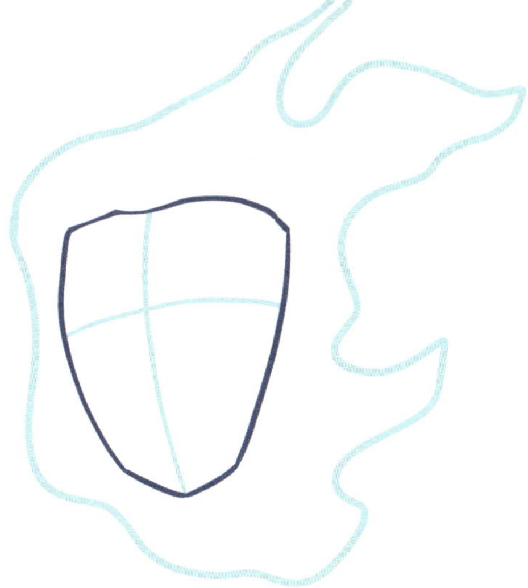

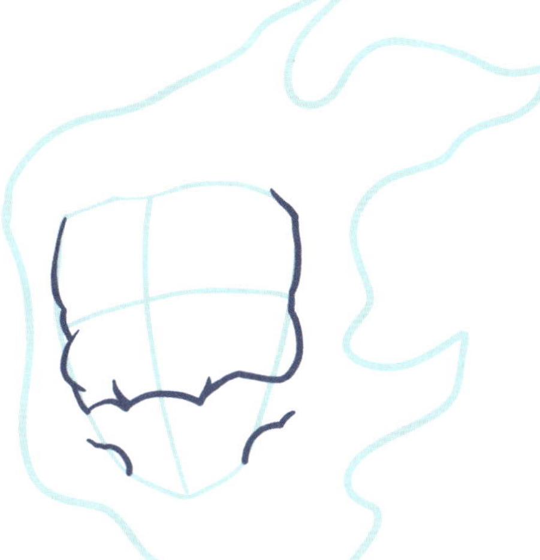

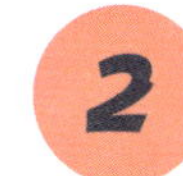

Refine the shape of the face. Add the bulging cheeks and upward, curved jawline. Draw the notches on either side of the lower jaw.

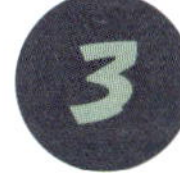

Using fire shapes similar to those in the chōchin-obake (page 22), draw the fireballs on the forehead of the mask. With upward curves draw thin, grinning eyes. Mirroring the top jawline, draw the lower jawline.

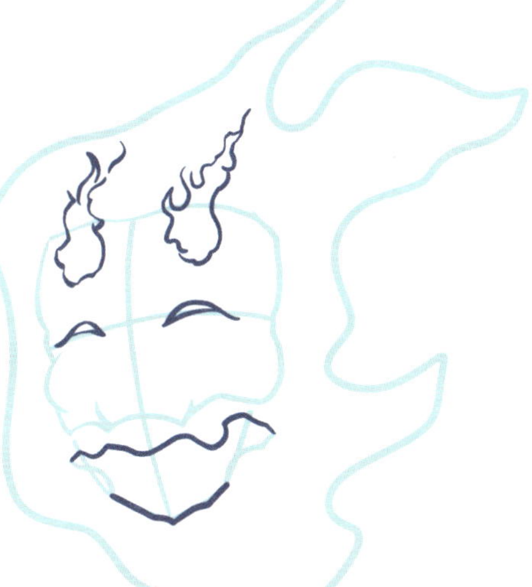

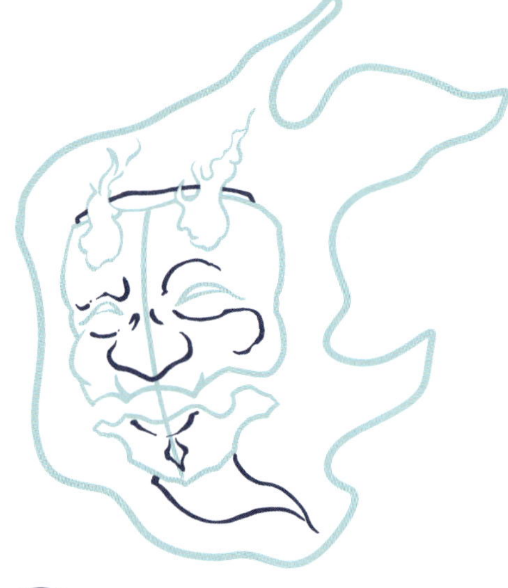

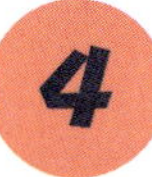

With a rounded V shape, draw the nose. As the menreiki is a mask depicting an old man, begin to add wrinkles to the face and a wispy beard flowing in the wind. Add a ridge along the top of the mask.

Continue to add wrinkles to the forehead and around the nose. Draw the hair of the beard with long, flowing curves. Draw two broken strings between the upper and lower jaws.

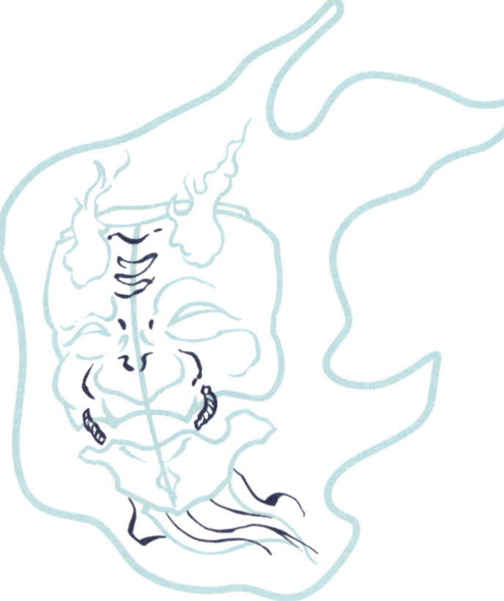

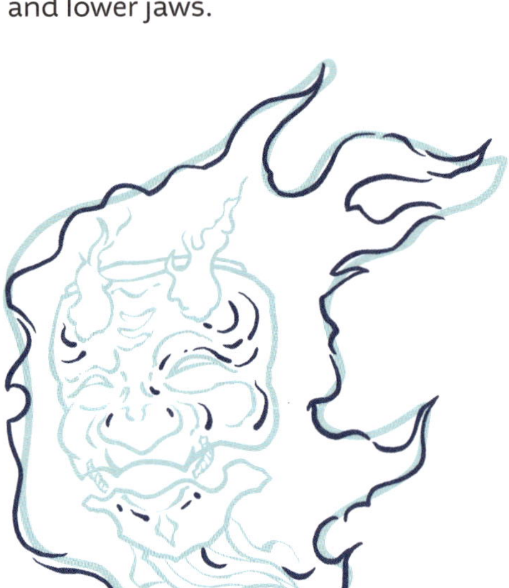

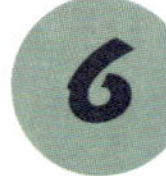

Add the final wrinkles to the face. With the mask mostly completed, turn your attention to the outer fire shape. Refine the loose shape so that it looks more like actual fire.

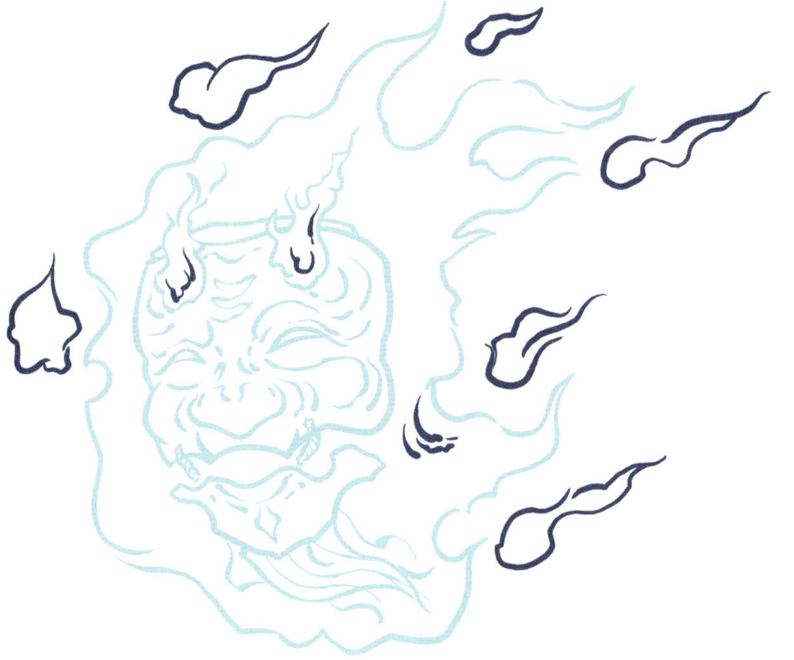
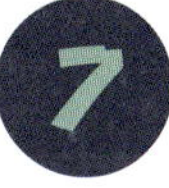
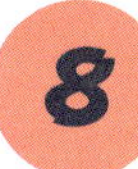

Using fireballs similar to those on the forehead, draw secondary, smaller fireballs between and around the tendrils of the larger fire shape. Keep in mind that the menreiki is flying forward, so the tails of the fire should flow backward. Add additional lines of detail to the fireballs on the menreiki's forehead.

Thicken the outline of the mask, especially the lines at the bottom of shapes like the chin, the upper jaw, and base of the nose.

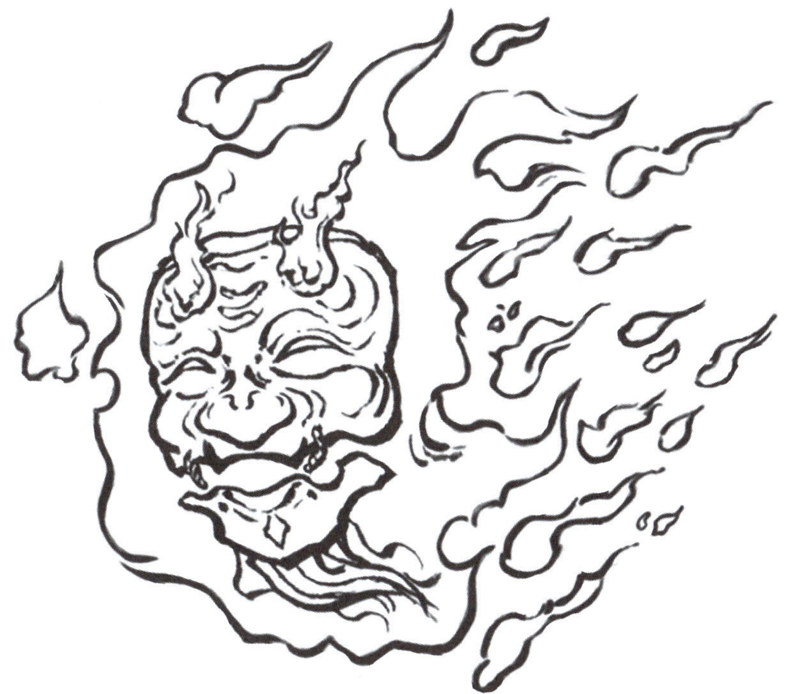

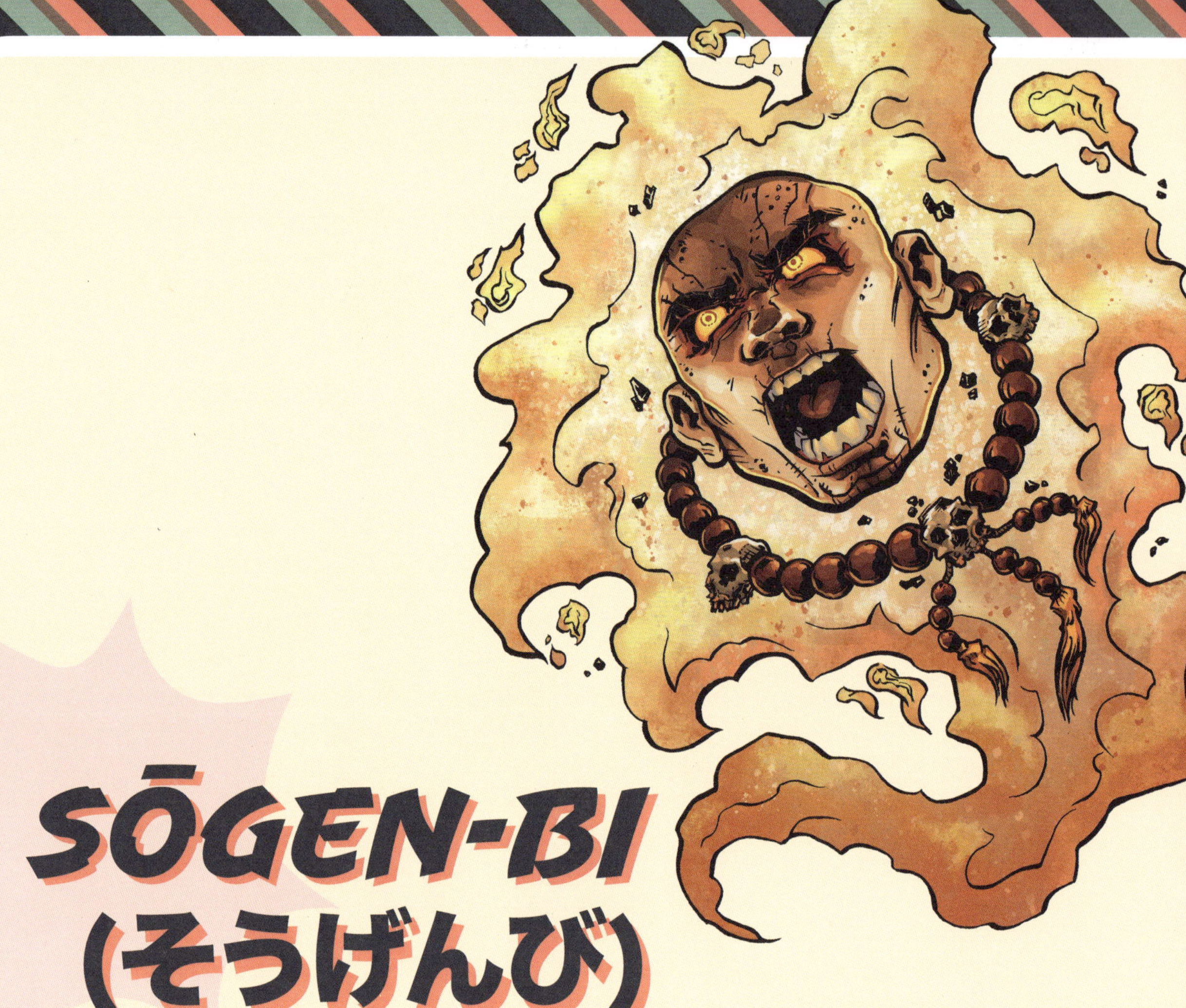

SŌGEN-BI
(そうげんび)

Sōgen-bi is a type of fireball yōkai and stems from a ghost story dating all the way back to 1683. Throughout his life, the wicked monk Sōgen stole money and lamp oil offered at his temple. As divine punishment for his crimes of stealing offerings in life, in death he is plunged in fire. He can be seen as a ghostly, anguished head wreathed in flames flying about the sky around the temple at night.

Drawing the Sōgen-bi will be similar to drawing the menreiki (page 122), but instead of a mask in the fireball, it will be a human monk's head.

Draw a tilted oval with center lines for the head. Lightly draw a much larger oval with a curving tail to block in the general fireball shape.

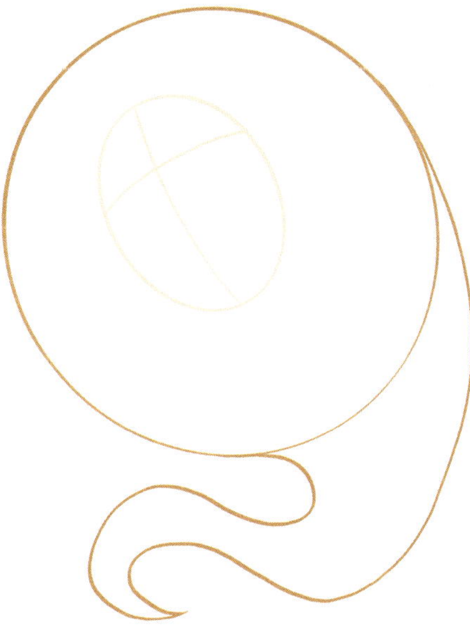

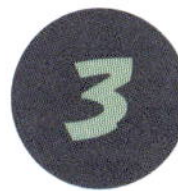

Start laying out the facial features by drawing the ears, a line to show where the nose will go, and a wide gaping mouth. Draw the eyes. Notice how the upper and lower eyelids slant toward the middle of the face to give the eyes an angry glare.

Draw the stretched hollows of the cheeks. Add the nose and eyebrows, slightly slanted inward to further push the angry expression. Lightly draw a large loop with three hanging strands to show where the necklace will go.

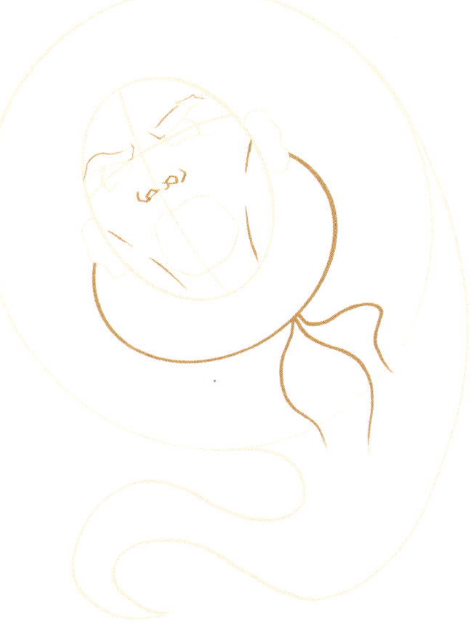

4

Refine the outline of the face. Add his teeth; make a few of them fang-like to enhance the rage on the Sōgen-bi's face. Draw the curves of the inner ear.

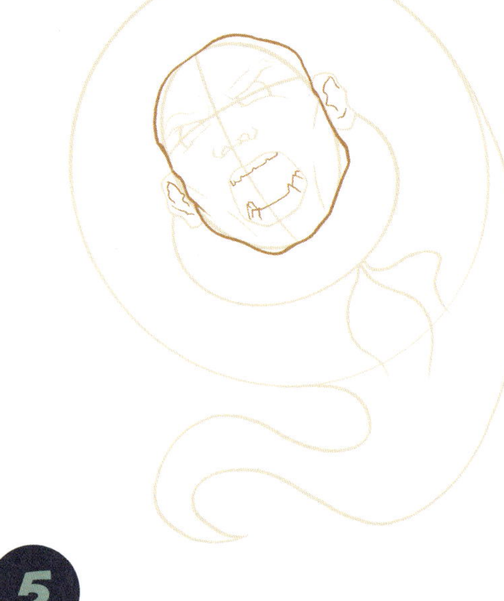

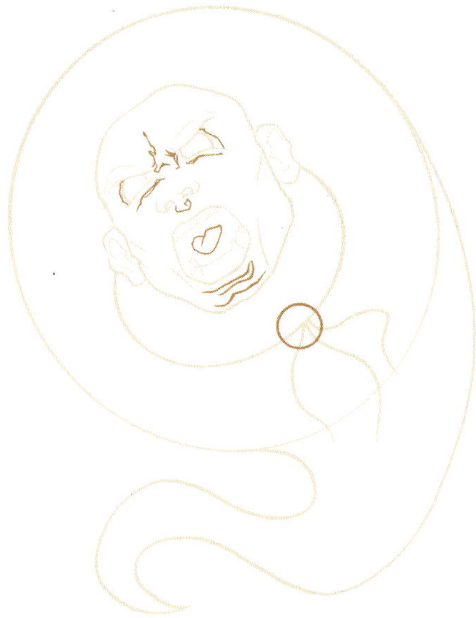

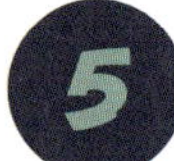

5

Add wrinkles to the face to push his expression: below the eyes, on the pinched nose bridge, and by the lower lip. Draw the tongue. Start the necklace by drawing a circle for the main bead in the center, where the three hanging lines connect.

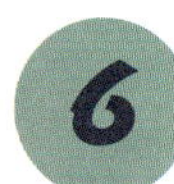

6

This step is all about circles and repeating shapes. Draw the round beads of the necklace by starting at the center bead and working your way up one side, overlapping slightly as you go. Add three smaller beads to each hanging line. Lastly, draw two circles in the eyes for the pupils.

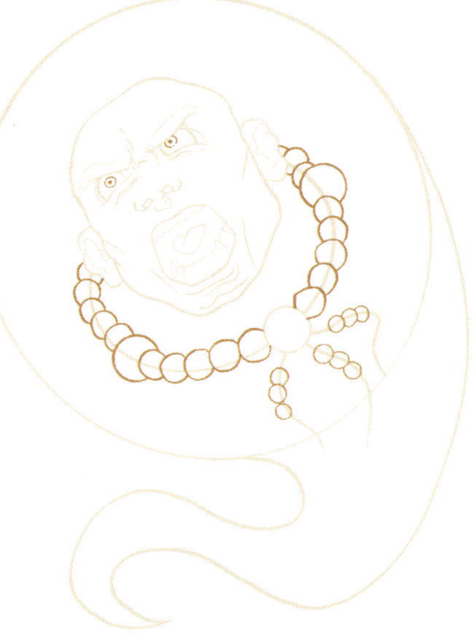

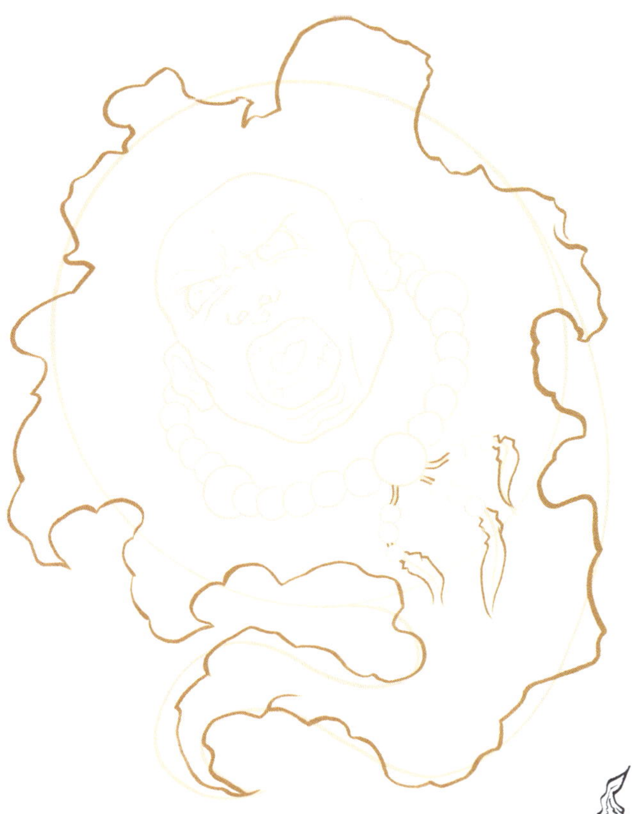

Just as with the menreiki (page 122), draw the outline of the fireball that surrounds the head of the Sōgen-bi. Drawing fire is mainly about knowing the direction it is going in and using a combination of curves and sharp angles that flow in that direction. Notice that the fireball is angled slightly to the left. Draw tassels at the bottom of each hanging line.

To finish, add as many details as you like, such as secondary smaller fireballs, debris floating around the monk's face, or a second row of fire lines around the head.

You can get more imaginative by turning the three larger beads into skulls to make the yōkai look scarier. This is where drawing can get really fun—use your imagination to push your ideas even further.

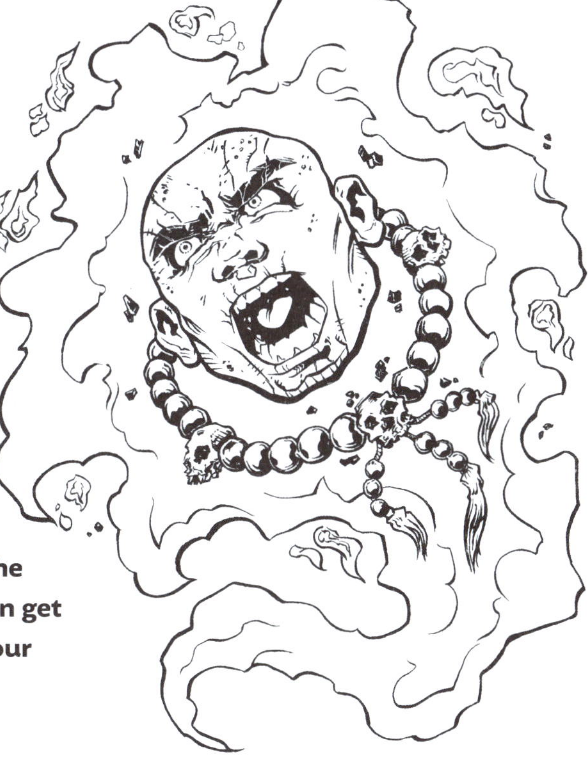

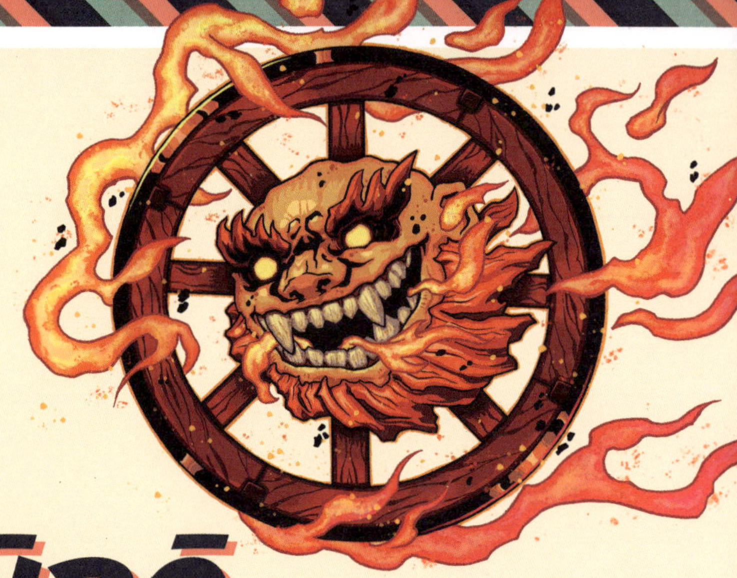

WANYŪDŌ
(わにゅうどう)

Written with the kanji for "wheel" and "monk," this yōkai features the head of a tormented man at the center of a giant oxcart wheel wreathed in flames. According to folklore, the wanyūdō is the condemned soul of an evil *daimyo*, or feudal lord, who had his many victims dragged on the ground by oxcart. The man's head is usually shaved like a monk's, supposedly in penance for the sins of his life.

It is believed that wanyūdō are servants of hell and guard its gates, wandering back and forth between this world and the underworld hunting victims. These fearsome yōkai steal the soul of anyone who gets too close, or even just glimpses the yōkai, and drag their soul to hell. The ferocious wanyūdō are also known to devour people, ripping them limb from limb, causing deadly fever with just a glance, and burning victims until nothing but a pile of ash remains.

Draw a circle for the head and two curved center lines. Be sure to leave enough room on the page to draw the larger wheel and fire.

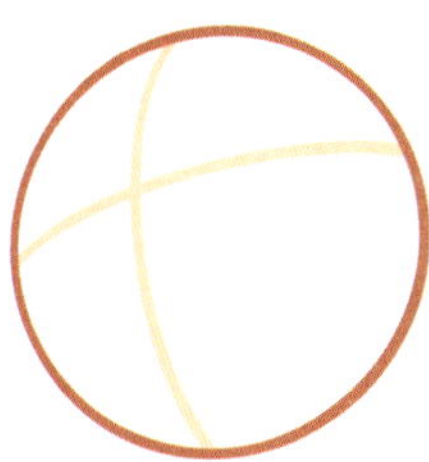

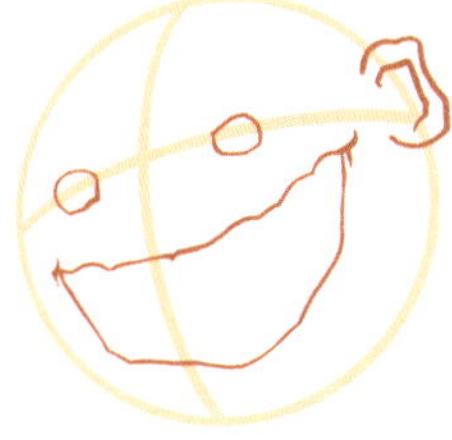

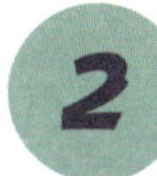

Start with the wicked grin of a mouth. Using two irregular curves, draw the top lip and deeper bottom lip. Do the same for the ear on the side of the face: larger outer curve and smaller inner curve. Draw the rounded shapes of the eyes.

Draw the bushy eyebrows whose shape mimics fire. Be sure to have the bottom of the eyebrows slant toward the center to create an angry expression. Draw the upturned nose, with its angled sides and flat nose tip.

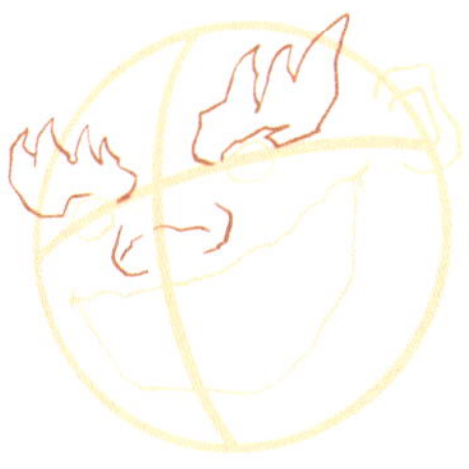

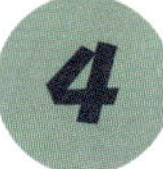

4

Starting with the top row, draw the teeth using an uneven, jagged line. Layer the bottom row behind. Like we did with the eyebrow shapes, draw the beard flowing back, mimicking fire.

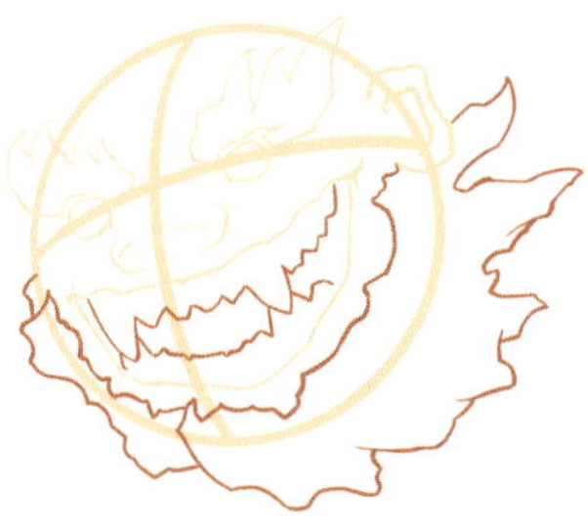

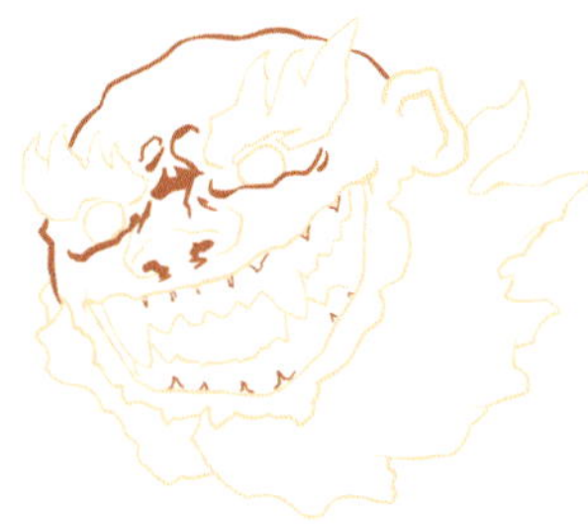

5

Add more details to the face: Draw the uneven, bumpy shape of the top of the head. Add the creases to the nose bridge and under the eyes to push the wanyūdō's fearsome expression. Draw the nostrils.

6

Draw three large concentric circles around the head to form the base of the wheel. A drawing compass is a good tool for this. To really enhance the expression, add shadow shapes on the eyebrows and deep wrinkles to the sides of the eyes and nose.

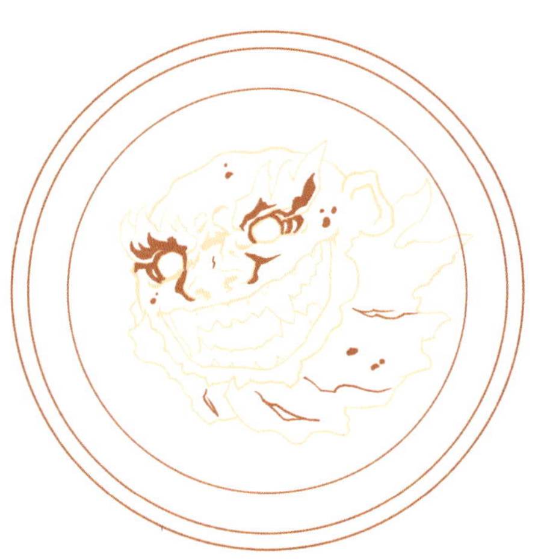

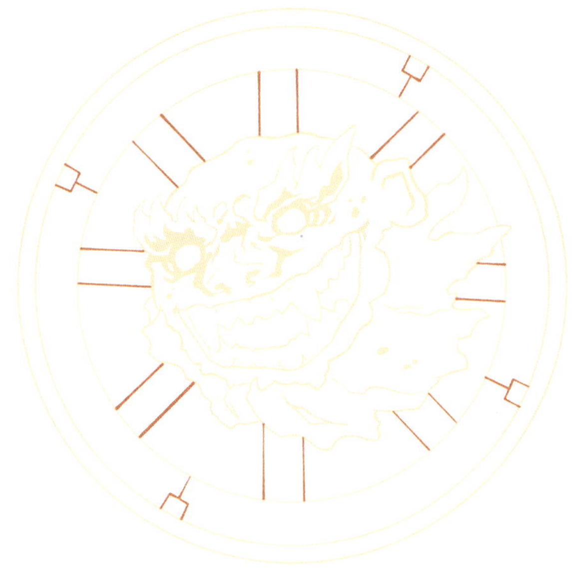

7

With a ruler, draw the eight wide spokes of the wagon wheel, behind the wanyūdō's head. Space the spokes evenly. Add the four boxlike joints to the inner wheel.

8

Using the same type of fire shapes from all the previous yōkai in this chapter, draw fire flowing around the wheel. Notice how they twine around the wheel and out of the wanyūdō's mouth.

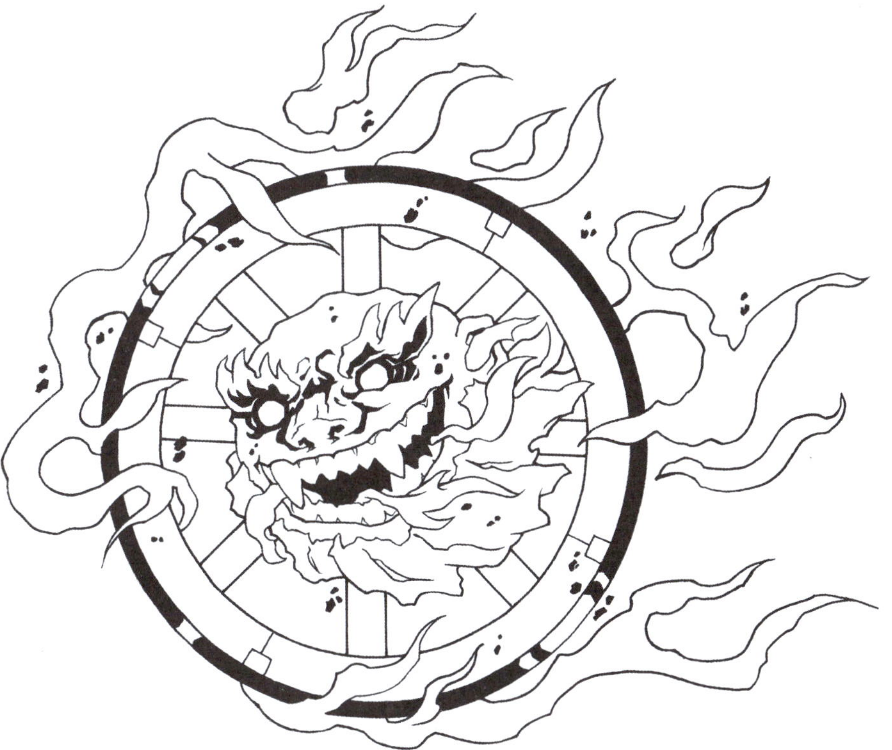

AO-ANDŌ (あおあんどう)

The ao-andō (which literally means "blue lantern") is a frightful spirit with twin horns, sharp teeth, and long hair emerging from a ghostly blue lantern. It is historically significant as it helped popularize yōkai, taking them from creatures to be feared to entertainment. This is because of this yōkai's ties to the Hyakumonogatari Kaidankai ritual, a popular game from the early Edo period. People would gather in a large, candlelit room at night to share scary stories with each other. After each story was told, a candle would be snuffed out, slowly letting the room grow darker and darker as the evening went on. It was believed that after the final story was told and the last candle extinguished, the room would be plunged into darkness and a yōkai, like the ao-andō, would appear.

Here we will draw the ao-andō as it is emerging from the lantern—the last candle of the Hyakumonogatari Kaidankai event. Drawing the face of the ao-andō will be similar to drawing the mask face of the menreiki (page 122), with the floating lower jaw and general face shapes.

Near the top of the page, draw an oval shape for the head. Add the center lines. Lower on the page, like with the haka-no-hi (page 114), lightly draw a line for the ground. Centered on this line, draw a tall vertical block, which will become the lantern.

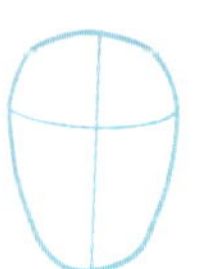

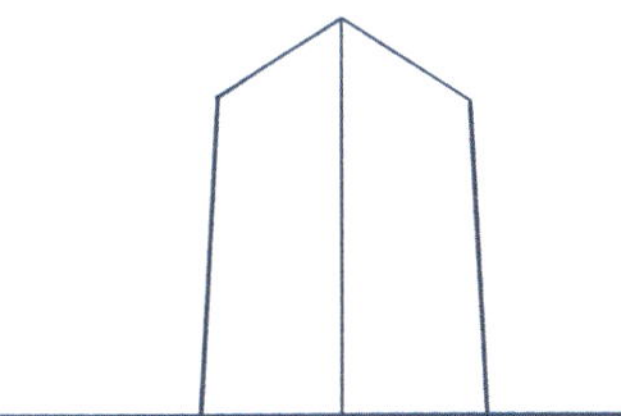

Imagine the scary face of the ao-andō rising up out of the lantern. To capture this, lightly draw the sides of the flowing, fiery body of the yōkai. To contrast with the flowing lines of the fire, use two angular lines to divide the face into the upper section and lower jaw. Add windows to the sides of the lantern.

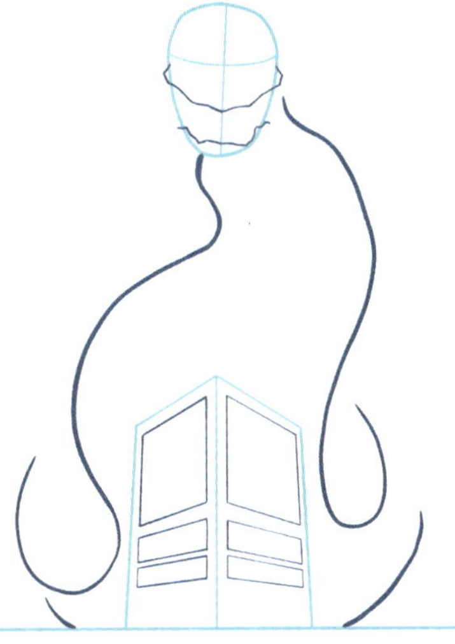

Draw two pointed ovals tilted inward to create the eyes. For the mane of fire around the face, draw curves for the longest tendrils of fire. To the lantern, draw a bamboo-rib pattern on the largest windows.

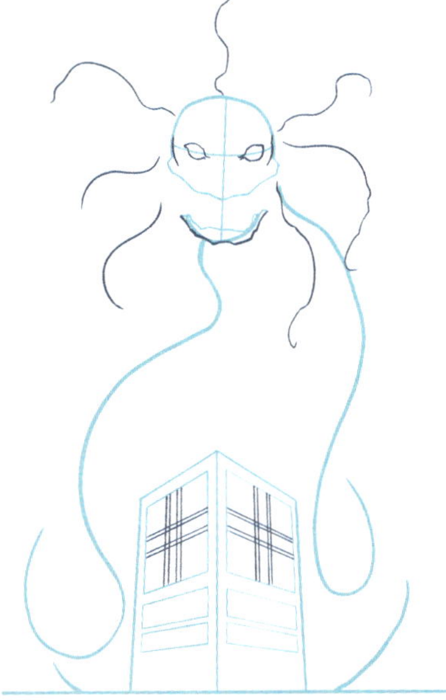

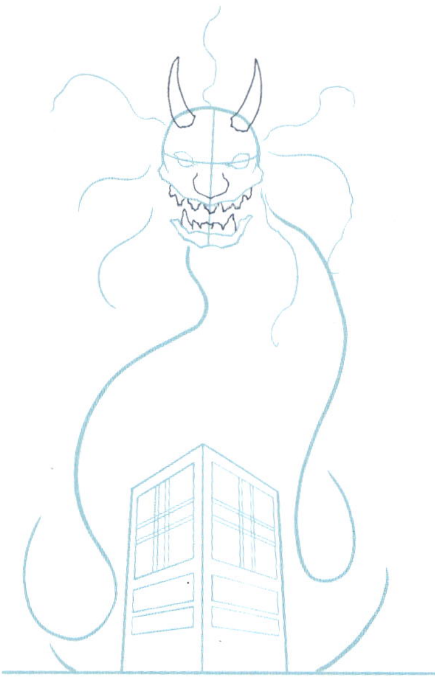

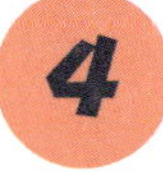

On the face, use a series of V shapes to draw two large horns, the wide nose, and jagged teeth.

In the same manner we've previously drawn in this chapter, refine the outline of the ao-andō's body to look like fire. For the face, draw the arched eyebrows and nostrils.

In these last steps continue to refine the fire body of this yōkai.

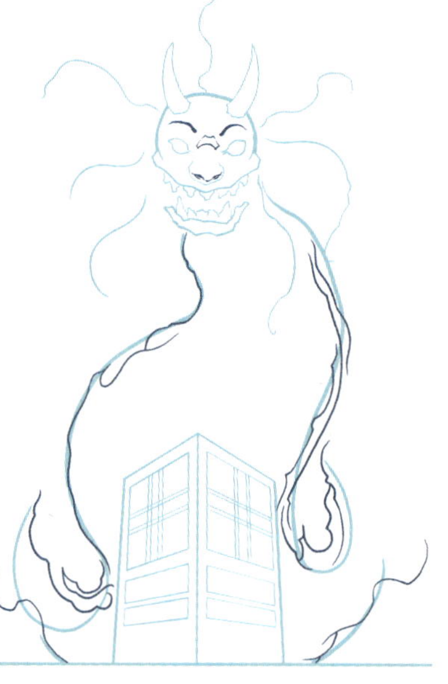

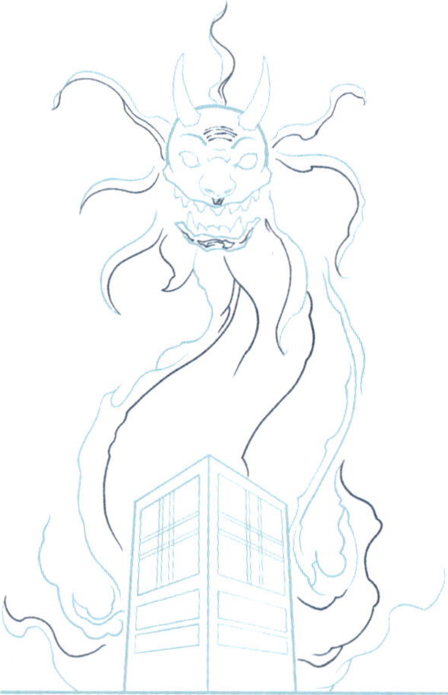

Draw lines within the body's shape to show the flow of the fire. Continue to build up the tendrils of fire around the face. Draw facial wrinkles on the forehead and chin areas.

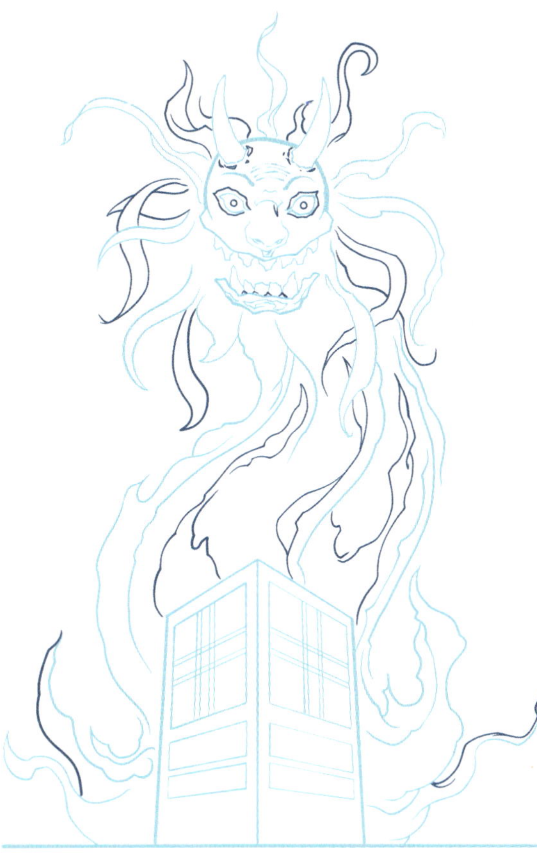

Add even more tendrils of fire to the mane, as well as more lines showing the flow of the fire to the body. Lastly, finish the details in the face by drawing the tiny pupils, smaller wrinkles, and widening the eye outlines.

Draw smaller secondary fire embers floating in the air between the larger tendrils of the mane. Add smaller broken pieces floating around the jaw. Shade in the lantern to pop it out from the fire.

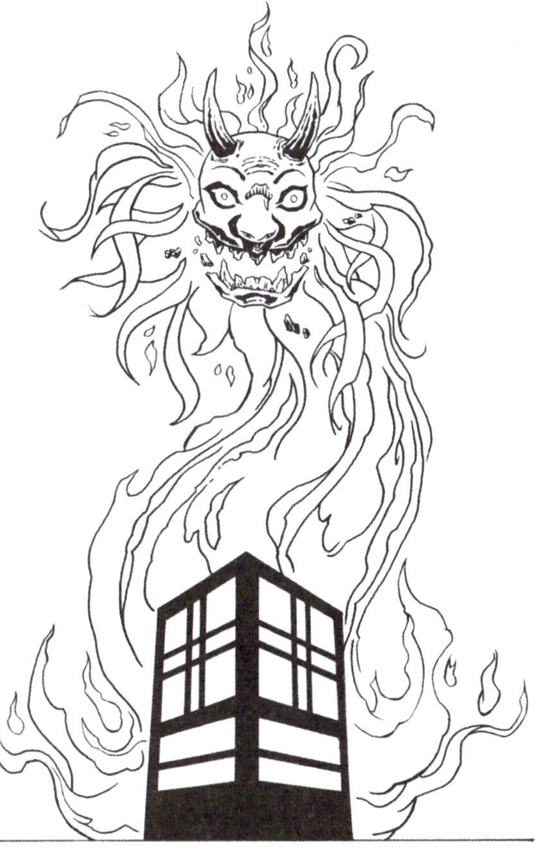

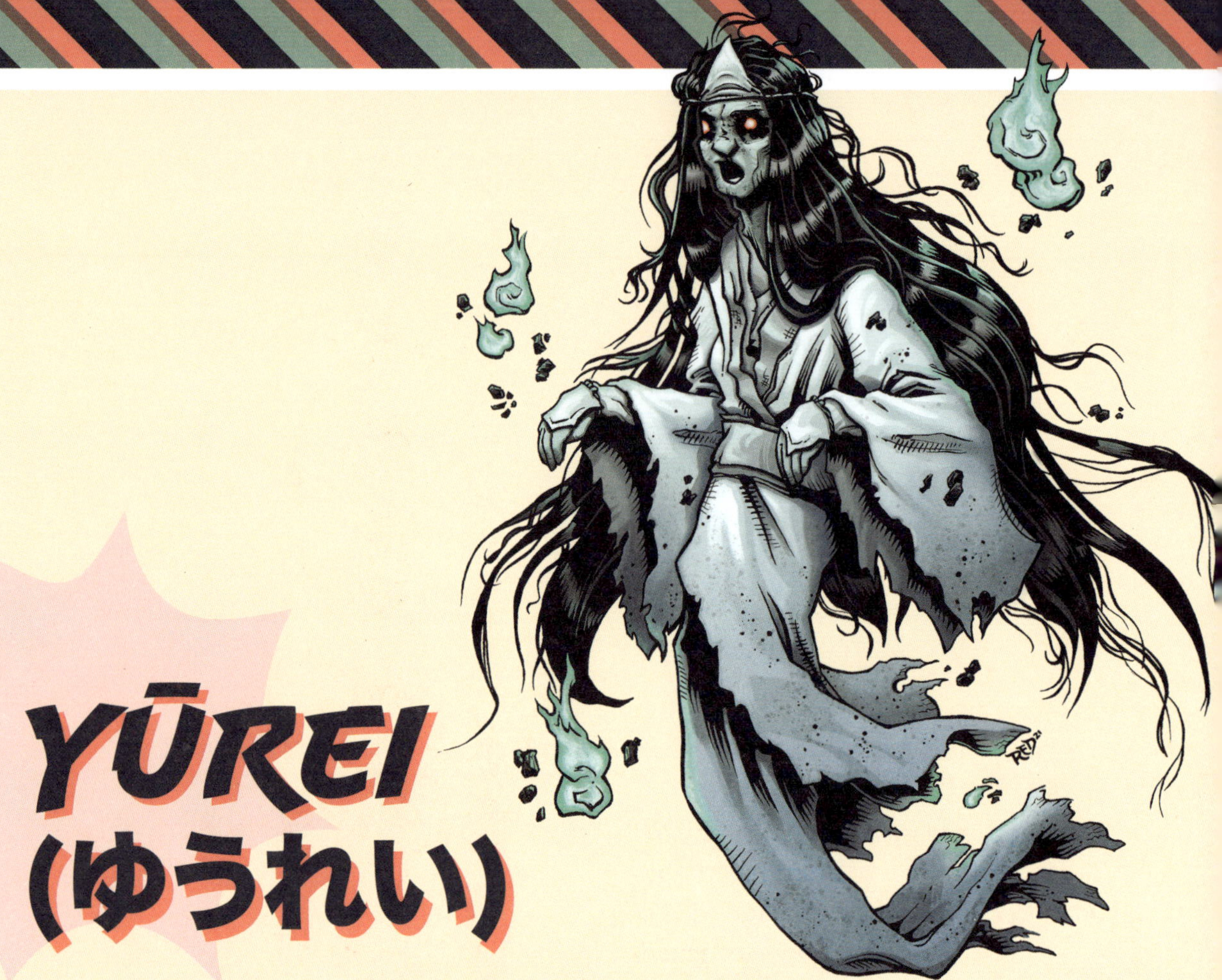

YŪREI
(ゆうれい)

In a general sense, yūrei are ghosts in Japan. Some haunt specific places, while others roam the lands freely. Most yūrei are deadly and extremely dangerous, driven by powerful emotions like revenge and anger, and often hold deep-seated grudges against the living. The revenge-seeking yūrei are the most dangerous!

Yūrei are typically shown wearing a traditional Japanese burial garment, the *kyōkatabira*, which consists of a white kimono, triangle headband, and arm and hand coverings. It is a Buddhist pilgrim's robe, stemming from the idea of the dead going on their final journey.

The term yūrei can be used to describe a particular ghost, and is also a classification of supernatural creatures unique to themselves.

Be sure to draw lightly for steps 1 to 4 as we block in the shapes of the figure.

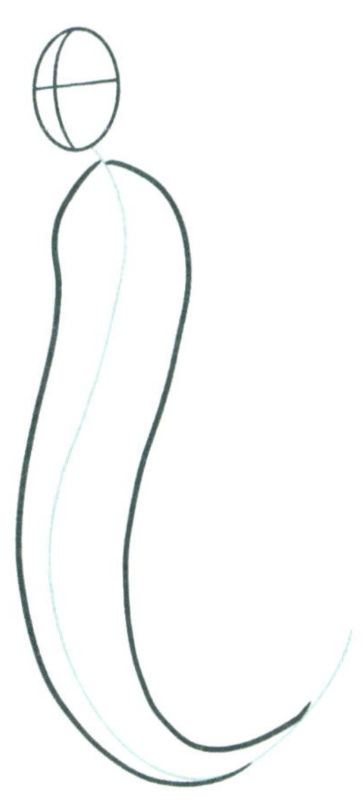

1

Draw an oval with center lines for the head. Flowing down from this, draw the line of action curving up at the bottom. Draw a tapered tube for the body centered around the line of action.

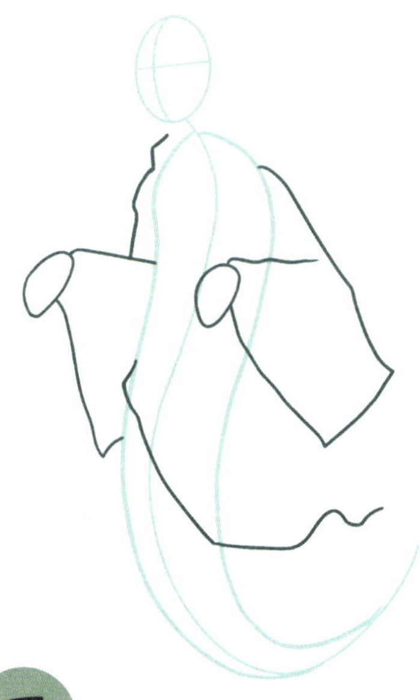

2

Draw rough ovals for the hands. Extending from these, draw the hanging, triangular-shaped sleeves of the kimono. Add a downward curve across the lower body to show the layers of the kimono.

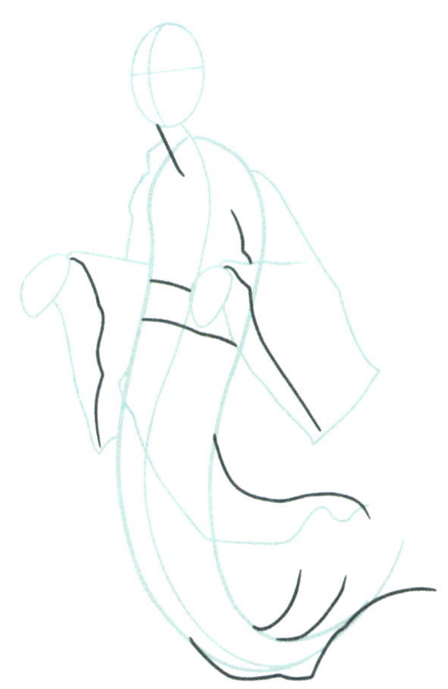

3

Continue to block in the basic shapes of the kimono. Add the open ends of the sleeves, the obi sash at the waist, and the frayed bottom blowing in the wind. Draw a line for the neck.

To complete the basic figure, draw in the wavy shape of the hair. Imagine the hair as a triangle, with the top point at the head and sides that billow out.

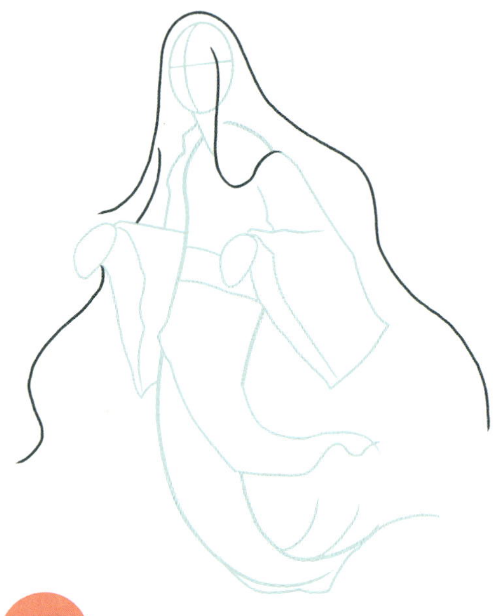

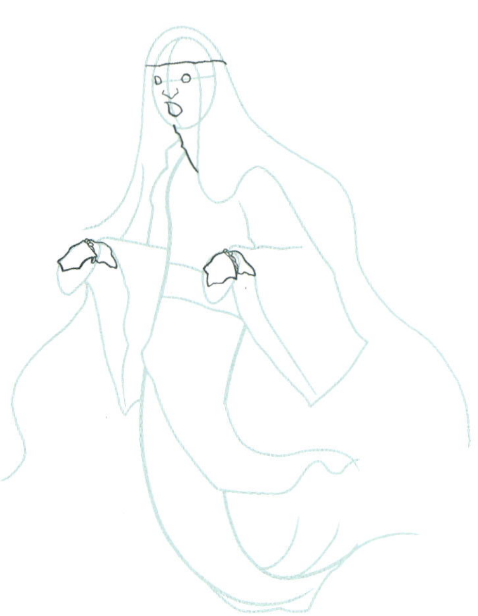

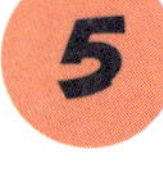

Draw the basic shapes of the eyes, nose, and mouth. Refine the neck. Draw the wrist coverings, which are cloth wrapped around the wrists and tied with thin rope.

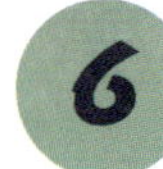

Complete the hands by drawing the fingers into the ovals. Draw the outline of the face, paying attention to the shape of the cheek and chin. Refine the obi so that it looks more like cloth by adding layers and an uneven outline.

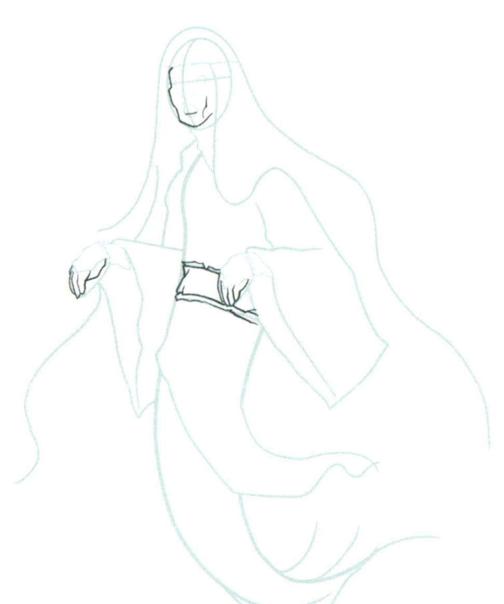

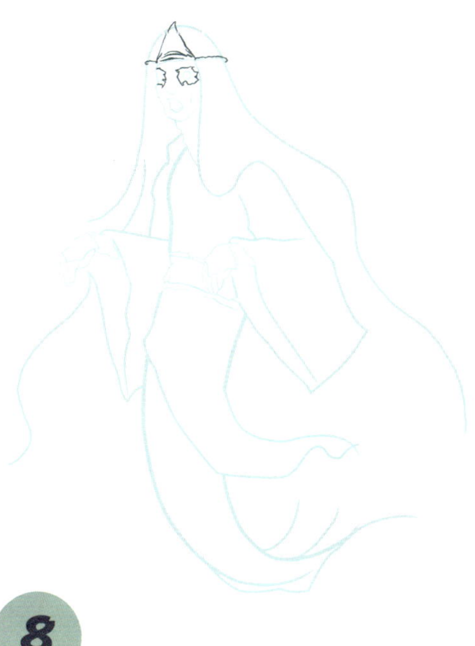

Draw the triangular headband, adding a few wrinkles where the cloth wraps around the string. Draw shadows around the eyes. Once these shapes are colored in, they will help to make the eyes pop.

Following the basic figure shapes already in place, draw the edges of the kimono fabric. As it is an old-worn burial garment, add tears and rips to the cloth to give the costume a tattered look.

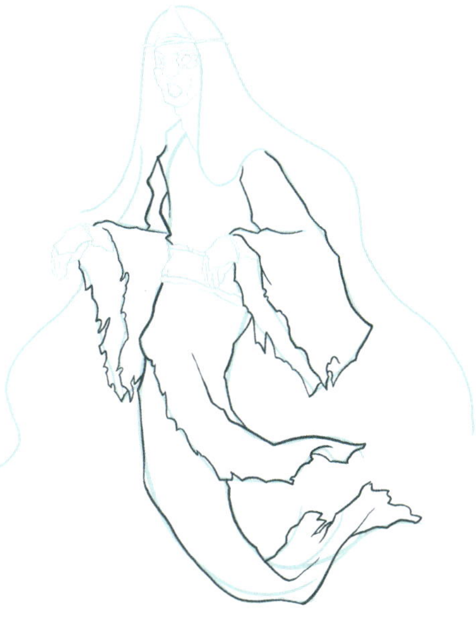

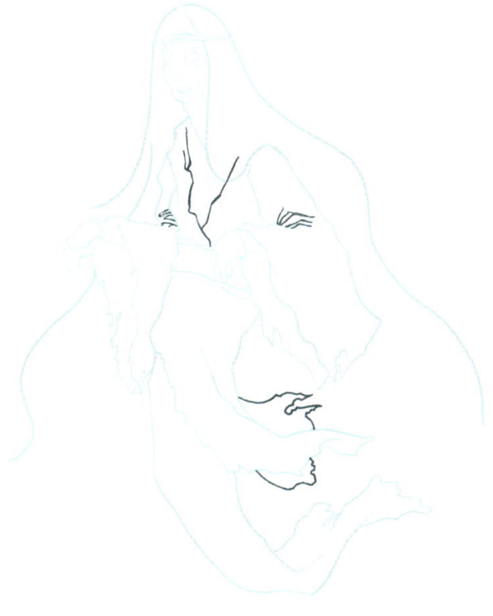

Continue to work on the kimono. Draw the V shape of the eri collar. Add wrinkles to the elbows. Draw more tattered ends billowing at the bottom.

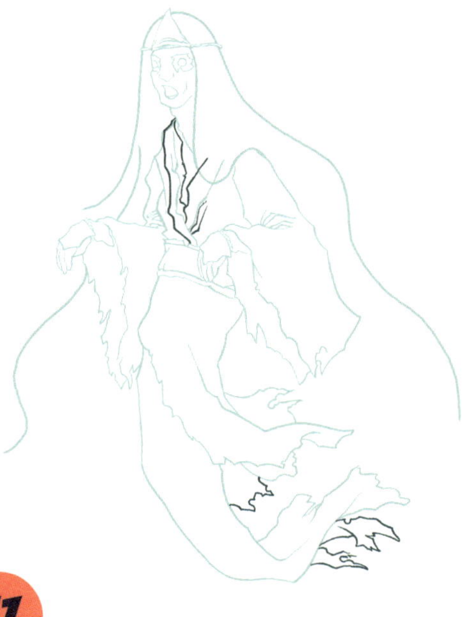

Building on the V of the eri from step 9, add more layers to the collar. Draw a few more tattered ends to the bottom of the kimono.

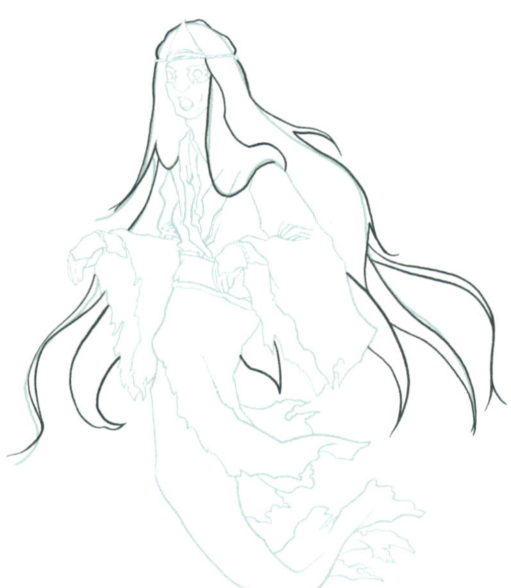

Now, to tackle the hair. Following the flow of the basic shape already in place, draw the major hair shapes. When drawing hair, it is best to think of it in terms of larger masses versus individual strands.

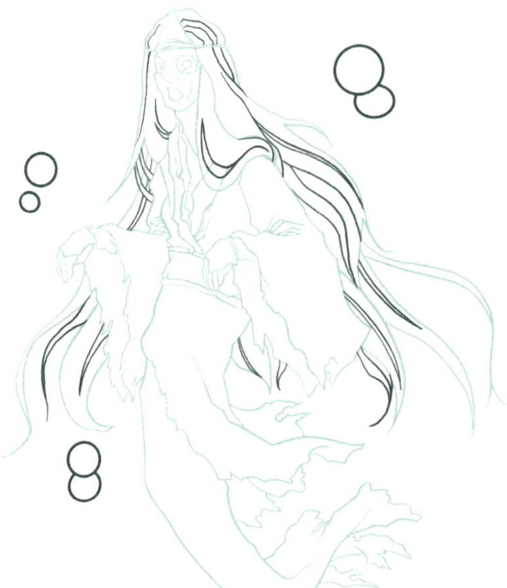

Inside of the larger masses of hair, draw smaller curved shapes to help give the hair more body. Lightly add circles floating around the figure to show where the fireballs will go.

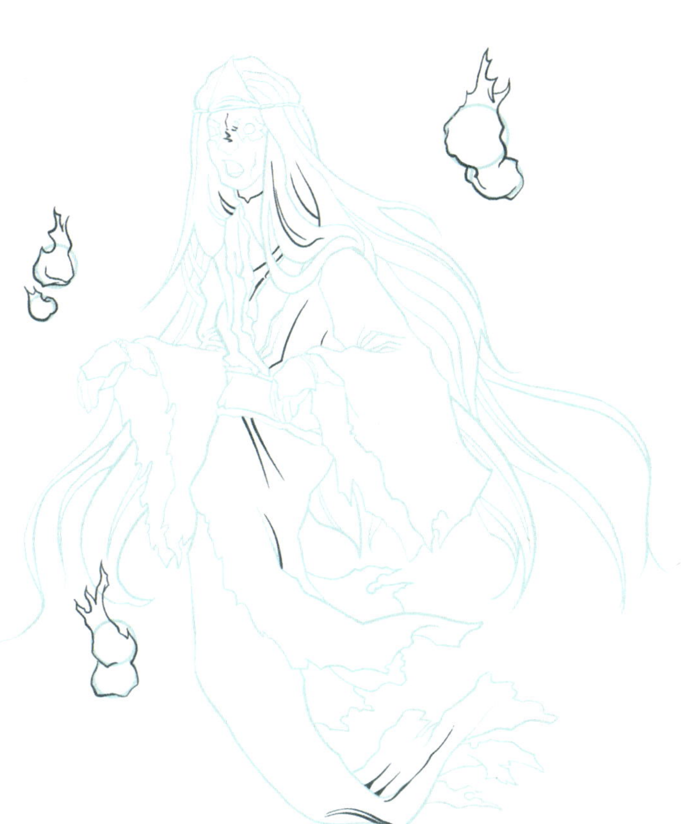

13

Add final details to the overall figure: a few wrinkles to the nose bridge, more curves to the hair around the face, and wrinkles to the kimono. Draw the fireballs like we've done in the other frightful yōkai.

14

To finish your yūrei drawing, add some final touches like debris floating around the figure. Shade in the mouth, around the eyes, and under the chin. To make the hair look more disheveled, draw loose strands waving in the air.

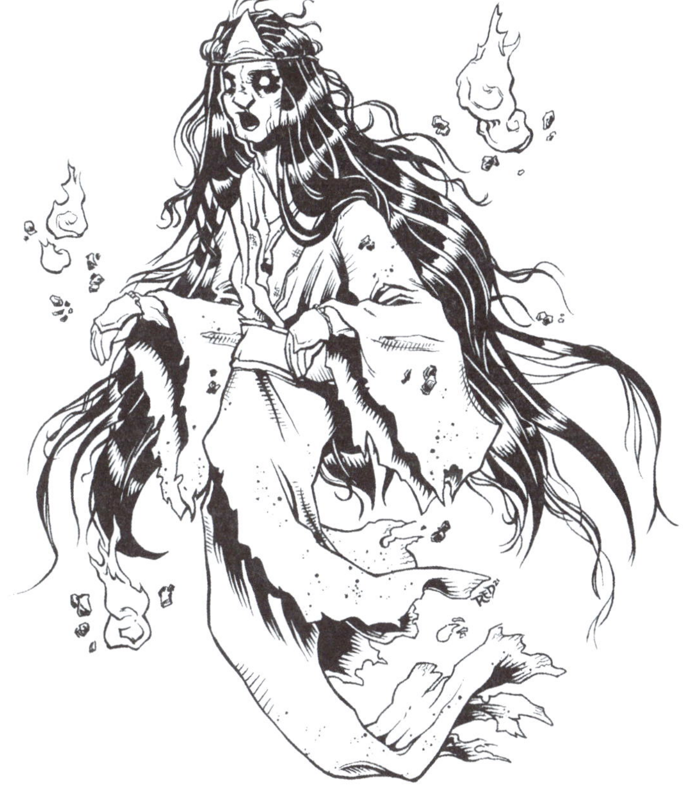

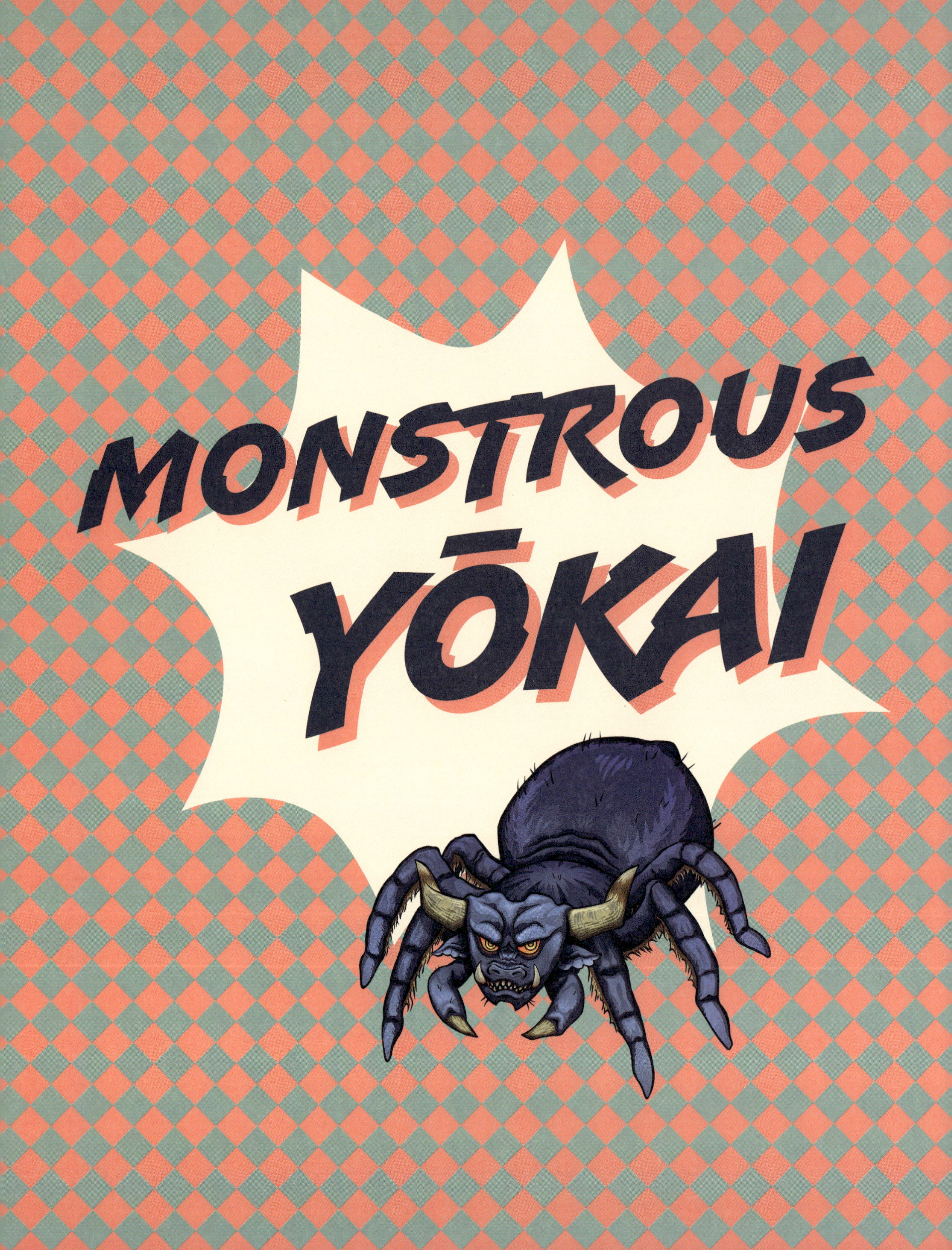
MONSTROUS
YŌKAI

Contained within this last section are the grotesque, the fearsome, and the bizarre. Here you will find tyrannical demons that feast upon human prey, bogeymen that stalk house to house stealing lazy children, and legendary calamities that torment the Japanese countryside. These are the monsters that have long stalked Japan's nightmares. They are the fears of the ancient Japanese people given life.

HYAKU-ME
(ひゃくめ)

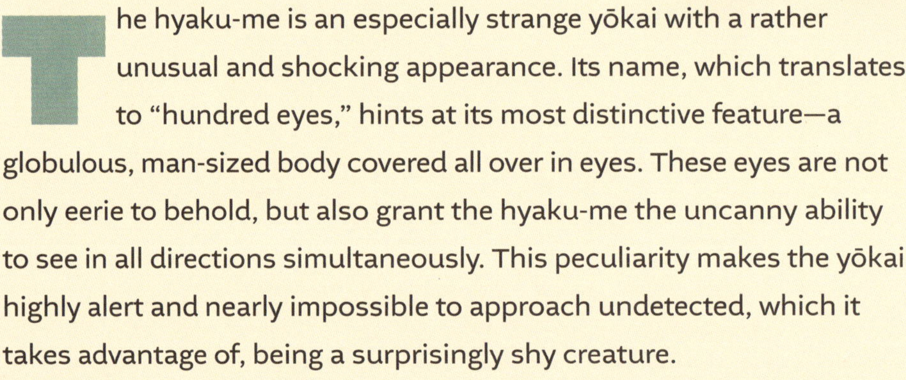

The hyaku-me is an especially strange yōkai with a rather unusual and shocking appearance. Its name, which translates to "hundred eyes," hints at its most distinctive feature—a globulous, man-sized body covered all over in eyes. These eyes are not only eerie to behold, but also grant the hyaku-me the uncanny ability to see in all directions simultaneously. This peculiarity makes the yōkai highly alert and nearly impossible to approach undetected, which it takes advantage of, being a surprisingly shy creature.

Despite its unsettling appearance, the hyaku-me is not inherently malevolent. It prefers to dwell in empty homes, abandoned temples, and graveyards. When a person enters its territory, it will extract one of its eyes that will then float and follow that person until they leave its territory. Should the hyaku-me feel threatened, it will jump out, relying on its hideous appearance to frighten the person away.

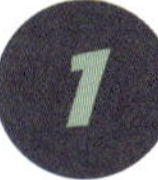

Lightly draw the curved line of action and the flat ground line. Draw a large bean shape for the body, with center lines.

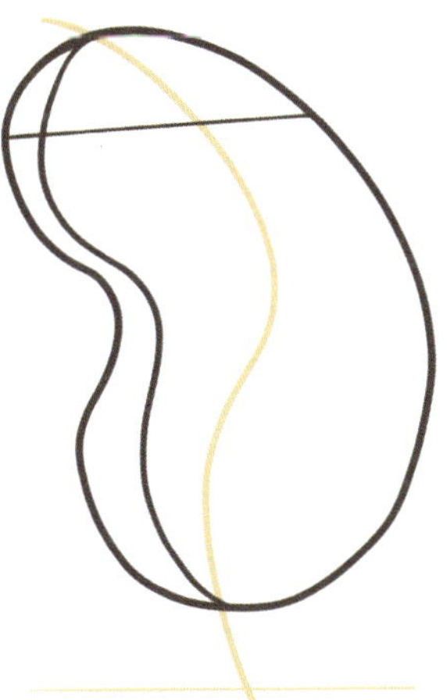

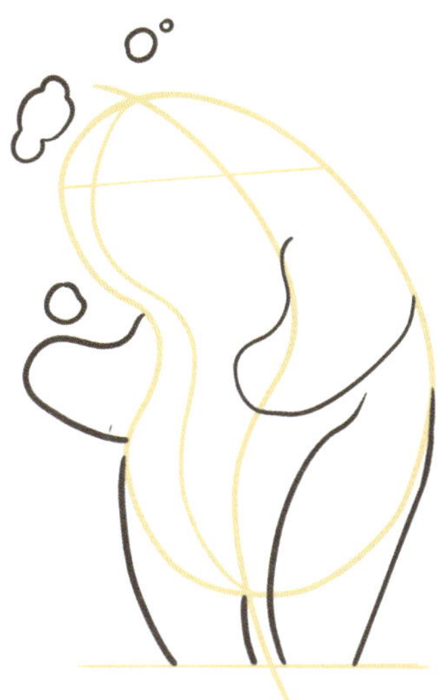

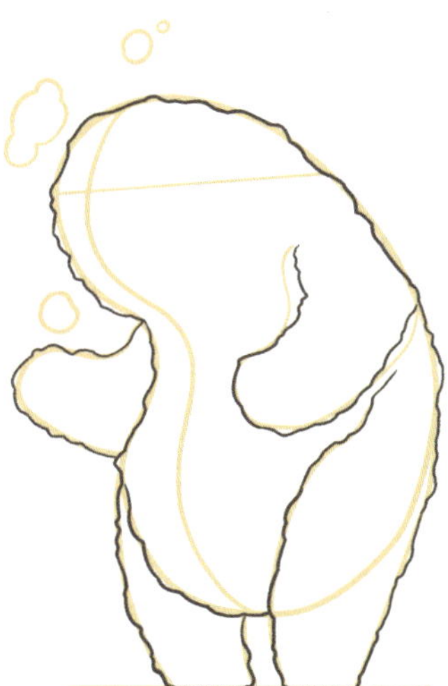

Draw the round forms of the arms and legs. Notice how the backs of the legs are straight, while the front sides are curved. Draw floating blobs around the head.

Following the outer edges of the body and limbs, draw their outlines so that it looks like the yōkai is made of flappy skin, or mud.

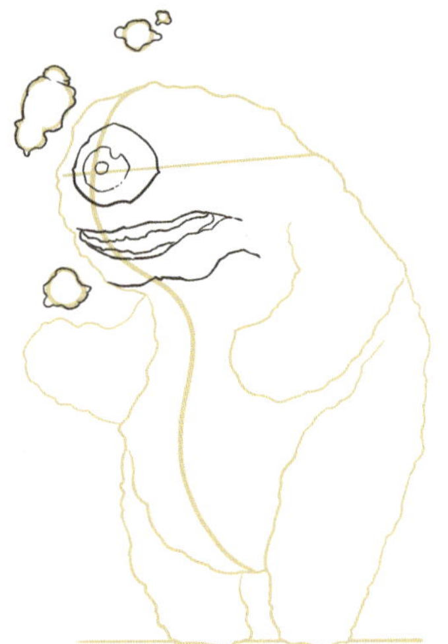

4

Draw the same flappy-skin outlines on the floating blobs. Use uneven circles to draw the large main eyeball. Add the mouth, continuing to use these uneven, irregular lines to convey the globulous nature of this yōkai.

Steps 5, 6, and 7 are all about the eyes. Here is a quick breakdown on how to construct an eye:

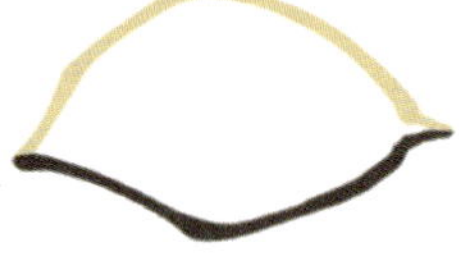
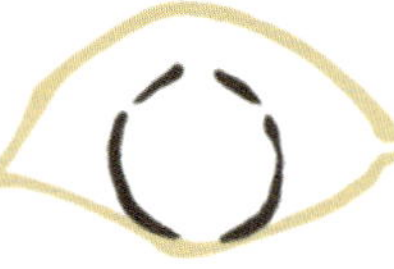
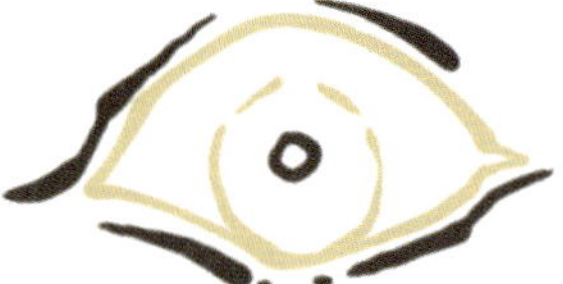

1. Draw the outline.

2. Draw a circle for the iris.

3. Add a smaller circle for the pupil. Lastly, draw wrinkles to indicate the eyelids.

5

This yōkai is not called "one hundred eyes" for nothing. This is an exercise in repeating shapes, so take your time. Draw the outlines of the eyes. Vary the size and width of the eyes to add interest to the design.

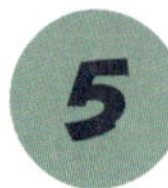
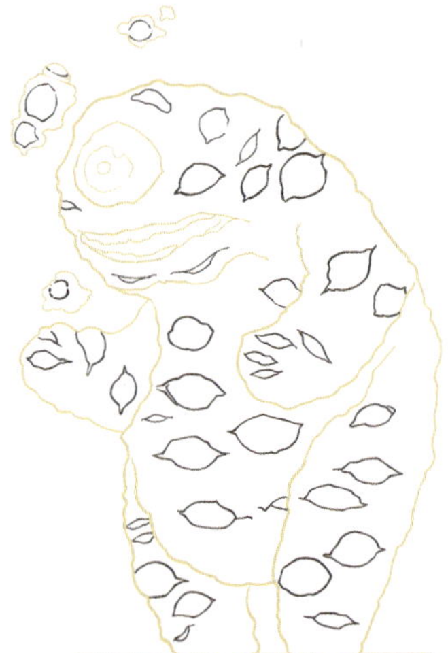

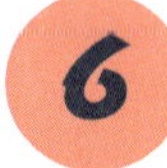

Draw the irregular circles of the irises inside each eye. Be sure they are not all centered, so that the creature is looking in different directions.

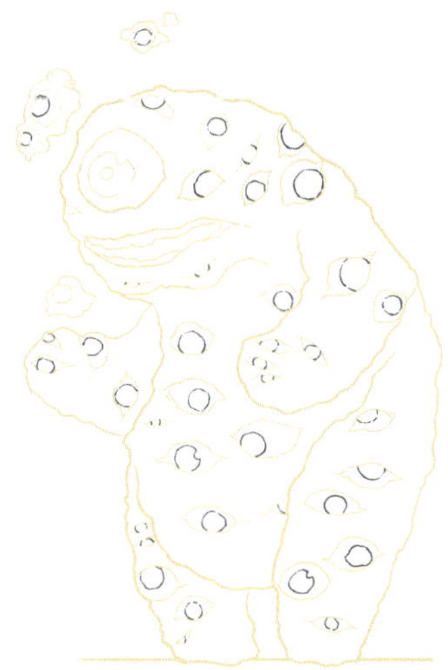

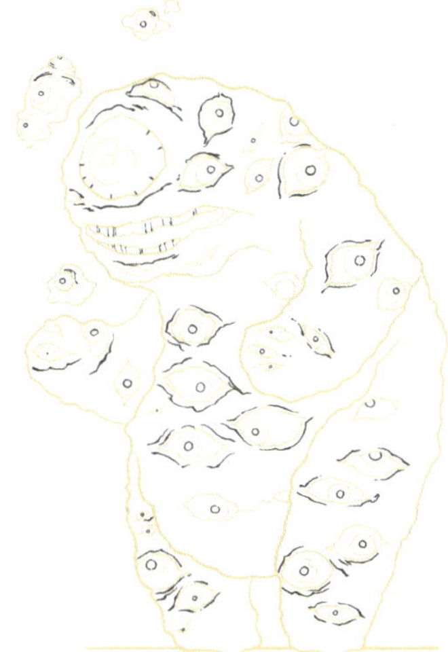

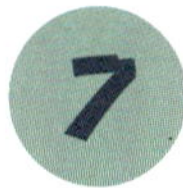

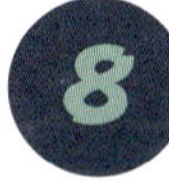

Draw the pupils and wrinkles around the eyes. You can shade in the pupils right away if you want. Use small dashes to add texture to the teeth.

For the final touches: shade in the mouth, around the main, large eye, and under the chin to make the face pop. Notice how these shadow shapes mimic the mud shapes of the hyaku-me's outline, which further enhance the blobby look of this grotesque yōkai. You could also add even more wrinkles to the body.

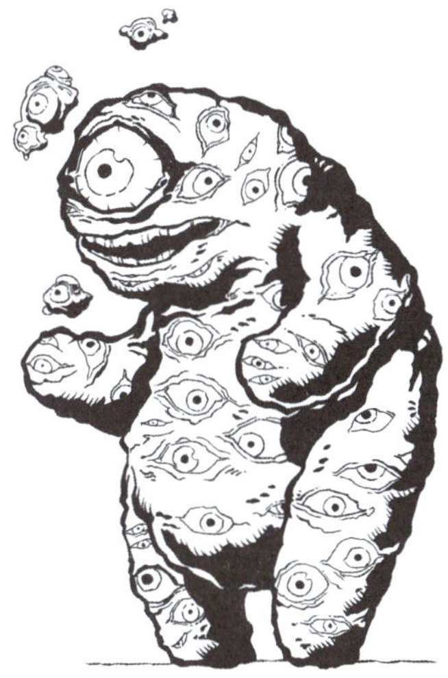

KAMIKIRI (かみきり)

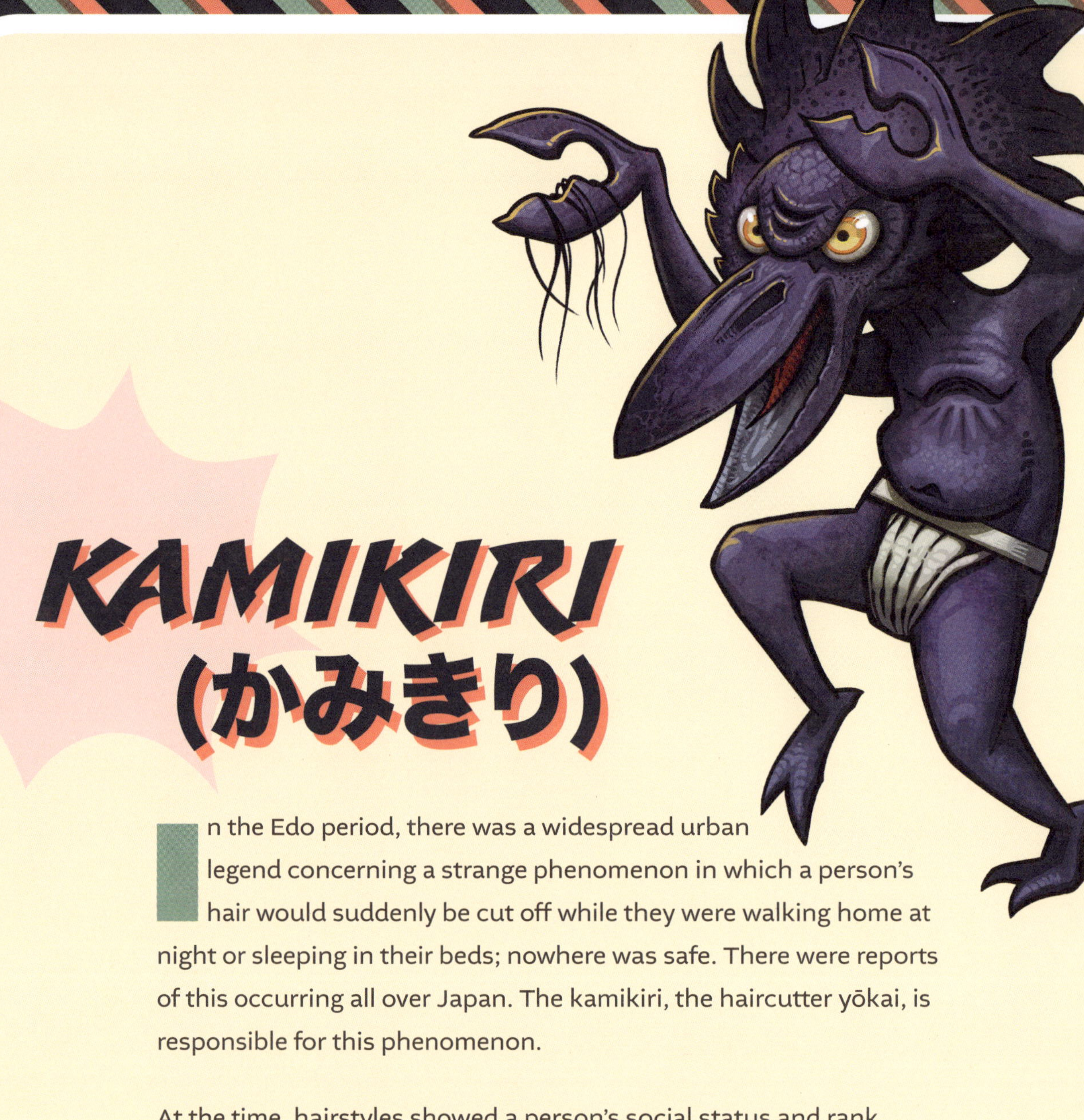

In the Edo period, there was a widespread urban legend concerning a strange phenomenon in which a person's hair would suddenly be cut off while they were walking home at night or sleeping in their beds; nowhere was safe. There were reports of this occurring all over Japan. The kamikiri, the haircutter yōkai, is responsible for this phenomenon.

At the time, hairstyles showed a person's social status and rank, including their profession or even marital status. People's hairstyles also served as symbols of beauty and power. So, to have one's hair suddenly cut off would be devastating.

The traditional appearance of this yōkai, and many others, can be found in the *Hyakkai-Zukan* picture scroll created by Sawaki Suushi.

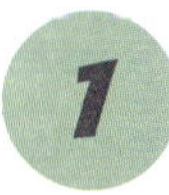

Lightly draw a curved line of action. Draw a circle for the head with center lines. From the head, draw two lines down for the body. Notice how the inner line curves in to form the kamikiri's pot belly.

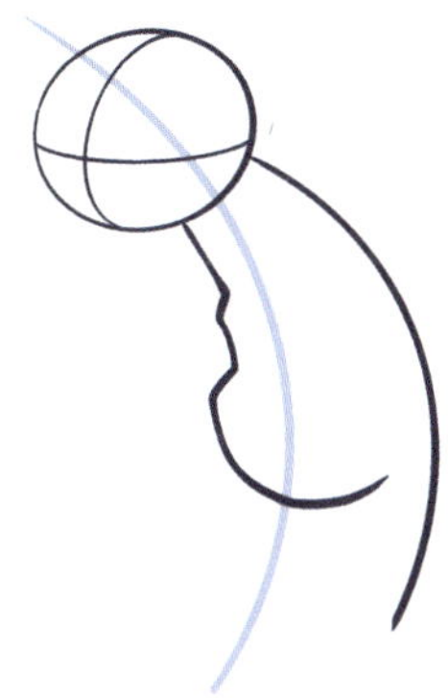

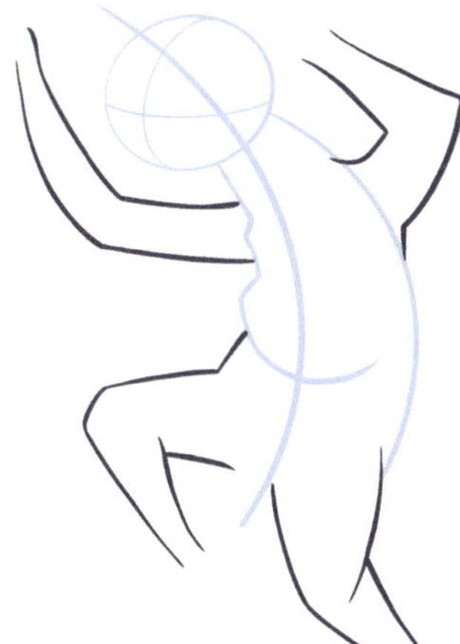

Using tubelike shapes, draw the arms and legs. Be sure to bend the limbs at the elbows and knees.

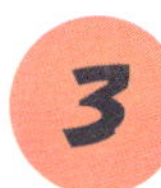

Draw the basic shapes for the claws, feet, and beak. Use large ovals for the claws and rounded triangles for the beak and feet.

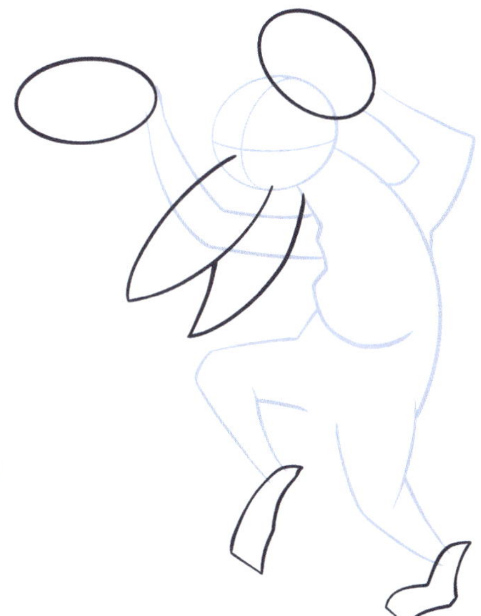

4

Using the same wavelike line, draw a fringe on each side of the face and a larger mane around the top of the head.

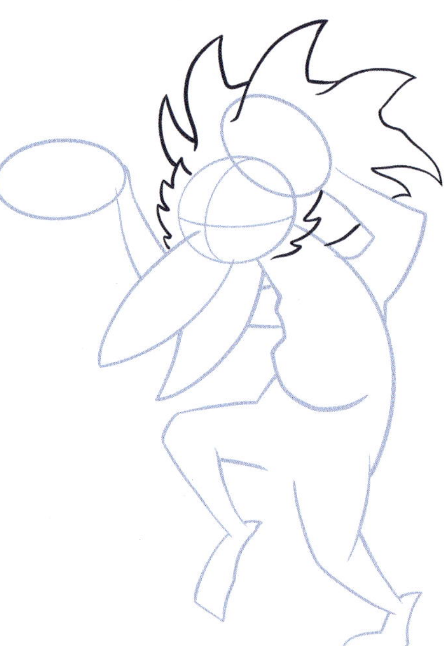

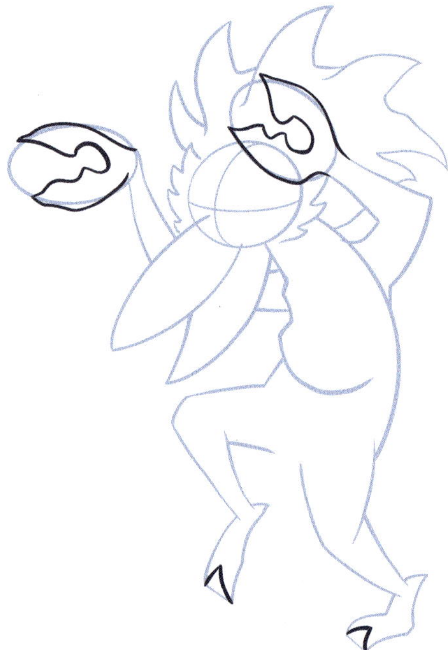

5

Draw the shear-like claws and add talons to the feet.

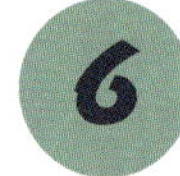

6

Refine the face by adding details: a pointed tongue, long nostrils, the uneven edge of the beak, and the brow ridge.

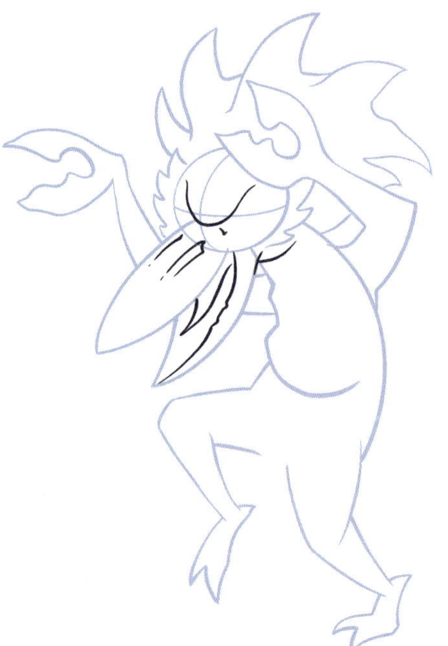

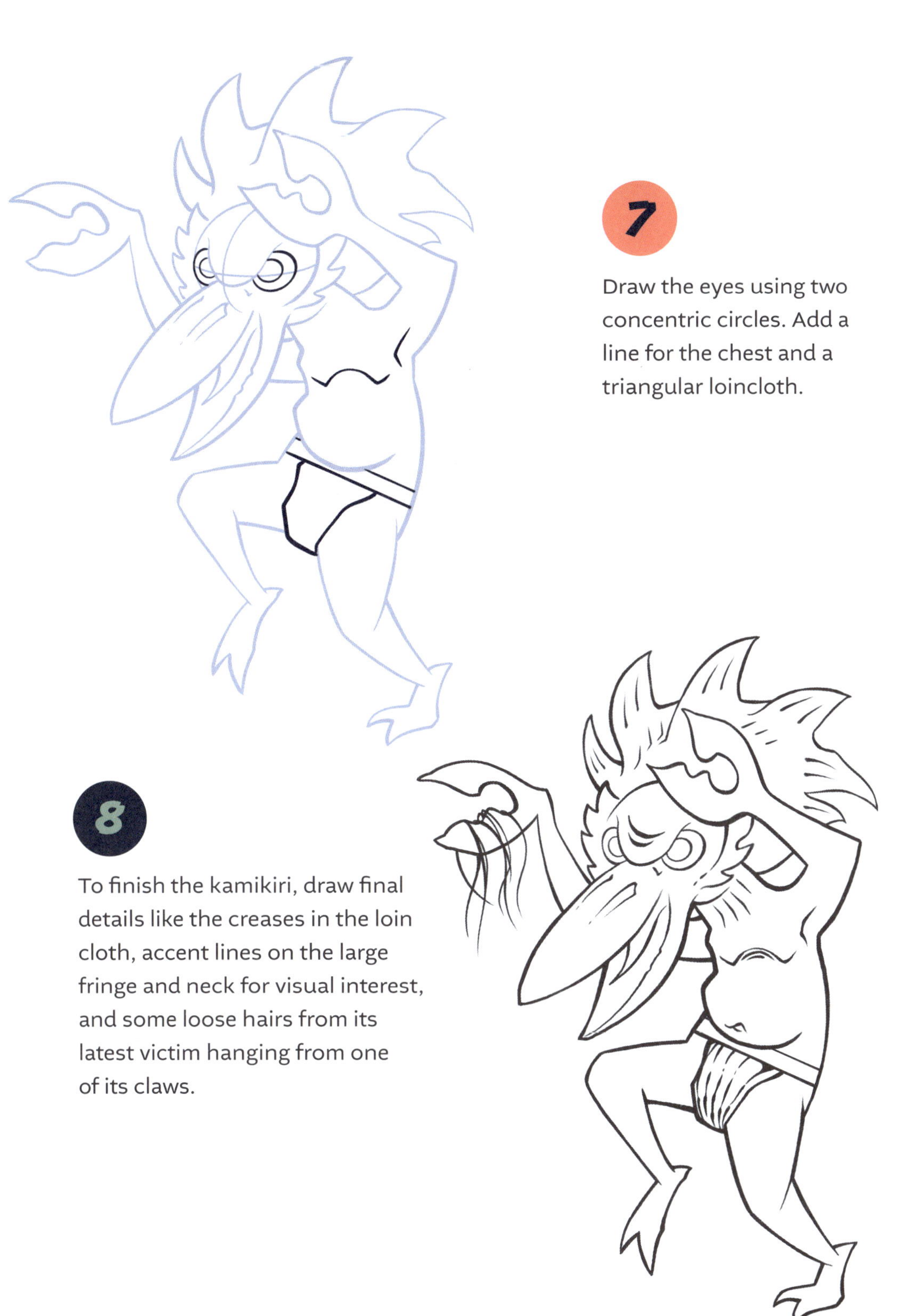

Draw the eyes using two concentric circles. Add a line for the chest and a triangular loincloth.

To finish the kamikiri, draw final details like the creases in the loin cloth, accent lines on the large fringe and neck for visual interest, and some loose hairs from its latest victim hanging from one of its claws.

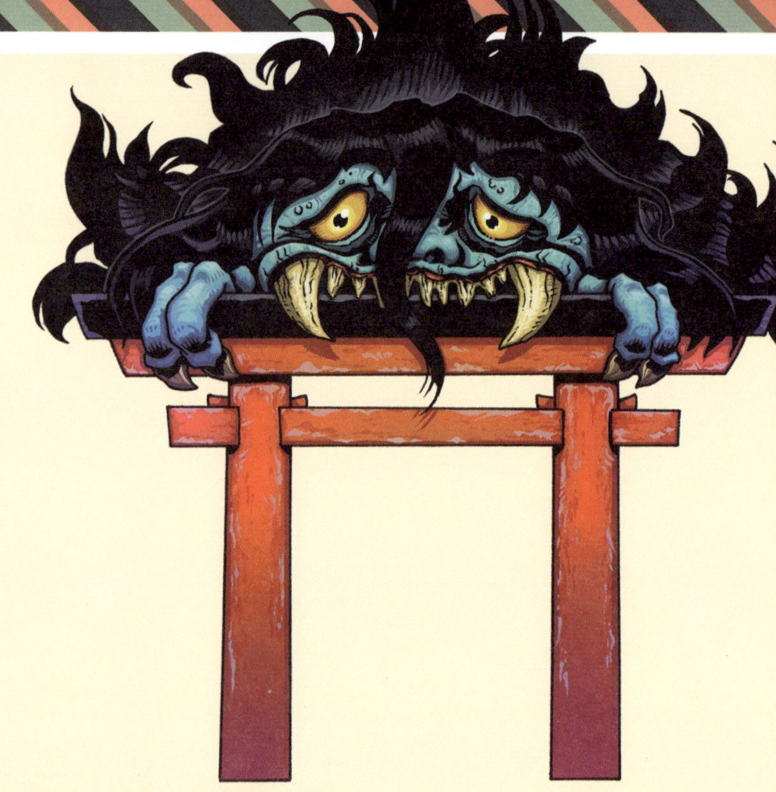

OTOROSHI
(おとろし)

The otoroshi is a hairy, fearsome guardian covered in a wild mane of long, black hair. This monster can most often be found perched above torii gates, on temple roof gables, and other high places. It serves as a protector of sacred ground and from its high vantage points will pounce down and devour any wicked individual who tries to enter.

Torii gates are an iconic feature of Japanese Shinto shrines and can be seen throughout the country. They mark the boundary between the normal world and the sacred world.

Start with a straight vertical line of action and center line. Draw three long rectangles, which will serve as the top and cross beams of the torii gate. The top two rectangles have slanted sides.

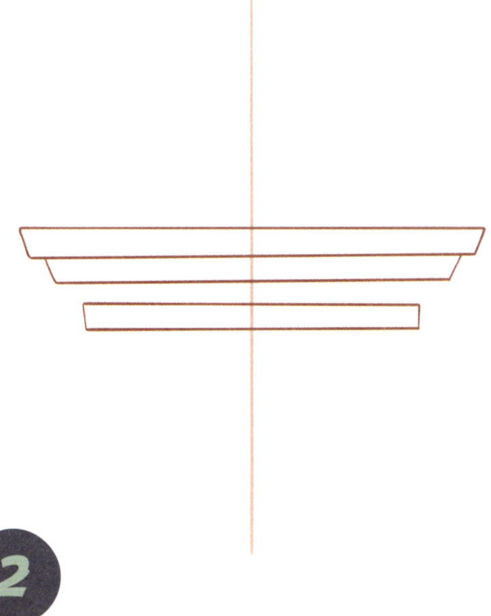

Draw two vertical columns under the rectangles. Draw four small half squares where the beam meets the columns. Erase the parts of the horizontal beam inside the columns so that it looks like the beam runs through them. (The tiny shadows under the beam help create this effect too.)

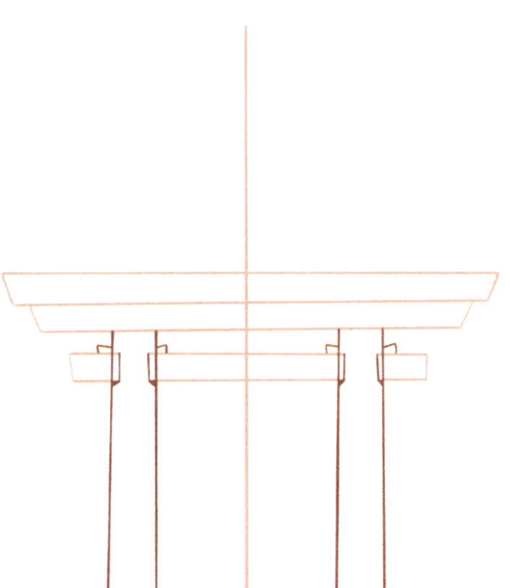

This otoroshi is a roughly symmetrical creature. Think of it in three layers: the face, the hair around the face, and the large mane. Draw the basic shapes of the yōkai: semicircles for face and eyes, irregular curved tubes for the fingers, and the downward, overarching curve of hair.

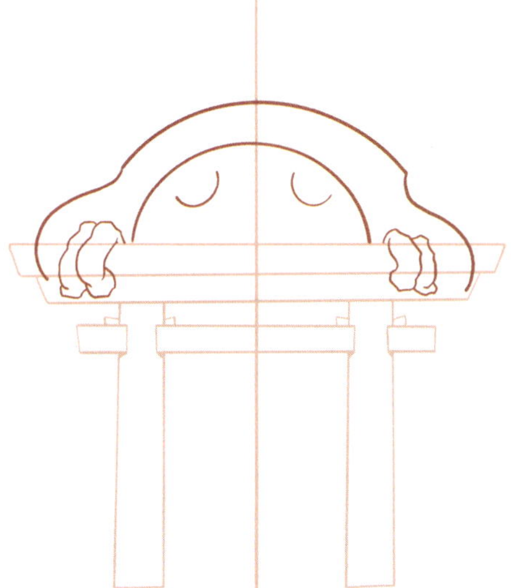

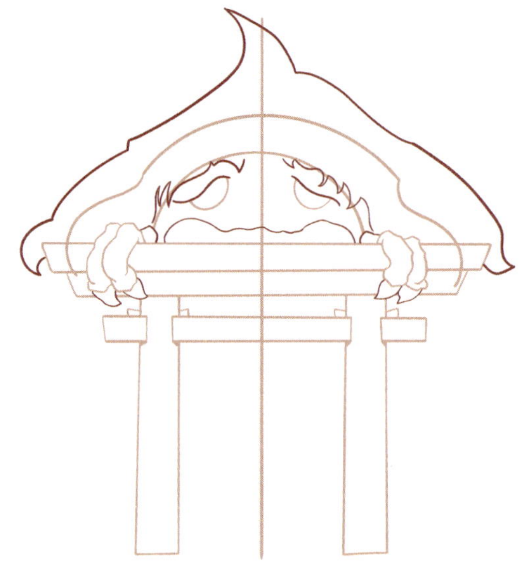

 **4**

Draw the loose, triangular shape of the mane flowing up to a point at the top. Draw the hair hanging over the face. The downward curves of the eyes help to capture the right expression. Add a gaping, open mouth, then rounded talons to the fingers.

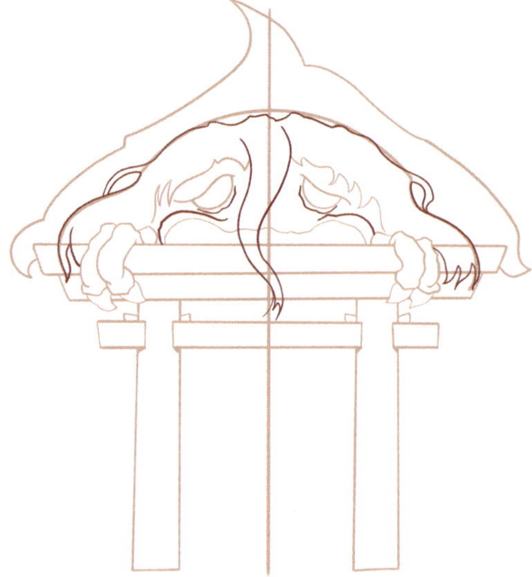

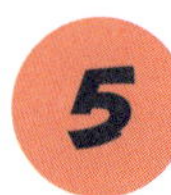 **5**

Refine the outline of the hair around the face. The otoroshi has a long, wavy lock of hair hanging down the middle of its face. Draw the curved cheeks and eye wrinkles.

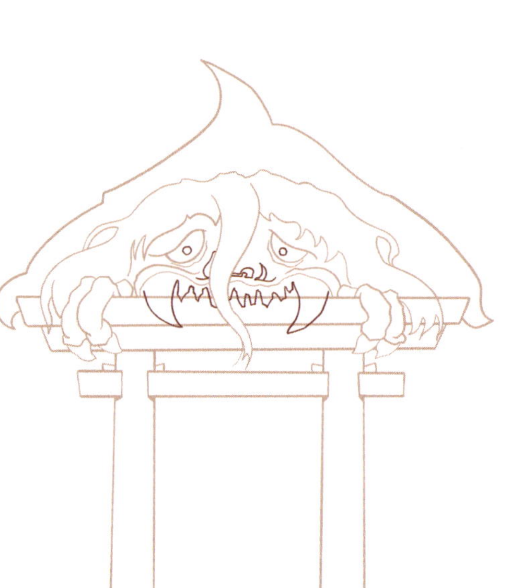

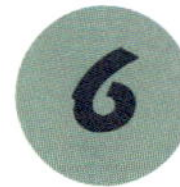 **6**

Draw the teeth and two large fangs with jagged lines. Add the tiny pupils to the eyes. Draw the curved sides of the nose and nostrils.

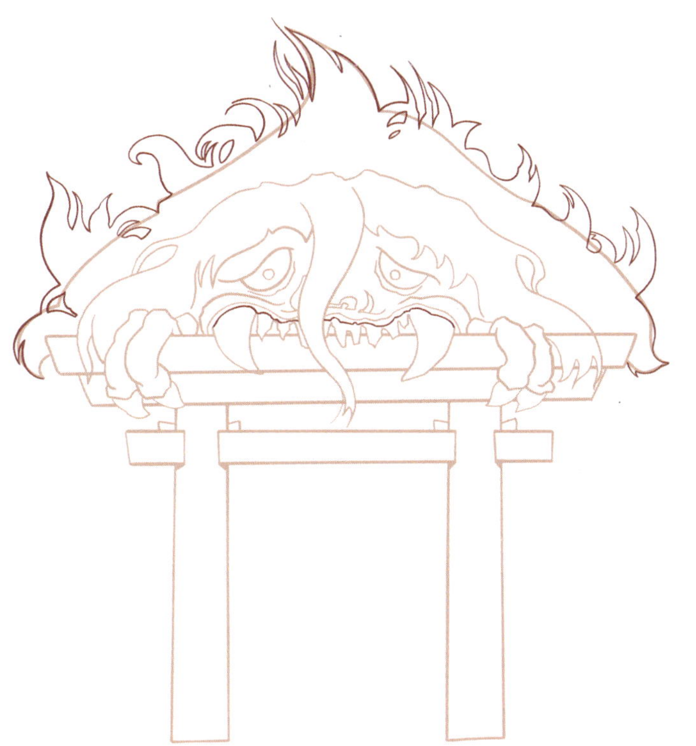

Draw the wavy, triangular hair of the outer mane. Unlike hair we've drawn before, make this mane look wild with locks flowing in different directions. Add a line for the gums.

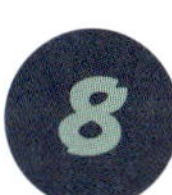

Draw a few final details such as the moles on the skin, deep shadows under the eyes, and broken lines inside the teeth to give them a more worn texture. Shade in the otoroshi's hair to make the face pop.

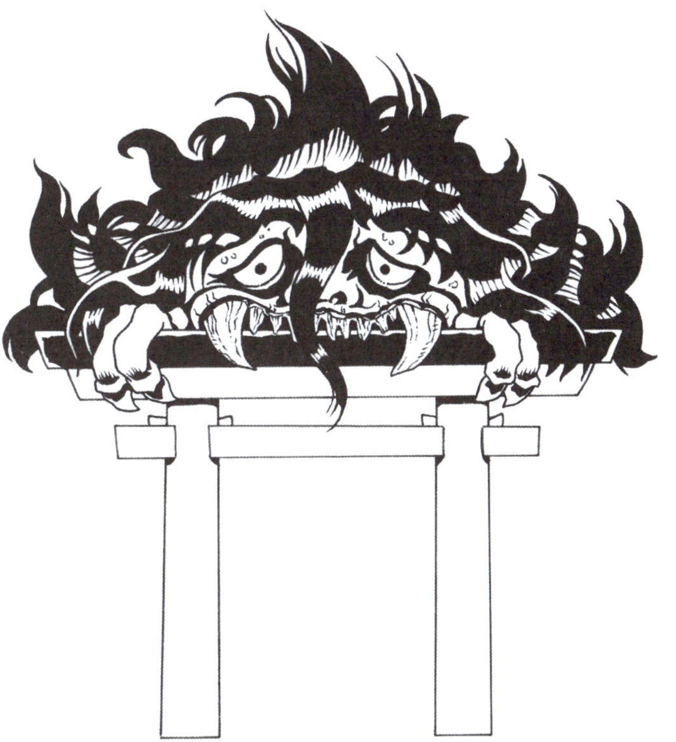

NURE-ONNA (ぬれおんな)

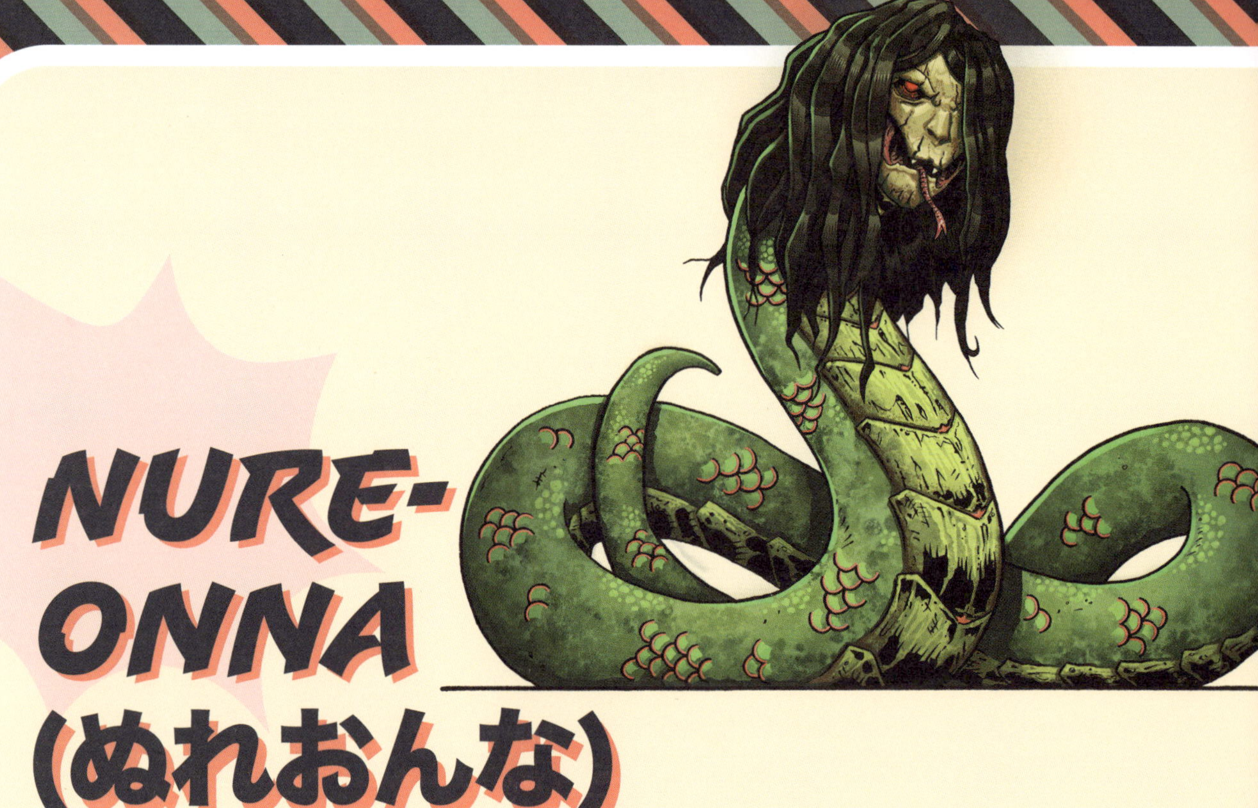

The nure-onna is a yōkai with the body of a snake and the head of a woman that stalks the shorelines and rivers of Japan, feeding on humans. She lures lonely travelers to the water's edge by feigning weakness, then pounces upon them.

Similar to the ningyo (page 76), there are variations in depictions of her appearance. At times she is portrayed with the lower body of a snake and the upper body of a woman. In more modern designs, a nure-onna is sometimes illustrated looking like a normal person except that she has snakes on her head instead of hair, resembling a gorgon in Greek mythology. This book features the more traditional design for a nure-onna, consisting of a snake body with the head of a woman.

In some regions there are tales of her partnering with the ushi-oni (page 162). In these tales they work together to hunt along the shore.

1

Draw the basic head shape using a circle and a V shape for the chin. Add the center lines. From the head, draw a flowing line of action slithering down in S curves, showing the coiled pose of the snake's body.

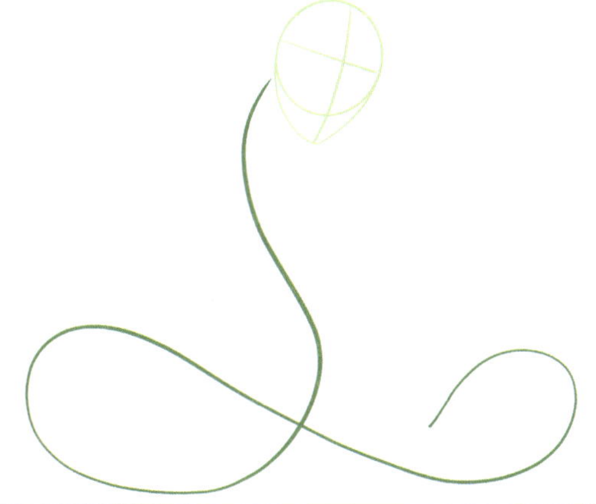

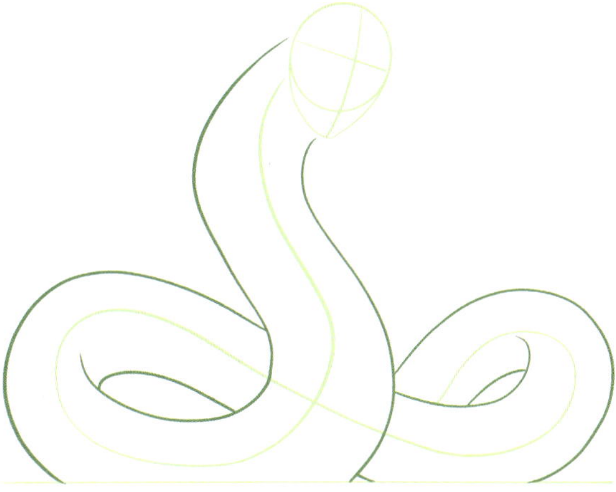

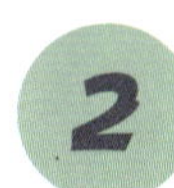

2

Starting at the head and following the line of action, draw the curved, tubular shape of the snake's body.

3

Draw the major masses of the hair hanging down over both sides of her head. This hair will be drawn in the same manner as the yūrei's (page 138) hair. Add the tail.

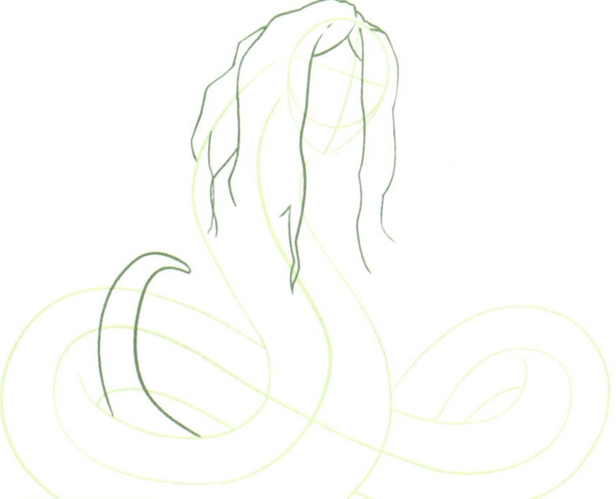

4

Continue to refine the hair by drawing the secondary shapes of hair inside the larger masses from step 3. Draw the curve of the belly following the shape of the body.

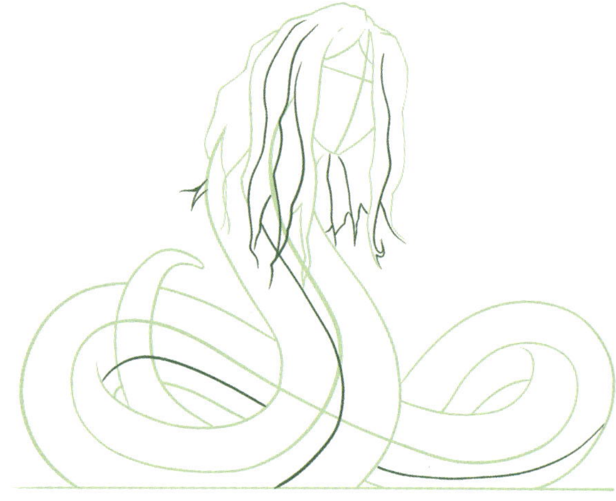

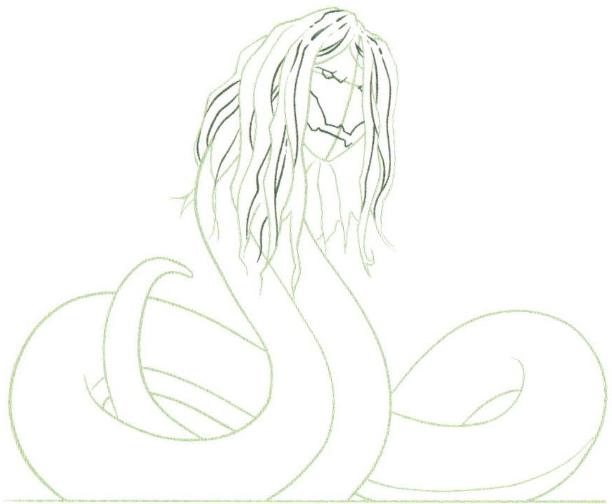

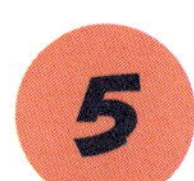

5

Finish the hair by drawing in more layers that continue to follow the downward flow. Begin the face by drawing the eyelid, slanted downward, and a semicircle eye. For the snake's mouth, draw lines that curve in on either side, then flatten in the middle.

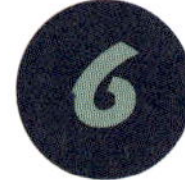

6

Draw the forked tongue. Add the slanted eyebrows, sharp nose, and pointed fangs. Use repeating shapes to draw the V-shaped belly scales that run down from the head following the curve of the body.

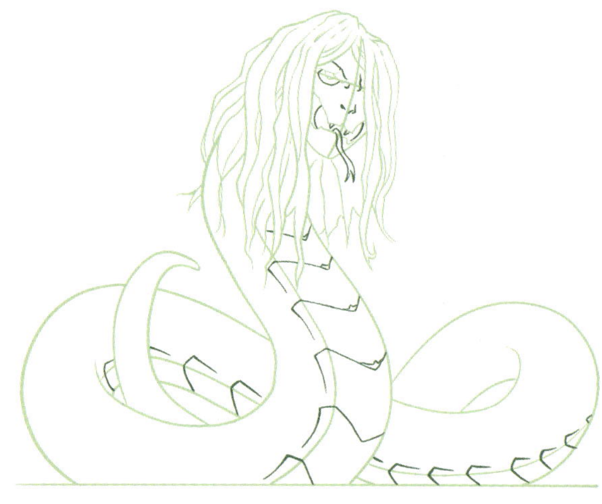

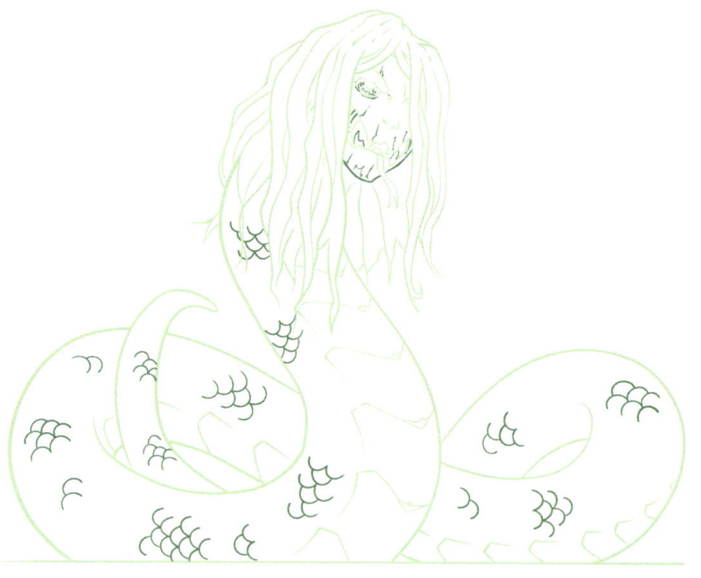

Using the same technique from the ningyo (page 81), draw small groups of scales along the snake body. Refine the outline of the face, giving the yōkai a more pointed chin. Add texture to the face and into the deep eye socket.

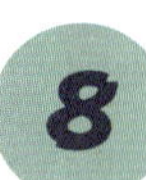

To finish the nure-onna, darken the inside of the mouth, under the eyes, and the hair in the back under the chin to really make the face pop. Using similar lines to those on the face, add texture to the belly scales.

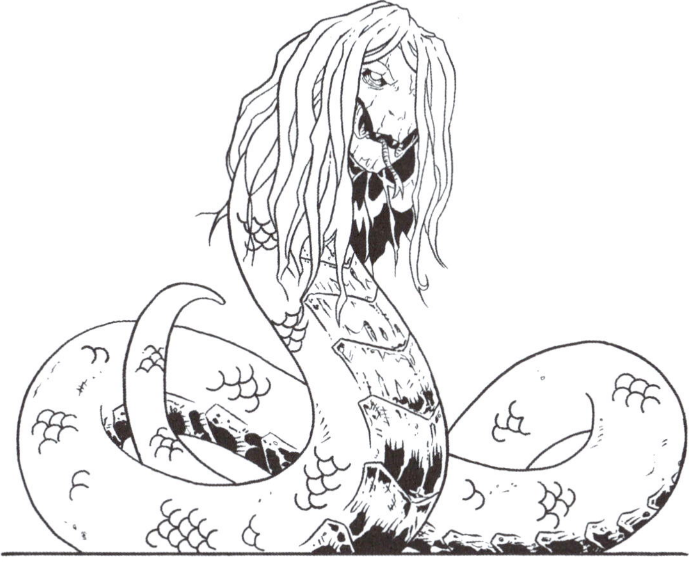

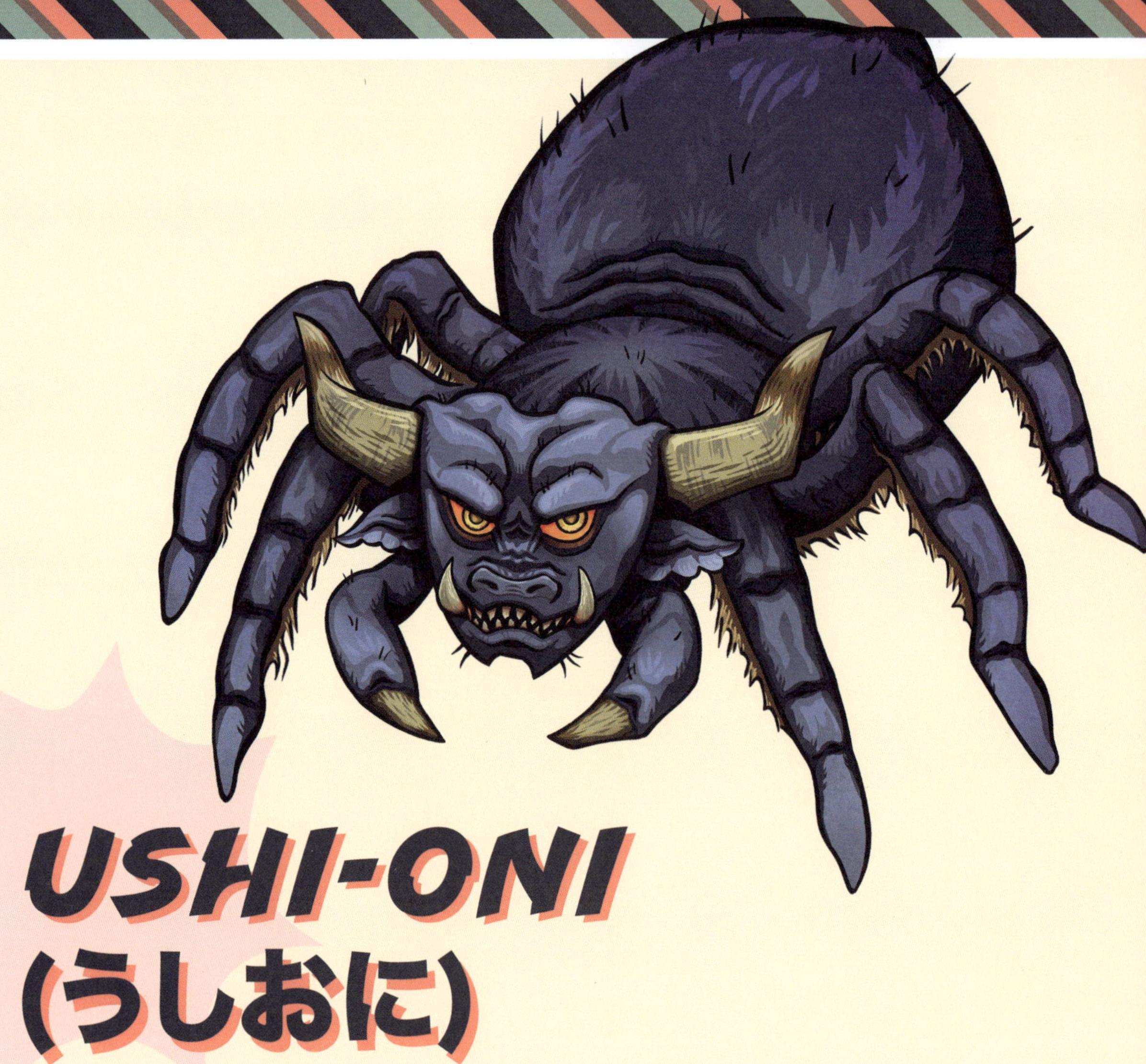

USHI-ONI
（うしおに）

The villain of many folktales, this ox demon is traditionally illustrated with the head of a bull ox and the body of a spider. This brute is known to lurk in coastal areas as well as in rivers and lakes, due to its partnership with the nure-onna (page 158). It is also known to wander farther afield into forests and mountains. The ushi-oni consumes people, torments villages, and spreads curses.

The process of drawing the ushi-oni will be very similar to that of the heikegani (page 62).

Draw an oval for the body. Extending outward from the body, draw lines of action for each of the demon's larger six legs. Pay attention to where they bend.

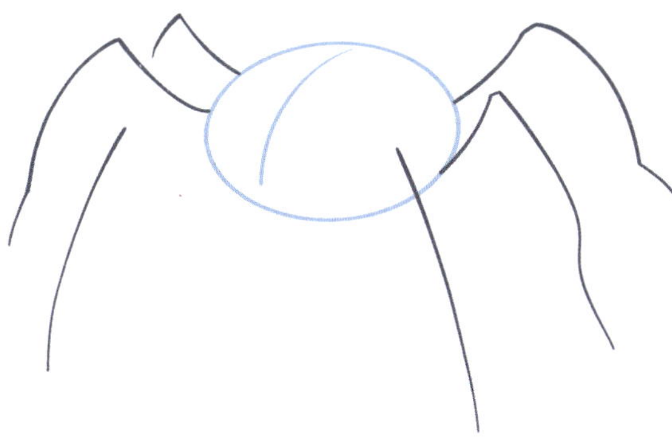

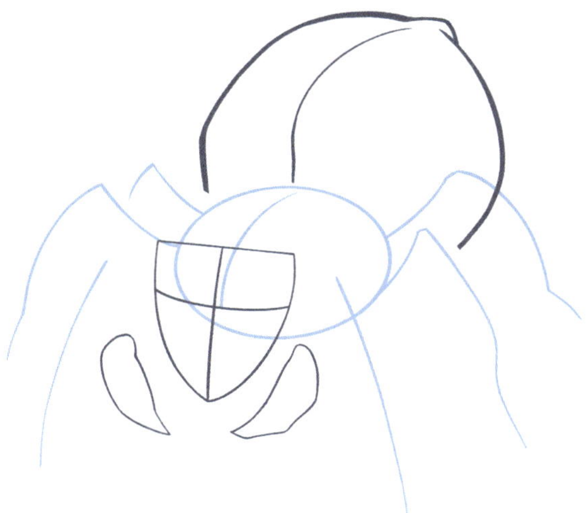

Draw the bulbous abdomen of the spider body, the triangular head shape, and pointed front legs.

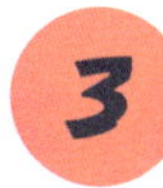

Refine the shape of the head: Draw bumps on top, a pointed chin, and two large, steer horns. Add lines that connect the spider's front legs to its abdomen.

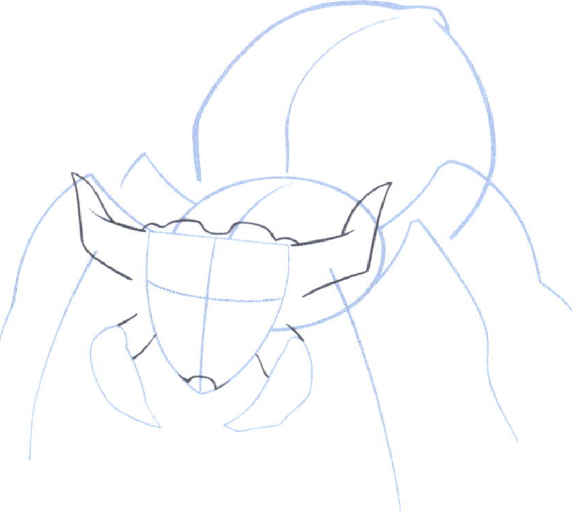

4

Following the lines of action, draw the segmented tube-like shapes of legs. Each leg should come to a rounded point.

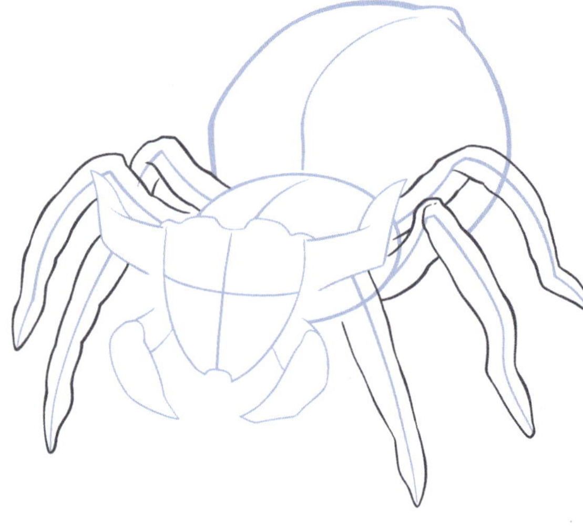

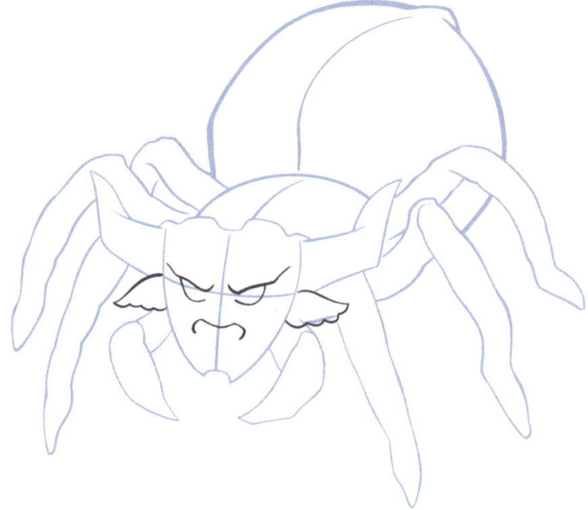

5

Draw in the basic shapes of the face: slanted brows that capture the fierce expression, the upward, curved bullnose, and ears that are hanging down.

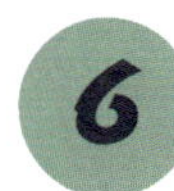

6

This step is all about wrinkles. Draw wrinkles on the face, capturing the rounded brow, angular mouth, and curved inner ears. Finish with the wrinkles at the base of the abdomen.

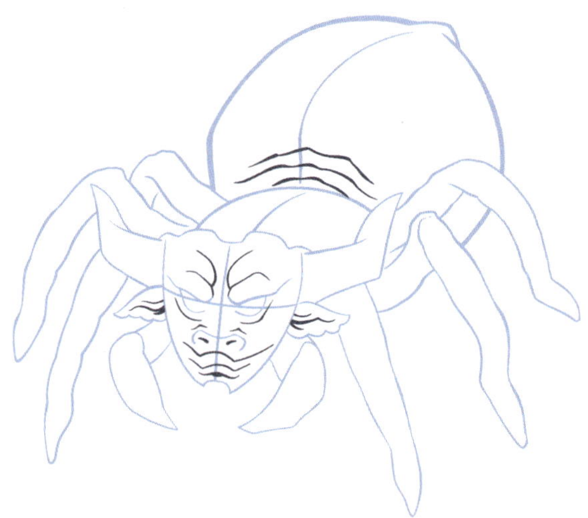

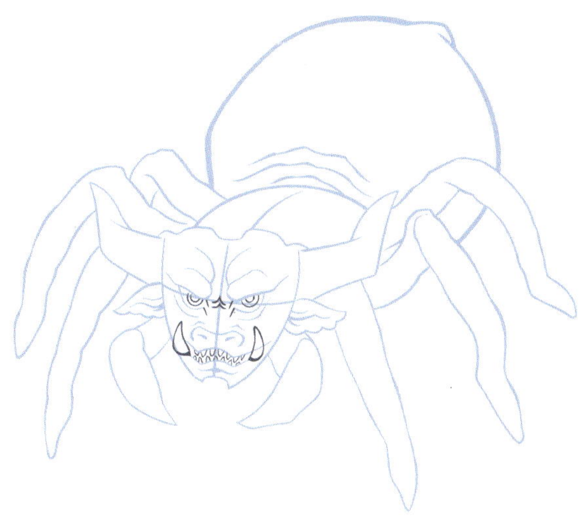

Draw the details of the face: pointed triangular teeth and large fangs, circular eyes, and pinched brow ridges to complete the expression.

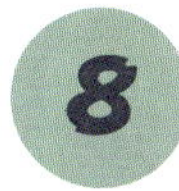

Draw hair hanging on the underside of the legs, as can be seen on a tarantula.

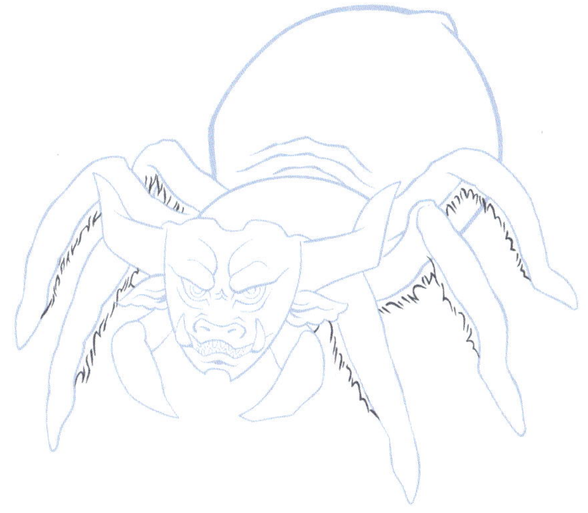

Add little hairs sticking up all over the body and thicken the main outline. Add shading around the ushi-oni's face to help push it forward from the body and limbs.

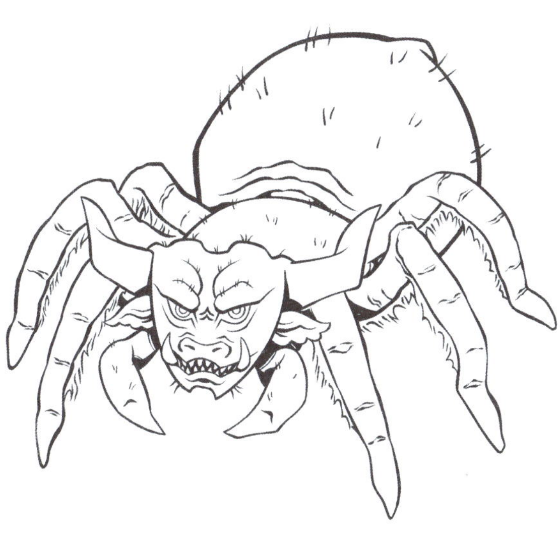

ONI (おに)

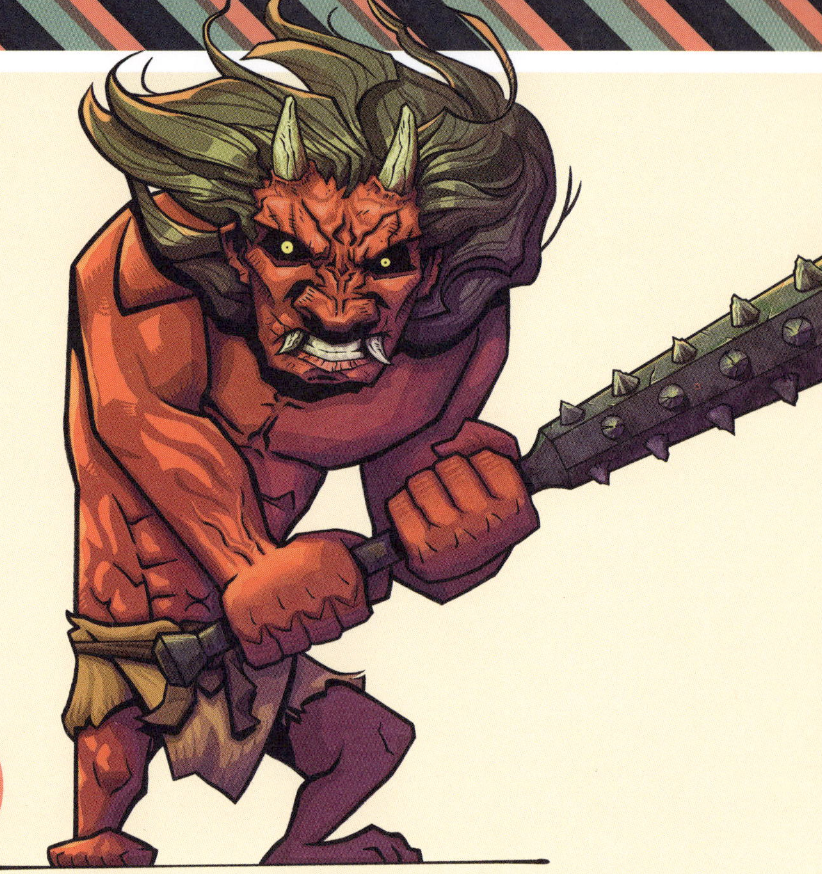

One of the most legendary yōkai in Japanese culture, oni are found throughout folklore, history, pop culture, anime, manga, and literature. These demon-ogres have plagued the Japanese countryside for centuries and are one of the most common villains in Japanese legends.

Oni come in a variety of forms. The most iconic oni are large, powerful, ruthless male ogres with red skin, two horns, and a tiger-pelt loincloth. They wield large, spiked clubs and live in remote mountains and caves. Oni are evil creatures, murdering, kidnapping, and eating people as well as enslaving them.

Oni can be used to describe a whole category of yōkai. Earlier in history it was used as a generic word for any demon, spirit, monster, or evil phenomenon.

Drawing the oni will be similar to drawing the spear-wielding ōgama (page 50), except with more detail, especially in the face and upper body.

Draw a long, curved line of action. At the base, draw a line for the ground and, near the top, the box-like shape of the head.

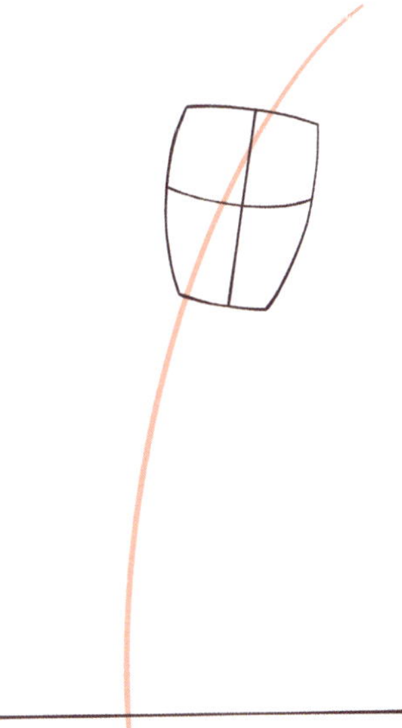

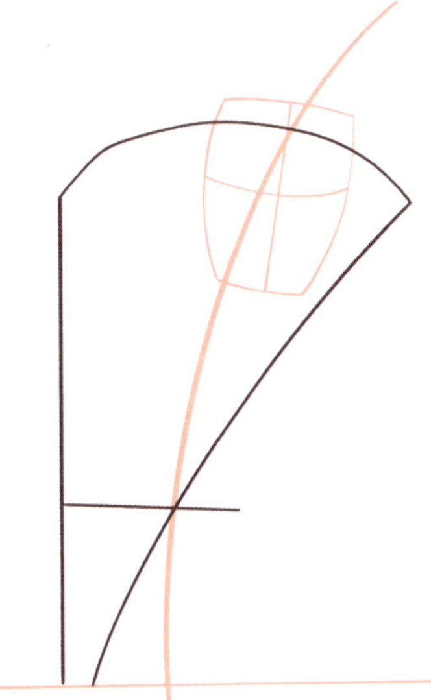

2

Draw a tall triangle for the body with a wide, rounded top for the shoulders. The horizontal line denotes the waist.

3

As with the ōgama, draw the short, bent legs and feet of the oni. Add a long, diagonal line showing where the oni's weapon will go.

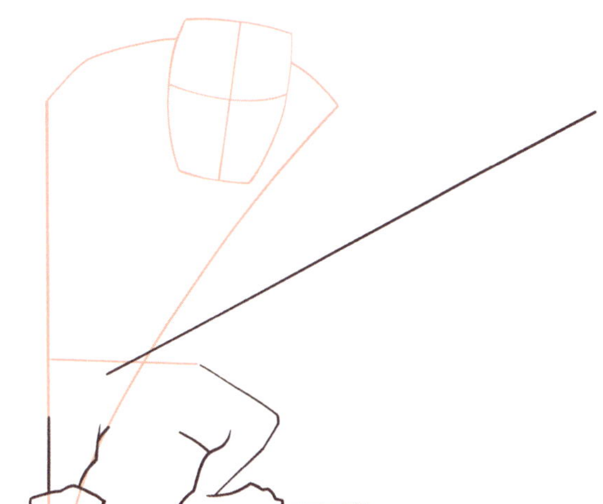

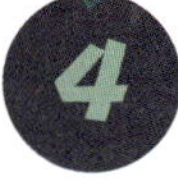

4

Draw rounded box shapes for the hands. Notice the bumps for the knuckles. Draw a large, swooping mane of hair around the head.

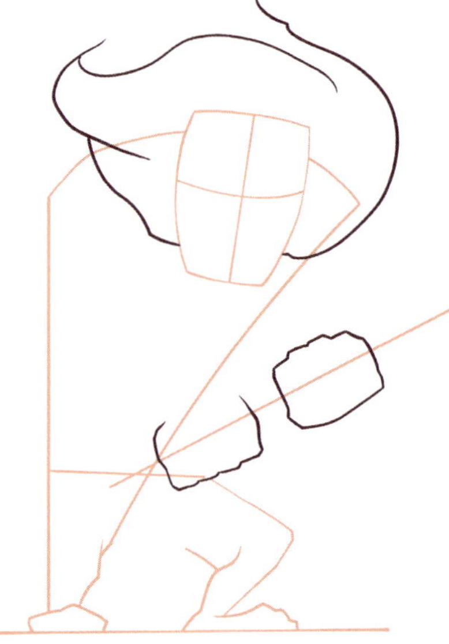

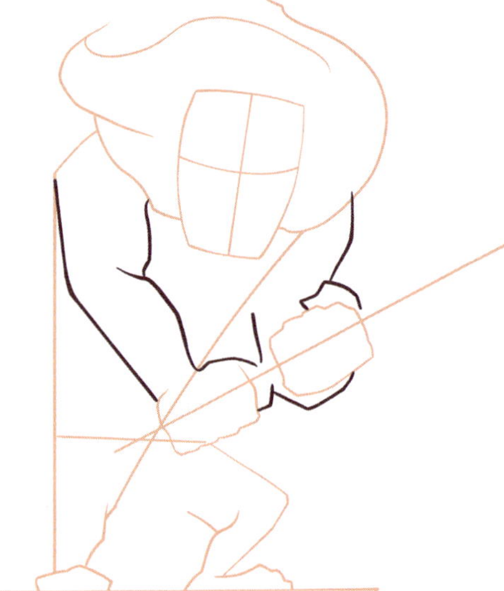

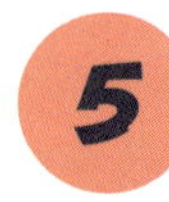

5

Connect the hands to the shoulders by drawing in the arms. Notice how the backsides of the arms are flat, while the front sides bulge with muscle.

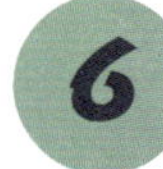

6

Draw the shapes of the oni's traditional weapon: the *kanabō*, which is a type of club. If needed, use a ruler to draw its straight edges. This kanabō has a narrower handle with a body that widens as it approaches the end.

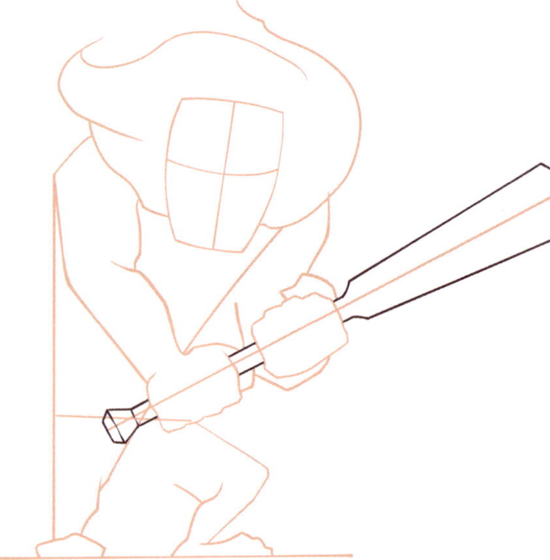

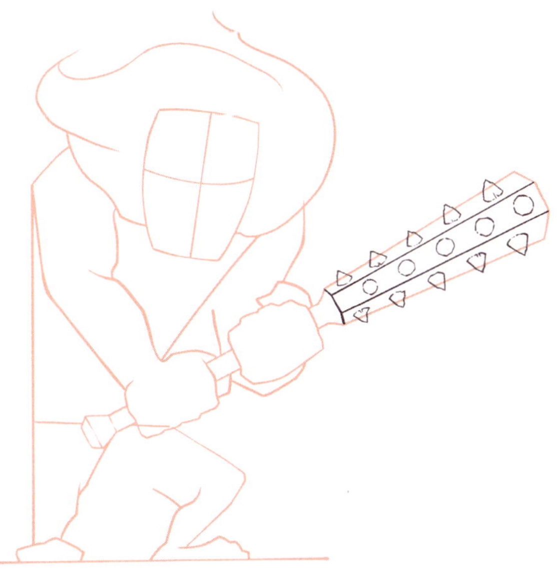

7

Add three rows of spikes to the kanabō using irregular triangles. For the center row use circles, since those spikes face directly out.

8

Refine the outline of the body, expanding the chest and using sweeping curves to block in the loincloth, the traditional costume of the oni.

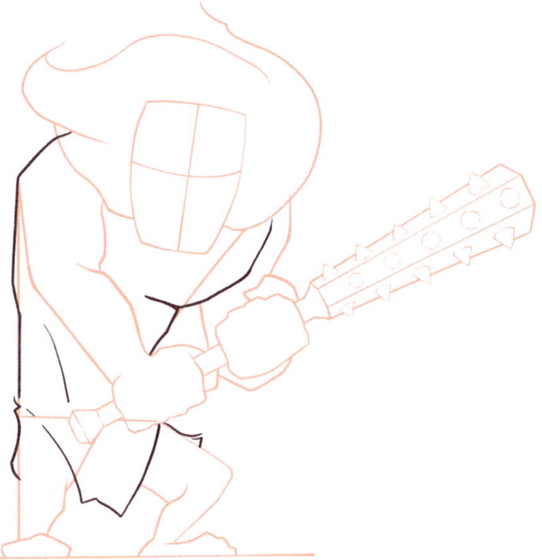

9

Draw in the rest of the loincloth using similar shapes to the ōgama's, including the band of fabric that serves as a belt, complete with a knot in the middle.

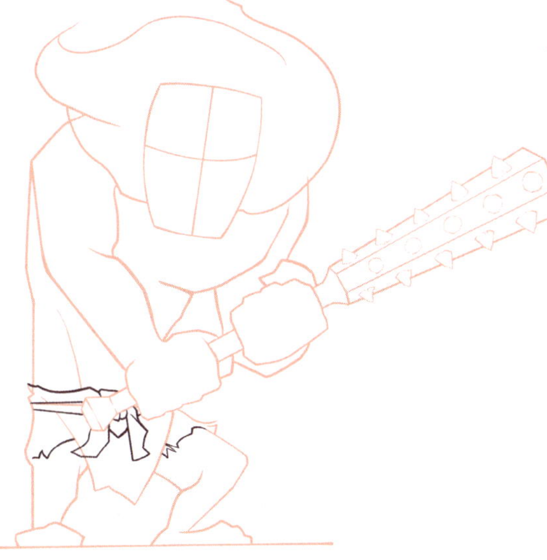

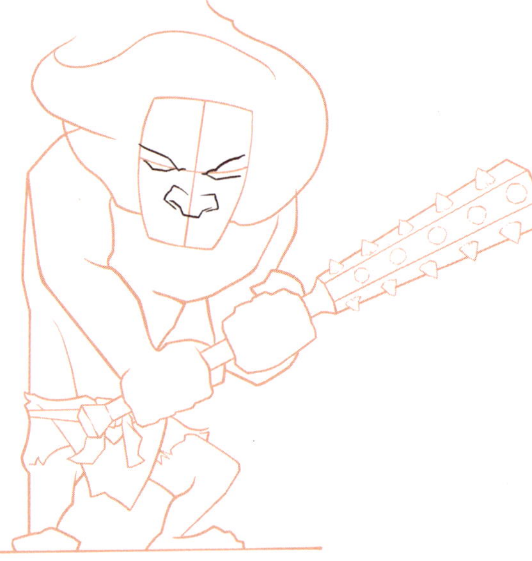

The next batch of steps will focus on rendering the face of the oni.

10

Draw the outline of the eyes and nose using sharp angles to push the oni's ferocious expression.

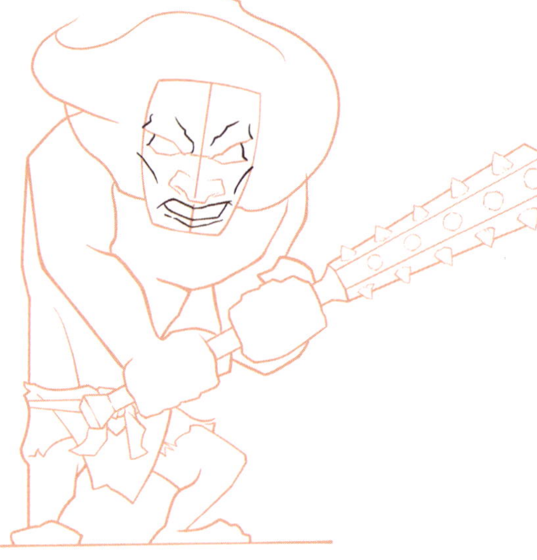

11

Draw the mouth, the hollows of the cheeks, and slanted brows.

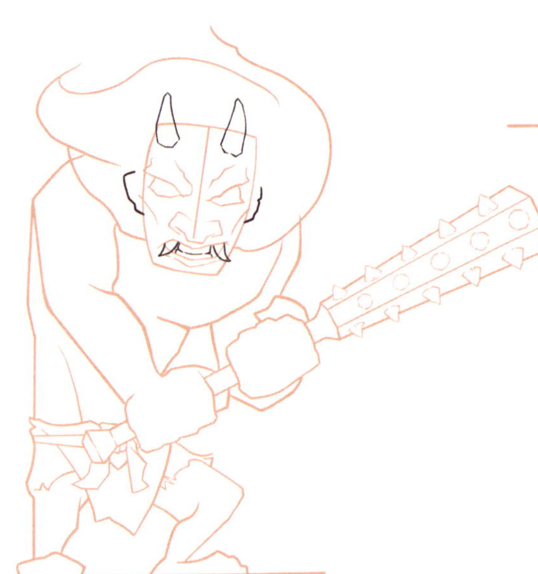

12

Add two long horns to the forehead and matching fangs to the mouth. Don't forget the simple ear shapes.

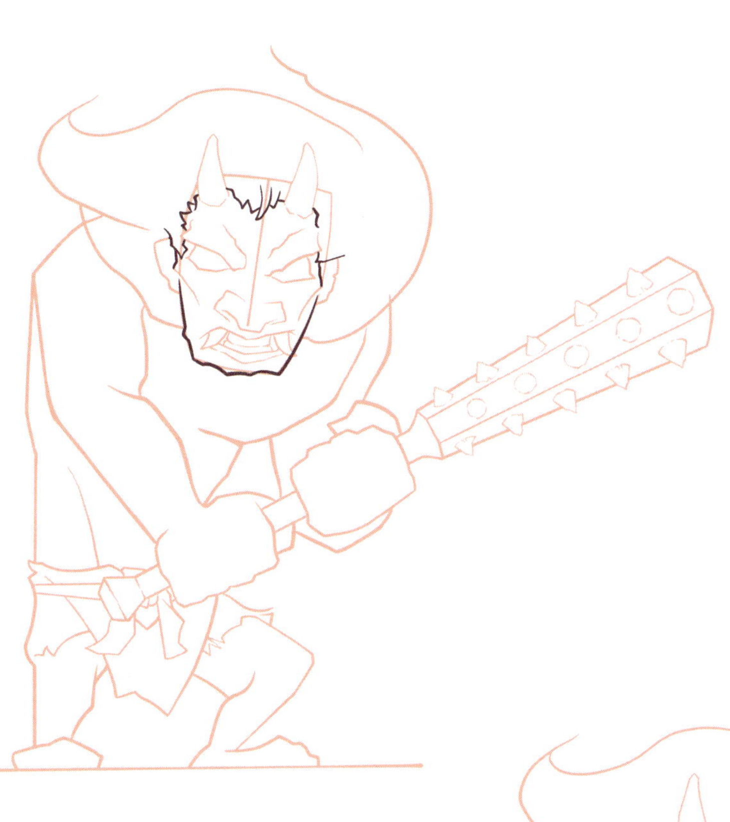

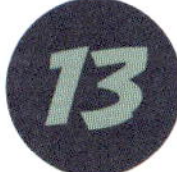

13

Refine the outline of the face by adding bulges for the chin and jaw. Draw the spiky hairline around the face.

14

When a face is contorted in anger, the brow is pinched. Draw these pinched wrinkles on the brow and between the eyes using sharp angles.

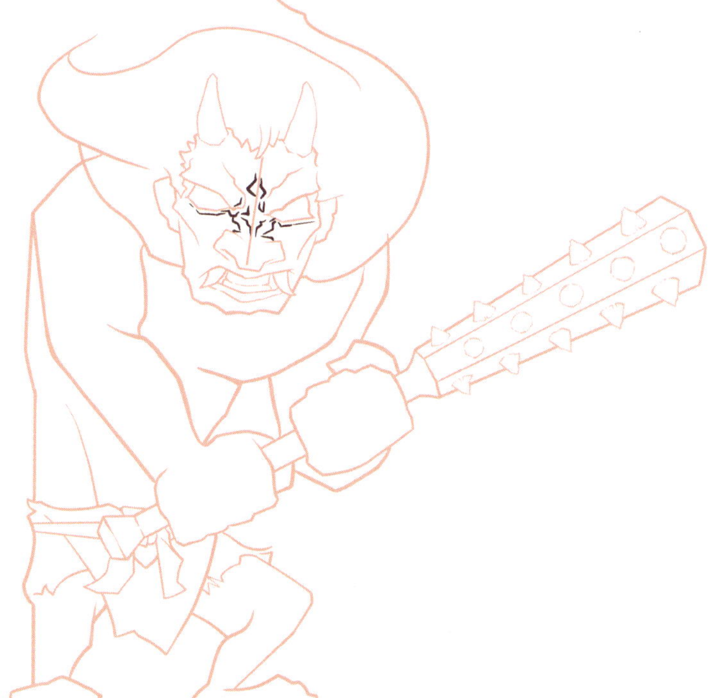

This last group of steps will focus on drawing the hair, then on final details to bring the oni to life.

Add complexity to the flowing mane of hair by drawing in larger, swooping masses, like we did with the otoroshi (page 154).

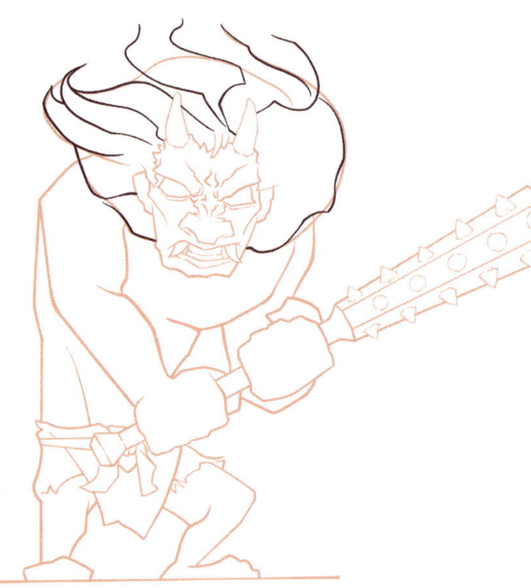

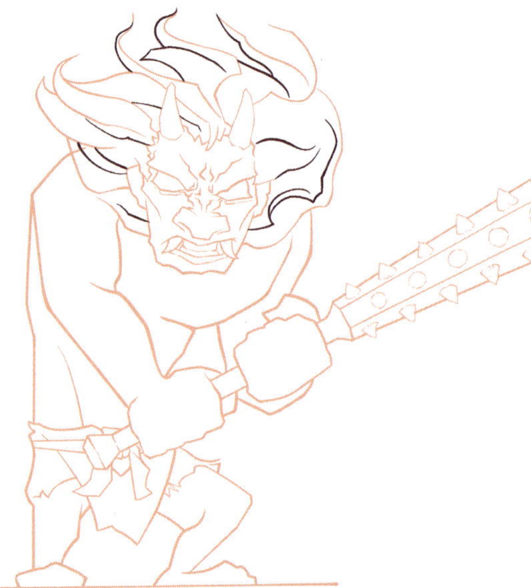

Continue to refine the hair. Like the otoroshi, the oni's hair looks wild, with it flowing out in different directions.

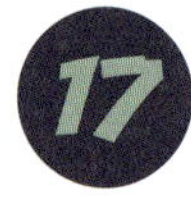

Add detail to the body by indicating the muscles of the chest, core, and shoulders using short, angled dashes.

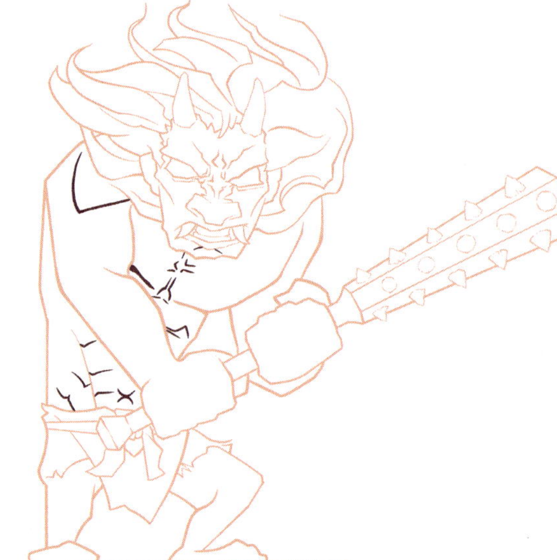

18

Refine the hands and feet by drawing in the fingers, toes, and triangular knuckles.

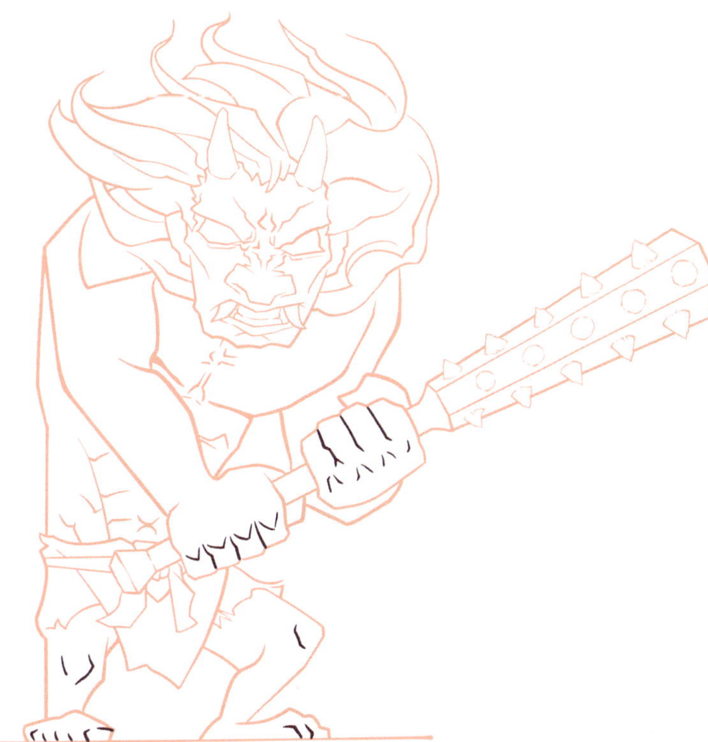

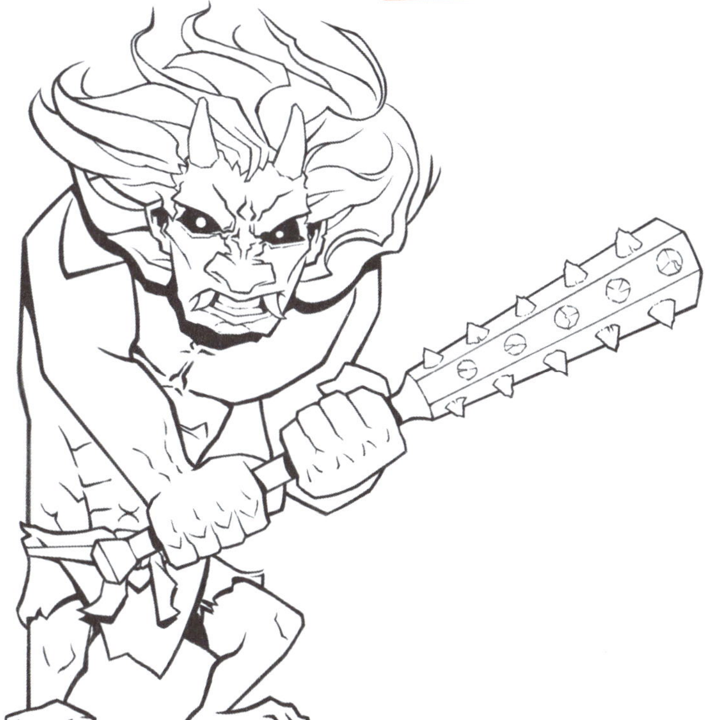

19

Finish the oni by thickening the outline of the body and adding a dark shadow beneath the head and hair. This helps the face to stand out from the body.

NAMAHAGE (なまはげ)

The namahage is a sort of Japanese bogeyman that steals away lazy children. Culturally, they are used to scare wayward children into behaving. While the namahage appears fierce, they mean well. If misbehaving children correct their ways, namahage are known to bless the household.

The origin of the namahage has to do with cautionary tales for children and lazy people who sat with their feet up by the warm hearth instead of working, so much so that they got blisters from the heat. The namahage would come, cut the blisters off their feet, collect the blisters, and steal that person away. This is why they are portrayed carrying knives and buckets.

For the final two "harder" yōkai, there will be more covered between each step, but don't let that intimidate you. Apply what you've learned in the previous sections and take your time with each step. Drawing tips like working outside to inside and large shapes to small shapes become very important when tackling more complex figures like the namahage and tengu (page 180). With complex drawing, it's all about creating layers of detail. Each layer can be simple by itself, but as you add more and more layers it will give the drawing a much more intricate look.

1

Draw the line of action. Add an oval and center lines for the head. Draw a larger wide oval for the upper body.

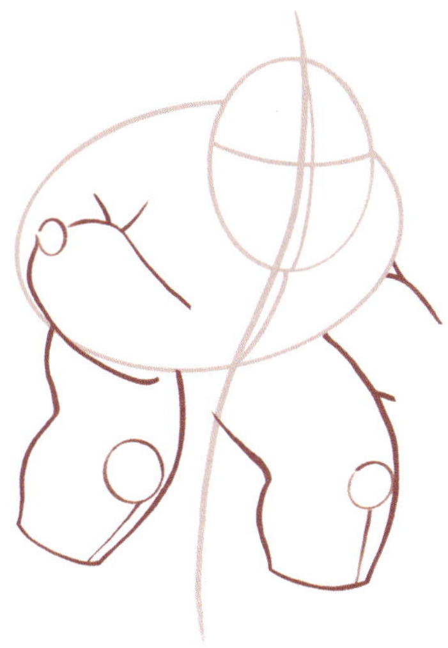

2

Draw tubular shapes for the arms and legs, with small bends at the elbows and knees. The namahage will be a wider, stouter figure, making him look all the more imposing.

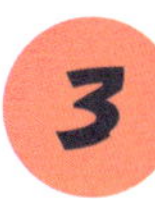

3

Add basic shapes for the hands and feet to the ends of the limbs. With the figure blocked in, draw the rigid outline of the face, as well as the namahage's two horns.

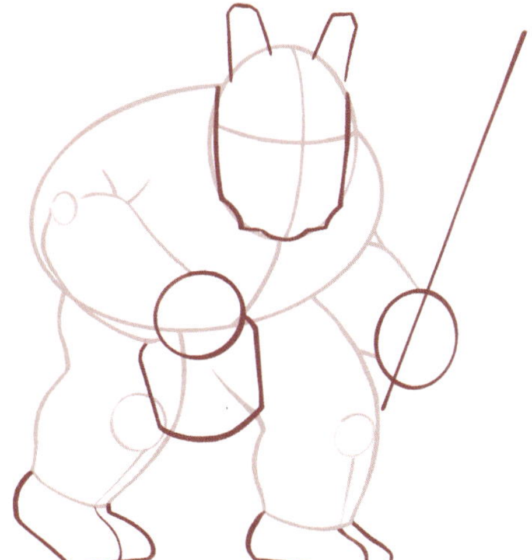

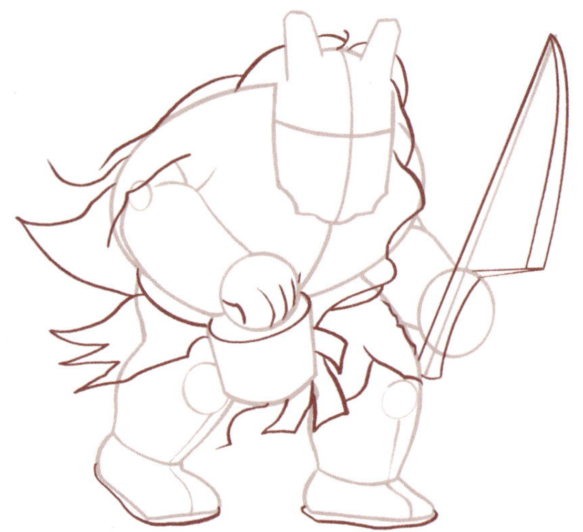

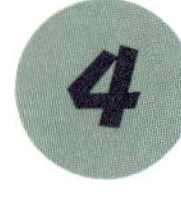

Use flowing lines to draw the outlines of the namahage's traditional straw cape, as if it were blowing in the wind. Draw his large knife, following the straight line from his hand. Use curved lines to indicate the top of the bucket he is carrying, as well as his fingers. Draw the bottoms of his zōri sandals following the outlines of his feet.

Work outside to inside. Add curved shapes for the eyes and growling mouth. Use repeating shapes to draw the straw arm and ankle wraps. These are mostly the same shape, just turned and curved to fit around his arms and legs, which are at different angles. These wraps consist of a straw base with two cords wrapped around it to hold the straw in place.

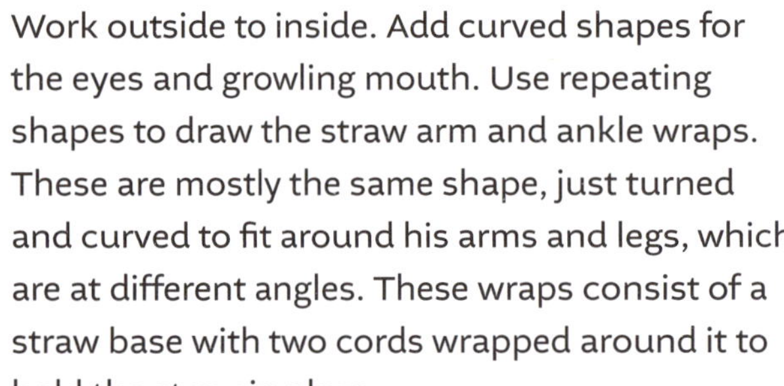

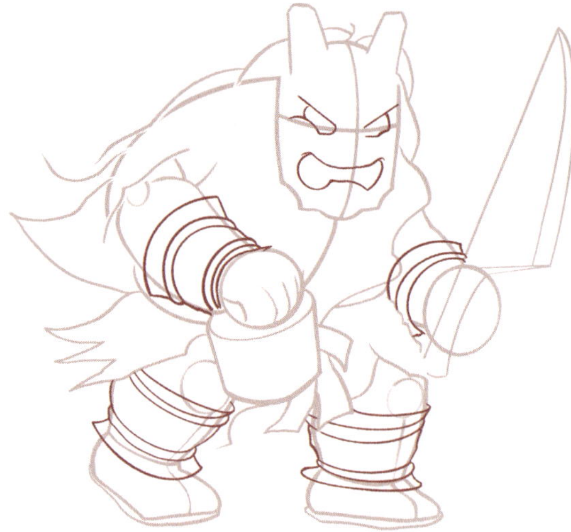

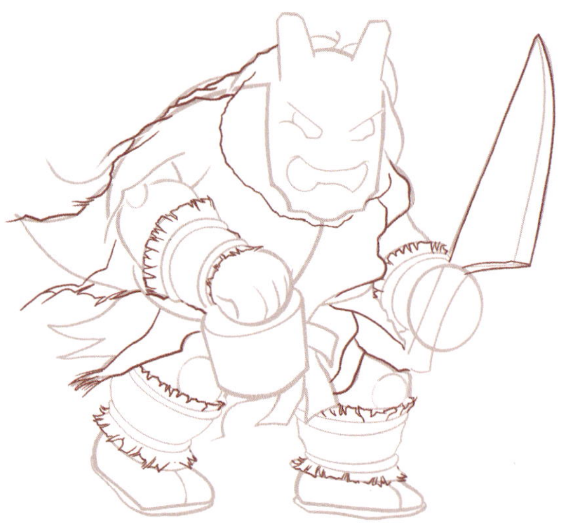

Now that the large shapes have been established, add details. Use short, wavy lines so that the outline of the straw cape looks like layered clusters of straw. Repeat these lines for the ends of the arm and ankle wraps. Give the ruled knife lines a slightly uneven, handmade look.

Refine the face: Draw the outline of the namahage's teeth along with the large fangs on either end. Draw the planes of the horns. Add the angled brow lines to enhance his fierce expression.

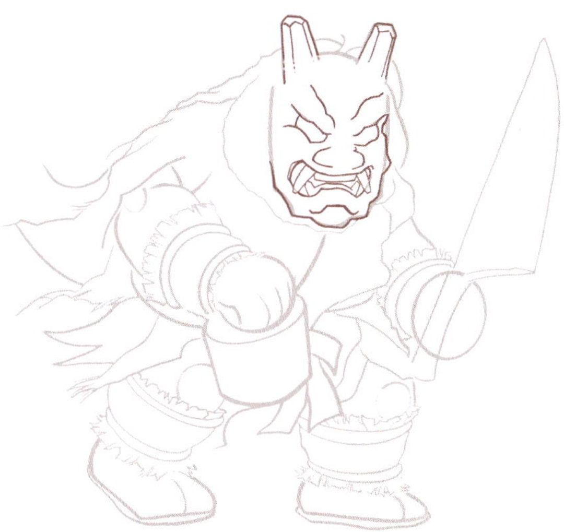

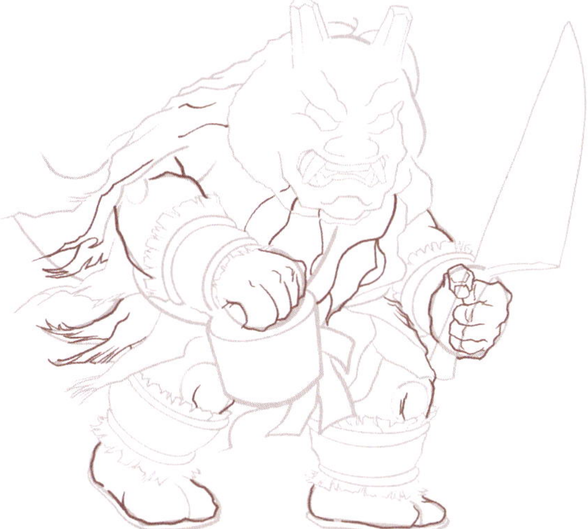

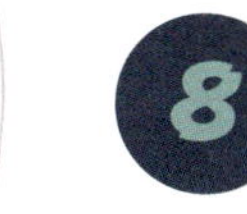

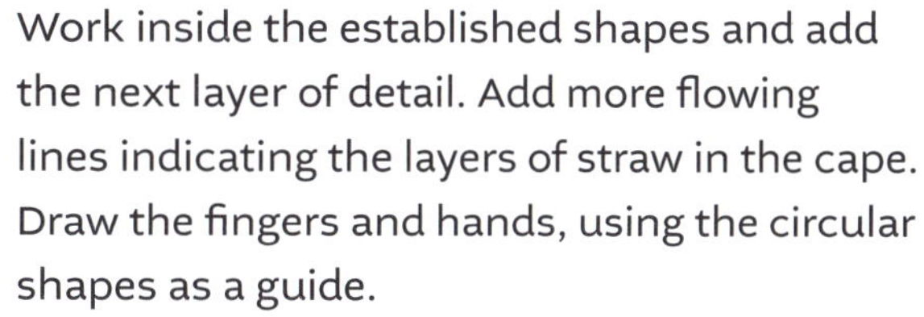

Work inside the established shapes and add the next layer of detail. Add more flowing lines indicating the layers of straw in the cape. Draw the fingers and hands, using the circular shapes as a guide.

Draw the tied knots on the cords of the arm and leg wraps: repeating shapes again. Begin drawing the front of his hair, which frames his face, and bring in some of the facial wrinkles, which help to enhance his ferocious expression.

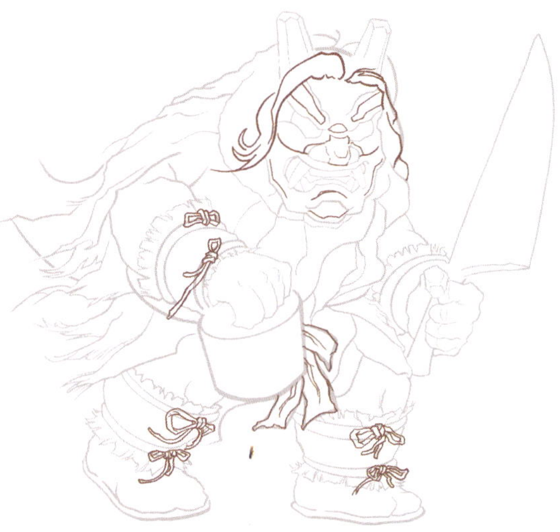

10

This next batch of steps may look complicated. Just tackle them one shape, one costume piece at a time. Add more hair strands around the face and additional layers of straw to the namahage's cape, building behind the lines from step 9.

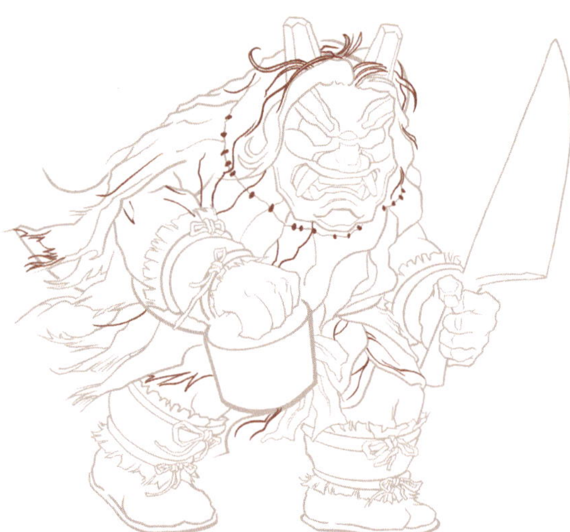

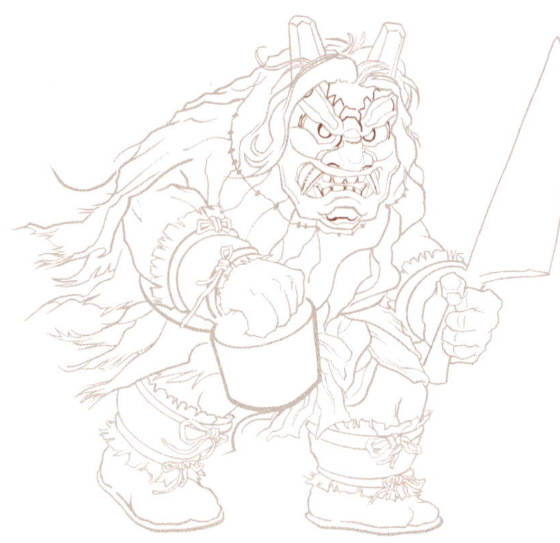

11

Draw in more facial details like the pupils, teeth, and the planes of the forehead.

12

Turn the larger tube shapes of the cords on the forearms and legs into actual twisted cord.

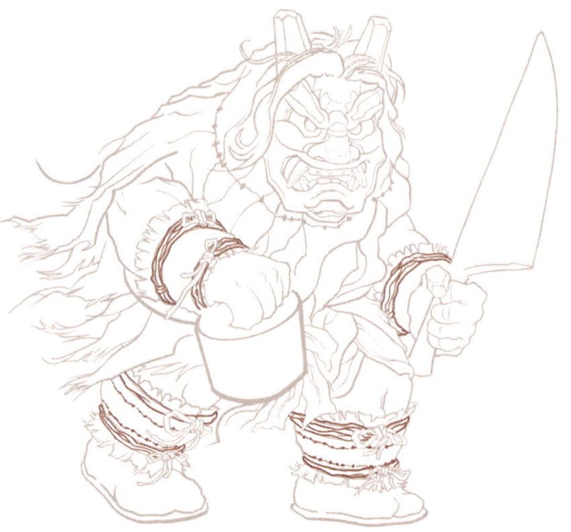

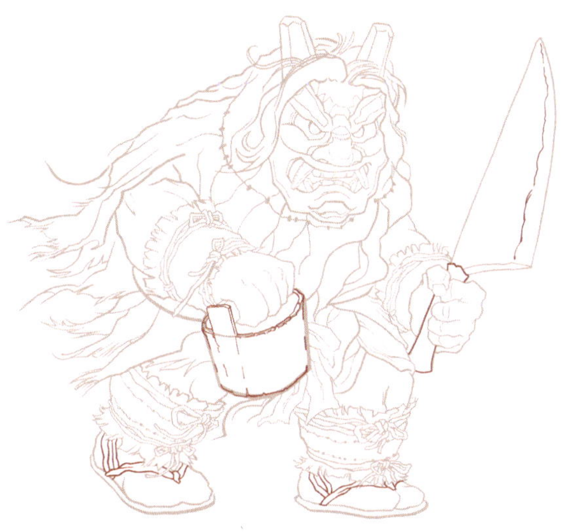

Add the straps to his sandals. Begin to show that the bucket is made of wood and refine the knife that he is holding.

Now for the smallest final details. Add interior texture lines, like the lines in the arm and ankle wraps, to show they are made of straw. Turn the tube shape of the waist tie into rope and add the straw ropes around the bucket. Draw some final strands of straw, blowing in the wind off the back of the cape.

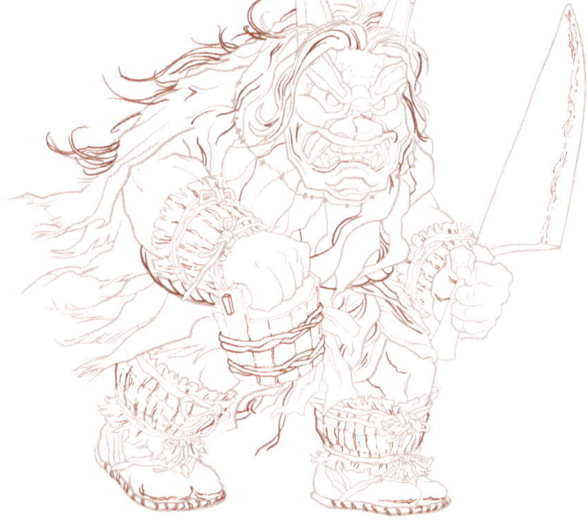

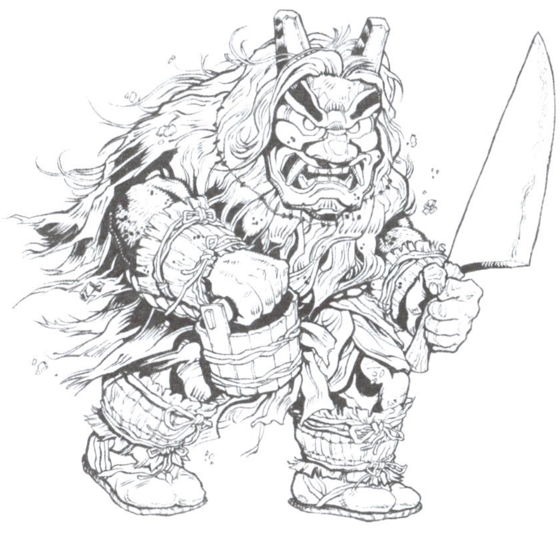

As a final touch, strengthen the outlines, such as the main outlines of the cape and arms. For more pop, you can add solid black shadows to help create separation, since there is a lot of detail in this drawing.

TENGU (てんぐ)

The traditional tengu embody mysterious dark forces from the mountains. They have crow-like features and the appearance of *yamabushi*, which are ascetic mountain dwellers. Tengu are wicked monk yōkai that seek to lead people off the path. In ancient Japan, monks used to call monks of other Buddhist sects "tengu" as an insult. These yōkai were blamed for spreading illness, war, torment, and other mysterious events plaguing the mountains upon which they lived. However, in modern interpretations they are portrayed as being more benevolent, living in clans that dwell on and protect their mountains.

As with the namahage (page 174), there will be more covered in each step since we have drawn dozens of yōkai at this point. Apply what you've learned in the drawings before this one and take your time with each step.

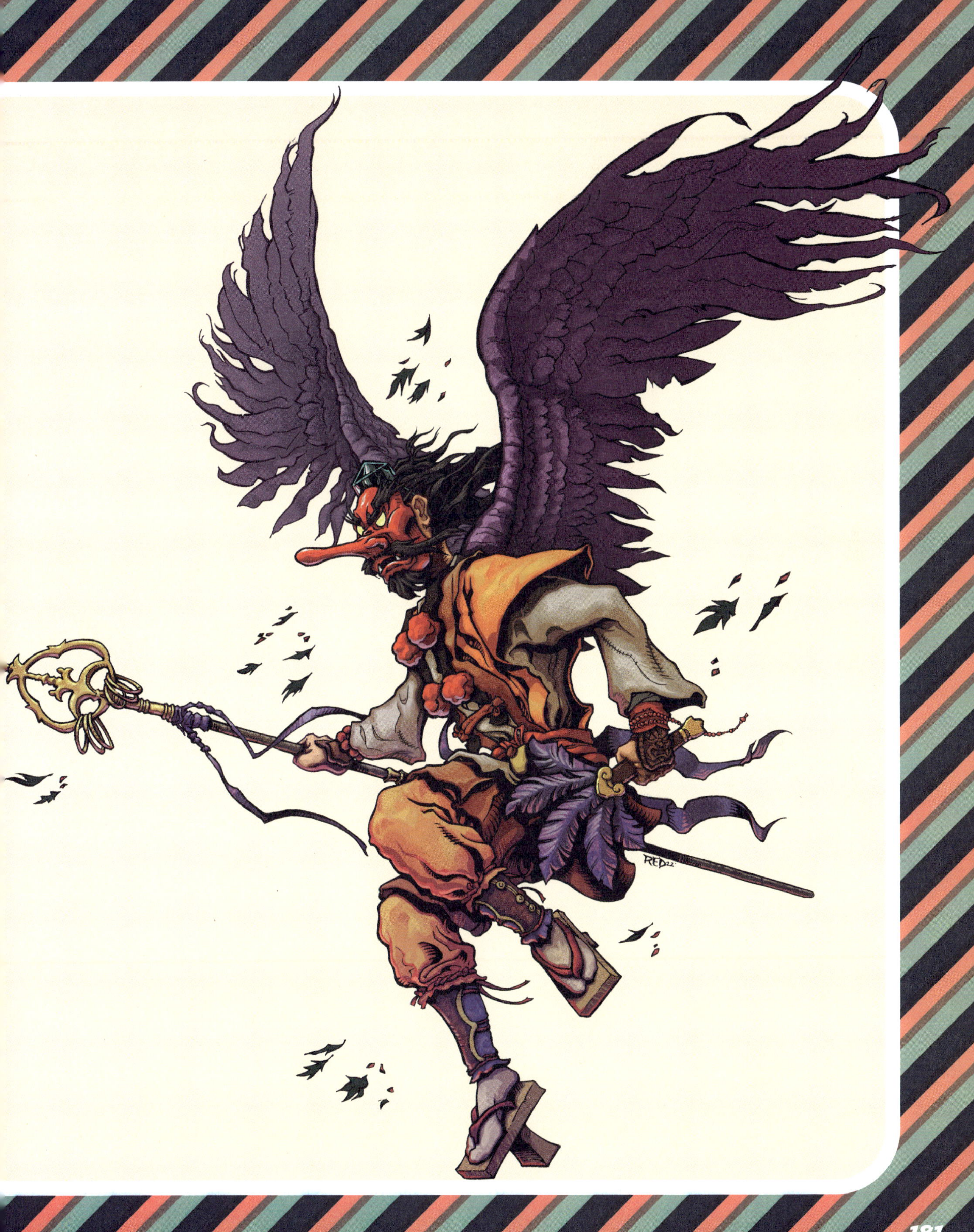

Sketch the line of action. Draw an oval for the head, then the curved center lines. Add a long eggplant shape for the body. Connect these shapes to create the neck.

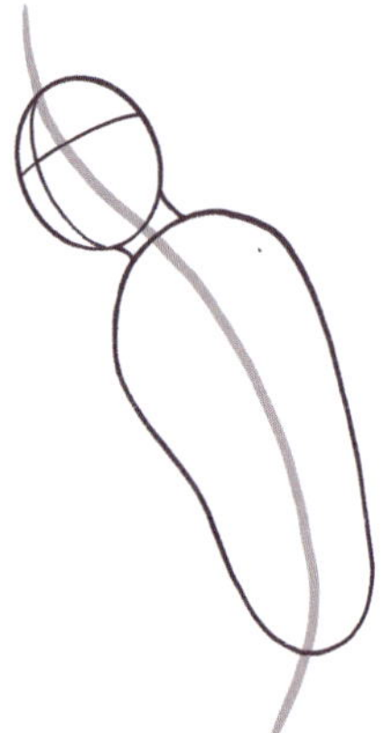

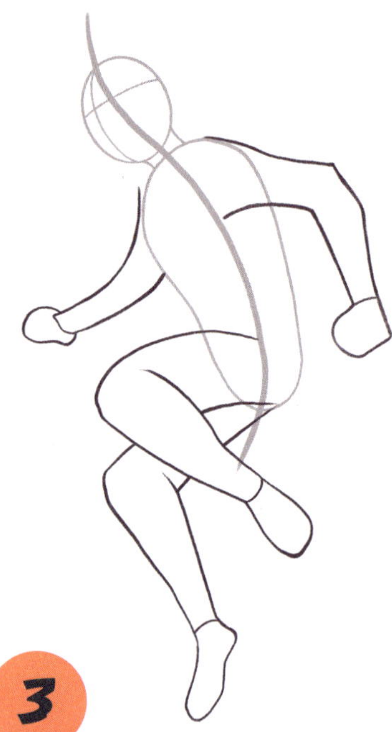

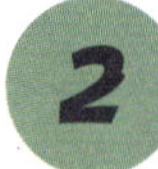

Draw curved, tubular shapes for the arms and legs. Following the direction and flow of the limbs, add on the basic shapes for the hands and feet.

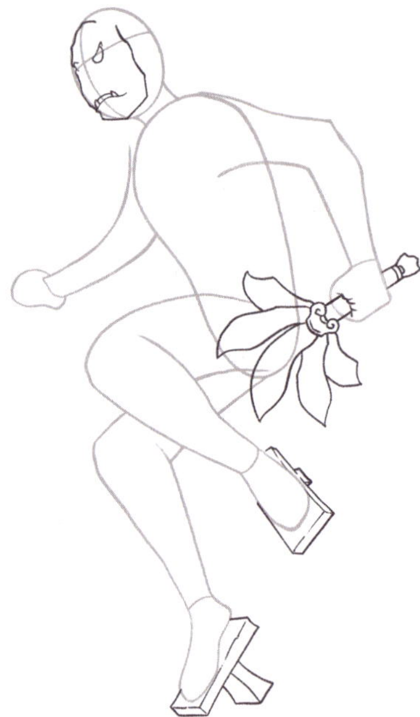

With the shapes of the basic figure in place, we can begin adding in costume pieces. Draw the outline of the tengu's face. Add his eyes and the basic shape of his mouth. Construct his geta sandals. Draw the basic shape of his fan. Use curved, leaf-like shapes for the feathers.

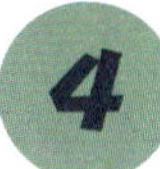

4

Start creating the layers of the tengu's traditional costume. Since he will be flying in the sky, use wavy lines to show that his clothes are blowing in the wind. Follow the overall shape of his limbs and body but allow the fabric to billow out when you draw it, versus sticking tightly to the leg and arm shapes.

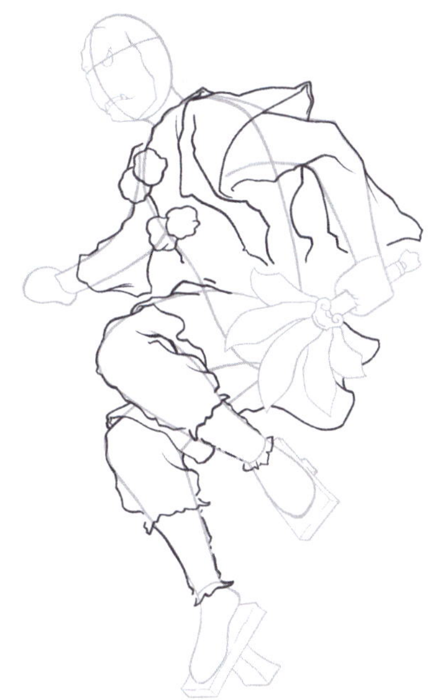

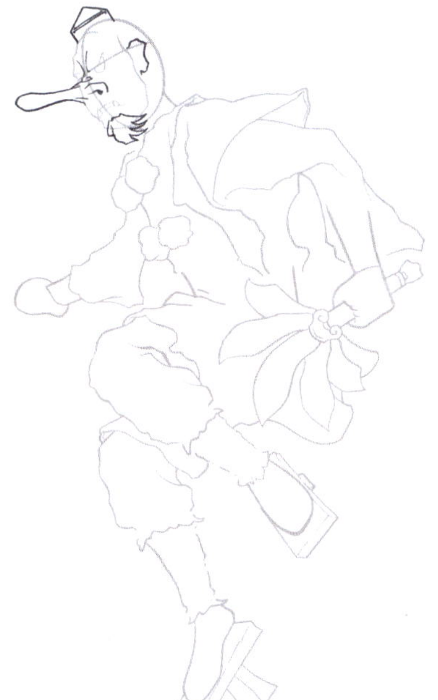

5

Continue to construct the face. Draw the tengu's nose, ears, and beard. Add the triangular box-shaped hat to the top of his head. This is called a *tokin* and is part of a yamabushi's traditional attire.

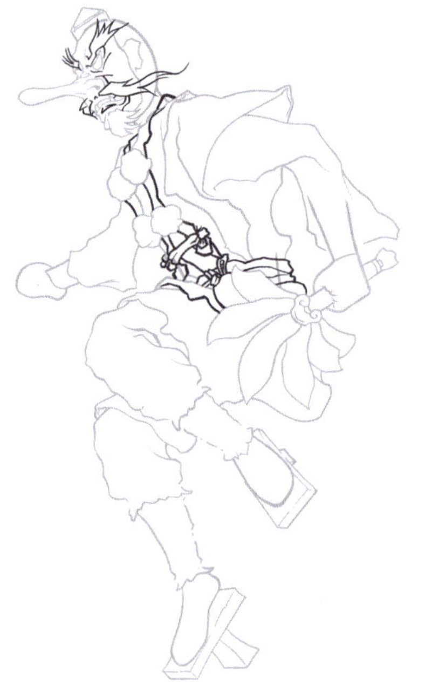

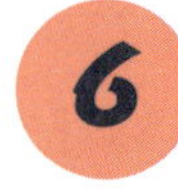

6

Finish off the face by drawing his mustache and eyebrows. Add more layers to the clothing. Pay attention to the wrinkles as you draw the tengu's obi sash.

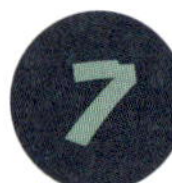

7

Draw the tengu's feet and hands. Add his wrist guards and the straps on his geta. Use circles to create the bracelet on his wrist.

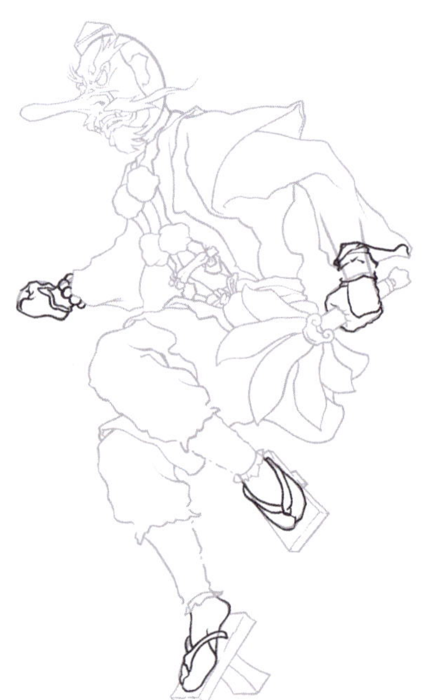

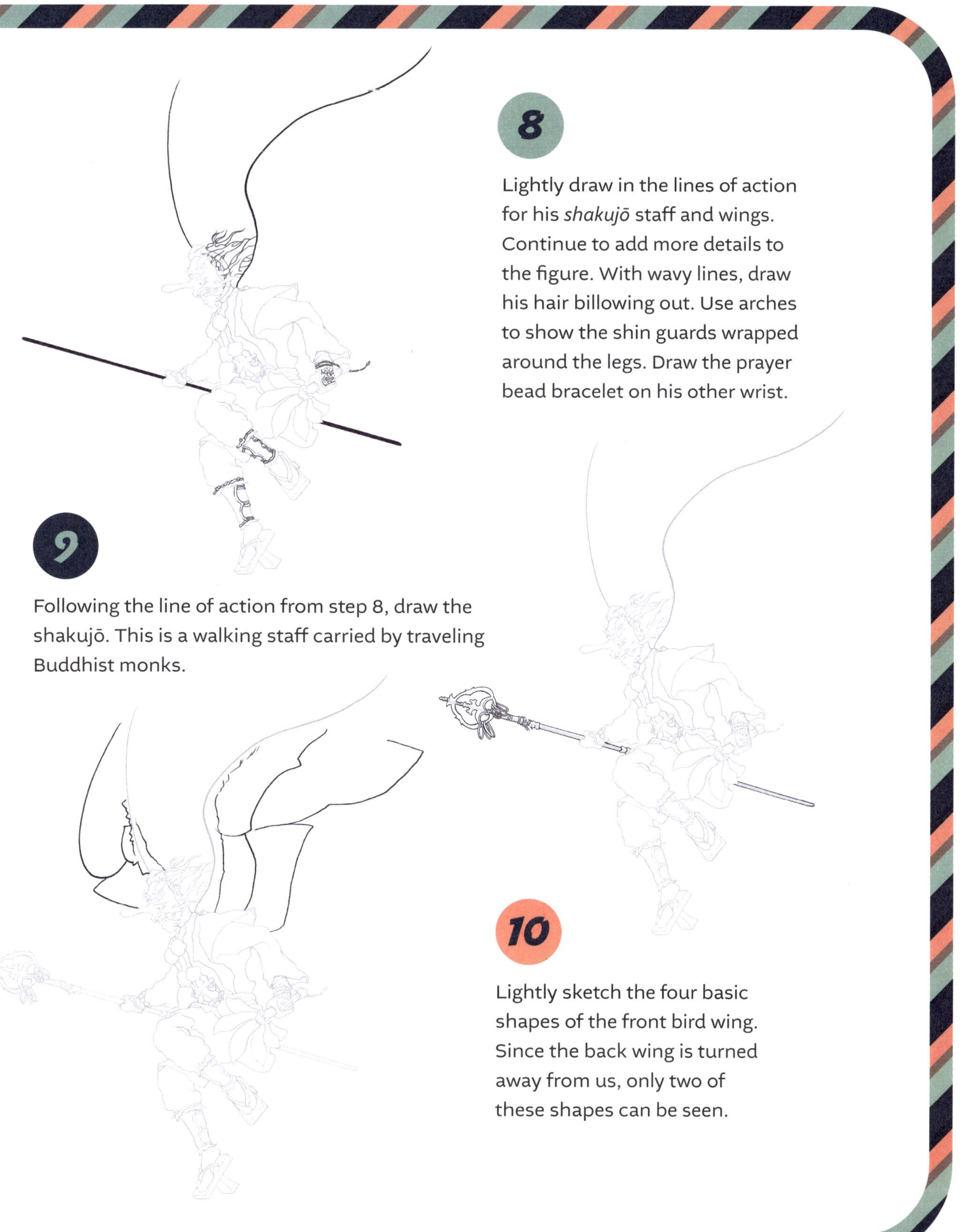

Lightly draw in the lines of action for his *shakujō* staff and wings. Continue to add more details to the figure. With wavy lines, draw his hair billowing out. Use arches to show the shin guards wrapped around the legs. Draw the prayer bead bracelet on his other wrist.

Following the line of action from step 8, draw the shakujō. This is a walking staff carried by traveling Buddhist monks.

Lightly sketch the four basic shapes of the front bird wing. Since the back wing is turned away from us, only two of these shapes can be seen.

Refine the leading edges of his wings. Start to add the final details of his costume. These include all the wrinkles in his clothing and the texture of the feathers in his fan.

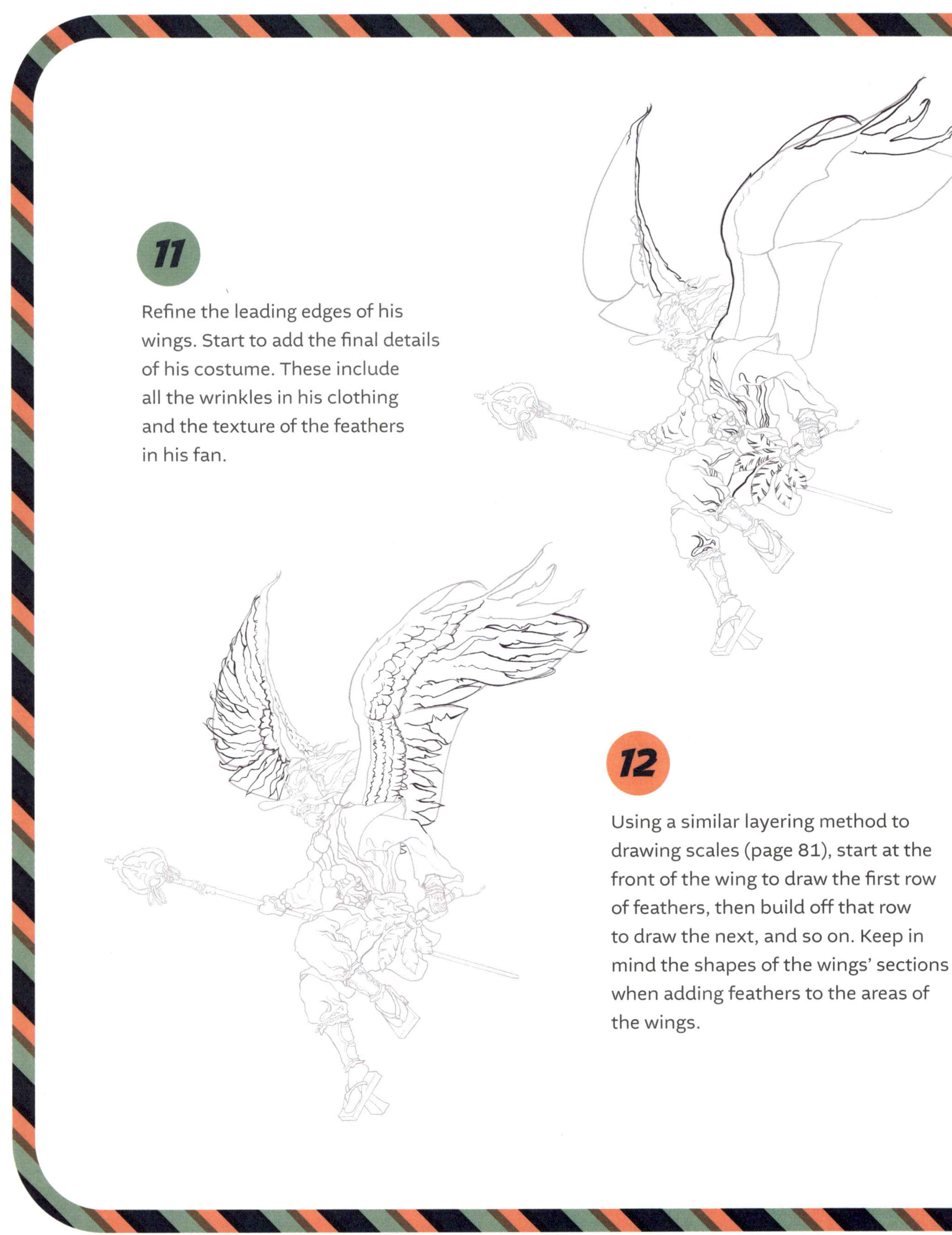

Using a similar layering method to drawing scales (page 81), start at the front of the wing to draw the first row of feathers, then build off that row to draw the next, and so on. Keep in mind the shapes of the wings' sections when adding feathers to the areas of the wings.

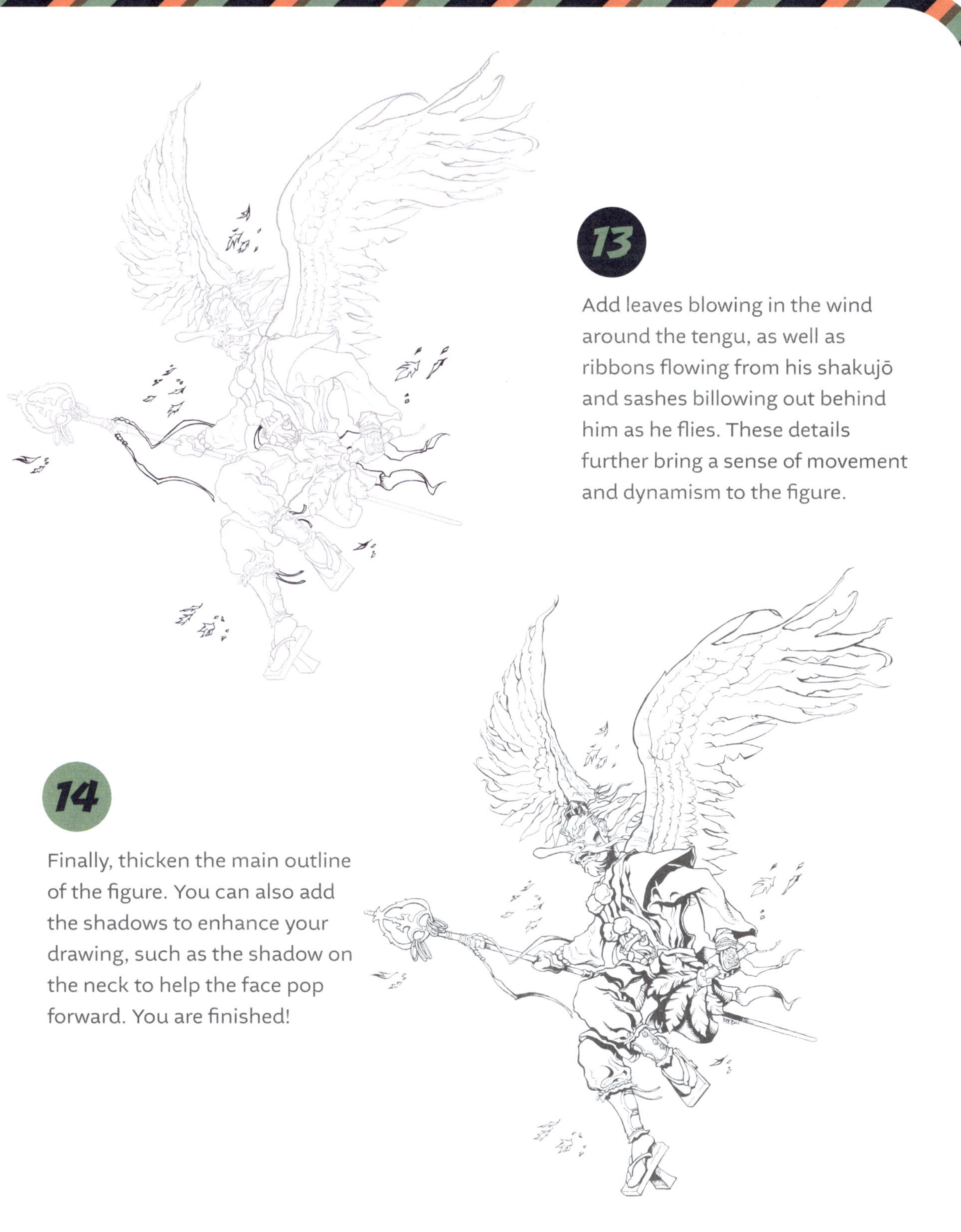

Add leaves blowing in the wind around the tengu, as well as ribbons flowing from his shakujō and sashes billowing out behind him as he flies. These details further bring a sense of movement and dynamism to the figure.

Finally, thicken the main outline of the figure. You can also add the shadows to enhance your drawing, such as the shadow on the neck to help the face pop forward. You are finished!

Want to dive deeper into the mysterious realm of yōkai? In this last section you'll find a glossary of key yōkai terms and artists, a list of yōkai-themed reading recommendations, and a little information about the author should you wish to connect.

Key Yōkai Terms

AYAKASHI: collective term for yōkai and supernatural occurrences.

BAKEMONO: monsters with the ability to transform. Literally meaning "changing thing," it is a term for yōkai that focuses on their transformative nature. However, the term is most often used to cover a much broader scope of supernatural creatures, being applied to monsters, ghosts, and other strange creatures.

EMAKI: long horizontal picture scrolls and hand scrolls that can be unfurled to show a series of events or images. Many of the yōkai artworks of the past were painted on emaki.

HYAKKIYAGYŌ EMAKI: *hyakkiyagyō* translates to English as "night parade of one hundred demons." This is a specific type of emaki whose subject is a parade of yōkai. It is a popular image composition for yōkai art.

HYAKUMONOGATARI: literally "one hundred stories." This term referred to a type of social gathering during the Edo period where people would gather to tell ghost stories, called Hyakumonogatari Kaidankai in Japanese. Many candles would be lit and after each story was told, a candle would be extinguished. After one hundred stories, the last candle would be extinguished, plunging the room into darkness and summoning a yōkai like the ao-andō (page 134). It is also used to describe a book or collection of supernatural stories.

KAMI: a general term for a god, deity, or strong spirit. This term is connected to Shinto beliefs, in that it is believed there is a spirit living in every object and every part of nature and can be found everywhere. Kami are not all-powerful gods in the way that we might understand the term in the West, and are also not necessarily worshiped.

KAMIKAKUSHI: a term that translates to "spiriting away" (and the term from which the famous Studio Ghibli film draws its name). It describes a traditional story in yōkai mythology where tengu or other yōkai would kidnap a person and take them to the realm of the yōkai. This story type continues to be a popular narrative in anime and manga.

MONONOKE: an older word for scary or unexplained things, which overlaps with being a word for yōkai and other supernatural subjects. This term was used before "yōkai" came into widespread use. In modern terminology it is often used interchangeably with obake, ayakashi, and bakemono in everyday speech, though in academia there are more distinctions between these terms.

OBAKE: monster. Another word used in similar ways to bakemono. It is used to describe monsters in general as opposed to more spirit-based creatures, but this distinction is not necessarily universal.

TSUKUMOGAMI: a specific type of yōkai. These yōkai are born from household objects and other items come to life. Usually, tsukumogami are born for two main reasons. Either they are objects that have existed for one hundred years, or they are items that have been neglected or thrown out.

Yōkai Artists

TORIYAMA SEKIEN (1712–1788) was the first artist to create an illustrated encyclopedic bestiary of the various yōkai in Japan entitled *Gazu Hyakkiyagyō,* or *The Illustrated Demon Horde's Night Parade* in English. His illustrations and designs set the visual standard for how many yōkai are portrayed, even to this day. He created many popular yōkai, such as the shami-chōrō (page 88), and served a major role in popularizing yōkai with the general public.

TSUKIOKA YOSHITOSHI (1839–1892) was considered the last great ukiyo-e master. Among his many wonderful artworks are collections of illustrations featuring yōkai.

Recommended Reading

Japandemonium Illustrated, translated into English by Hiroko Yoda and Matt Alt. An essential read for those interested in yōkai, this book compiles the artwork of artist Toriyama Sekien.

The Book of Yōkai by Michael Dylan Foster. One of my favorite books on yōkai. It dives deep into the world of yōkai, exploring such themes as their cultural origins, historical roots, and yōkai in literature as well as in art.

Yokai Museum, *Yokai Wonderland*, and *Yokai Storyland* by Yumoto Koichi. A wonderful trio of books that showcase numerous yōkai art and objects collected by yōkai scholar Yumoto Koichi over the course of his career. The objects in this collection mainly originate from the Edo period to present day. As a commercial illustrator I find the art produced over the centuries for the yōkai games and products shown in these books fascinating. An essential yōkai visual resource.

Yoshitoshi's Strange Tales, *Tsukioka Yoshitoshi Ghost Stories of Ukiyo-e*, or any other book focusing on the artwork of Tsukioka Yoshitoshi. He was an ukiyo-e master artist. I love the dynamic compositions of his art and his use of beautifully detailed patterns.

Japanese Yokai and other Supernatural Beings by Andreas Marks. This is a well-put-together modern encyclopedia of yōkai, with each yōkai entry featuring wonderful pieces of artwork from Japanese history.

Yokai Attack! by Hiroko Yoda and Matt Alt. This is a yōkai encyclopedia written like a survival guide for younger readers and contains pages full of fun, colorful illustrations.

Strange Japanese Yokai by Kenji Murakami. Another modern yōkai encyclopedia for younger readers featuring many unique and lesser known yōkai.

Yokai.com by Matthew Meyer. A wonderful, extensive online database of yōkai. He also publishes his database in a collection of print and electronic books.

Acknowledgments

For my parents, with their infinite patience and full-hearted encouragement. And for all the growing artists out there who may use this book to learn and improve their craft. **THANK YOU ALL.**

Thank you for purchasing this book.
I hope it helps you on your own artist journey.
Welcome to the wonderful world of Japanese yōkai!

About the Author

Lance Red is an illustrator and graphic designer with a love for animated colors and clean line art. He has had fun for years creating fantasy illustrations in the tabletop games and RPG industries. As an artist, Lance paints both digitally in Photoshop and Procreate and traditionally in oil paints, but, either way, all his art starts with a pencil, paper, and a good drawing: his first love in art.

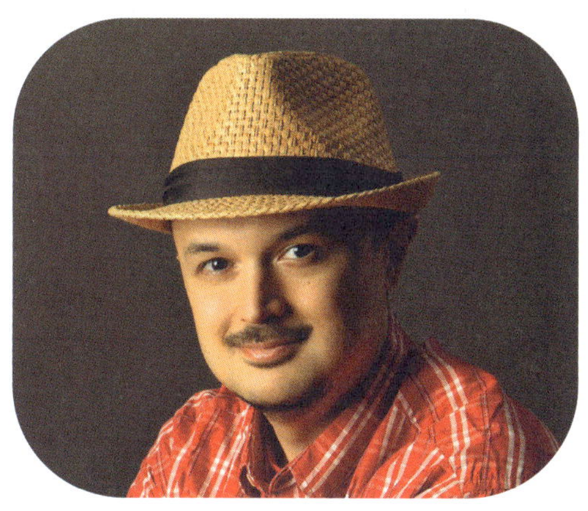

Find the Author Online

Want even more drawing and painting tutorials?

Have art questions?

Lance shares monthly art tutorials and talks about the craft of making art with his community on Patreon:
www.patreon.com/LanceRed

More art, prints, and other fun things at:
www.Lance.Red

First published in 2024 by Wellfleet Press,
an imprint of The Quarto Group,
142 West 36th Street, 4th Floor,
New York, NY 10018, USA
(212) 779-4972
www.Quarto.com

Wellfleet Press titles are also available at discount for retail, wholesale, promotional, and bulk purchase. For details, contact the Special Sales Manager by email at specialsales@quarto.com or by mail at The Quarto Group, Attn: Special Sales Manager, 100 Cummings Center Suite 265D, Beverly, MA 01915 USA.

10 9 8 7 6 5 4 3 2 1

ISBN: 978-1-57715-445-7

Digital edition published in 2024
eISBN: 978-0-7603-9021-4

Library of Congress Cataloging-in-Publication Data

Names: Red, Lance, author.
Title: Yōkai bestiary : how to draw eerie and enchanting Japanese ghouls
  and monsters / Lance Red.
Description: New York, NY : Wellfleet Press, 2024. | Summary: "Yokai
  Bestiary presents detailed step-by-step drawing projects featuring
  ghouls, monsters, and demons from Japanese folklore"-- Provided by
  publisher.
Identifiers: LCCN 2024010586 (print) | LCCN 2024010587 (ebook) | ISBN
  9781577154457 (trade paperback) | ISBN 9780760390214 (ebook)
Subjects: LCSH: Yōkai (Japanese folklore) in art. | Drawing--Technique.
Classification: LCC NC825.M6 R43 2024 (print) | LCC NC825.M6 (ebook) |
  DDC 743/.893982--dc23/eng/20240403
LC record available at https://lccn.loc.gov/2024010586
LC ebook record available at https://lccn.loc.gov/2024010587

Group Publisher: Rage Kindelsperger
Editorial Director: Erin Canning
Creative Director: Laura Drew
Managing Editor: Cara Donaldson
Editor: Elizabeth You
Art Director: Scott Richardson
Interior Design: Brad Norr Design

Printed in China